苏州发展研究丛书

主编 王国平

苏州外文史料译编
（第一辑）

主　编　卞浩宇
副主编　孟祥德　徐　冰
参　编　黄洁婷　戴　莉　蔡　骏　余利霞

图书在版编目(CIP)数据

　　苏州外文史料译编.第一辑:英汉对照/卞浩宇主编.--苏州:苏州大学出版社,2022.11
　　(苏州发展研究丛书/王国平主编)
　　ISBN 978-7-5672-4102-2

　　Ⅰ.①苏… Ⅱ.①卞… Ⅲ.①苏州-地方史-史料-汇编-英、汉 Ⅳ.①K295.33

　　中国版本图书馆CIP数据核字(2022)第215168号

Suzhou Waiwen Shiliao Yibian(Di-yi Ji)

书　　名：苏州外文史料译编(第一辑)
主　　编：卞浩宇
责任编辑：沈　琴
装帧设计：刘　俊
出版发行：苏州大学出版社(Soochow University Press)
社　　址：苏州市十梓街1号　邮编:215006
印　　刷：苏州工业园区美柯乐制版印务有限责任公司
邮购热线：0512-67480030
销售热线：0512-67481020
开　　本：700 mm×1 000 mm　1/16　印张:19　字数:351千
版　　次：2022年11月第1版
印　　次：2022年11月第1次印刷
书　　号：ISBN 978-7-5672-4102-2
定　　价：78.00元

图书若有印装错误,本社负责调换
苏州大学出版社营销部　电话:0512-67481020
苏州大学出版社网址　http://www.sudapress.com
苏州大学出版社邮箱　sdcbs@suda.edu.cn

苏州发展研究丛书

编委会

主　任　芮国强

副主任　周玉玲　黄涧秋　王国平　沈慧瑛

编　委（按姓氏笔画排序）

　　　　　王　芹　王黎明　卞浩宇　朱　跃

　　　　　朱从兵　汤哲声　孙中旺　李　峰

　　　　　吴恩培　张海洋　陈其弟　徐　静

　　　　　高　峰　曹培根　蔡晓荣

序　言

苏州是首批国家历史文化名城,是吴文化的重要发祥地之一,有"人间天堂"的美誉。从2 500多年前建城至今,任凭风吹雨打、时光流转,苏州保留了中国城市最完整的肌理,勾勒着承载诗意栖居的都市梦想。历史赋予生命,活力创造未来。苏州的名片不仅是"人家尽枕河"的江南好景,更是依托强有力的工业基础而迅速崛起的现代化强市。改革开放以来,从"小康构想"印证地到"勾画现代化目标"地,"强富美高"美好蓝图正一步一个脚印在苏州大地化为美好现实。站在全面建设社会主义现代化国家的新起点,一向敢为人先的苏州人再次拿出当年创造"三大法宝"的魄力,努力将全面小康阶段的"曾经先发"变为现代化新征程上的"再度领先"。

"苏人以为雅者,则四方随而雅之"。苏州是一座被文化浸润的城市,长江文化、运河文化、吴文化、古城文化、江南文化等在此交会融通。历史给苏州留下的不仅是园林文化、精致文化,更是一种追求卓越、胸怀天下的文化。追溯历史、放眼全国,苏州是一种独特的文化现象,中国式现代化的重要特征在苏州都有更为集中的体现,苏州理应成为中国区域经济、社会和文化研究中一个独具魅力、独领风骚的重要研究对象。党的二十大报告指出,要推进文化自信自强,铸就社会主义文化新辉煌。"全面建设社会主义现代化国家,必须坚持中国特色社会主义文化发展道路,增强文化自信,围绕举旗帜、聚民心、育新人、兴文化、展形象建设社会主义文化强国,发展面向现代化、面向世界、面向未来的,民族的科学的大众的社会主义文化,激发全民族文化创新创造活力,增强实现中华民族伟大复兴的精神力量。"站在"两个一百年"奋斗目标的历史交汇点,把苏州城市发展作为一门学科来探索和打造,是一个城市增强历史自觉、坚定文化自信的体现。文化自信是一种态度，是苏州的信心和决心；文化自强是一种行动，是推进中国式现代化的重要支撑。近年来，苏州全力推进文化自信自强，增强历史责任、时代责任，高标准高质量推进苏州地域文明探源工程，加强太湖流域文明、史前文化、吴越文化等研究力度，扎实做好"苏州全书"编纂等工作，着力填补苏州历史研究缺环，进一步发扬光大苏州优秀传统文化，为推动中华文化更好走向世界做出更大贡献。

对苏州发展的研究，应当立足于苏州在中华文明发展历程和世界城市发展史中的地位和贡献，突出城市文脉、城市品质、城市精神、城市叙事的一体建构，从根本上回答苏州何以成为苏州、苏州将成为什么样的新苏州等重大命题。当前，要把文献开发研究摆在突出位置，编纂汇聚分散在世界各地有关苏州的文献，再通过出版向世界各地传播苏州历史文化，钩沉文献原著的全貌，探寻我们的精神原乡，重建文化高地的辉煌。

当前，苏州社科界各路"大军"都在为推动城市文化的基础性工程建设群策群力、添柴加薪。作为苏州唯一的市属公办本科院校，苏州城市学院责无旁贷、奋勇争先。苏州城市学院在建校伊始就成立了苏州发展研究院，旨在就深入挖掘、传承、保护、利用苏州历史文化资源方面做出自己的努力和贡献，为城市的数字化转型、城市更新和创新发展进一步集智汇力、建言献策。为此，苏州城市学院苏州发展研究院隆重推出"苏州发展研究丛书"，近期主要包括苏州历史文化与当代苏州研究系列、苏州文献史料编研系列，希望能为讲好苏州故事、展现苏州风采而绵绵用力、久久为功。

聚沙成塔、集腋成裘，我们期待大家的共同参与！

是为序。

芮国强
2022 年 11 月

"Beautiful Soo" The Capital of Kiangsu
姑苏景志　　1

Some Notes from the History of Soochow
苏州历史见闻　　81

Eighteen Capitals of China
中国十八省府　　147

My Holidays in China
在华度假记事　　197

China: Its Marvel and Mystery
中国：神奇而又神秘的国度　　237

The Travelers' Handbook for China
游历中国闻见撷要录　　247

Alas Poor Soochow! Thy Beauties Are in Shanghai
可叹啊，苏州！美人都去了上海　　261

The Venice of the Far East
东方威尼斯　　269

Trifles of Travel
旅行琐记　　281

译后记　　292

"Beautiful Soo" The Capital of Kiangsu

姑苏景志

(杜步西 著 卞浩宇 译)

《姑苏景志》("Beautiful Soo" The Capital of Kiangsu)系杜步西(Rev. Hampden C. Du Bose,D. D.,1845—1910)撰写的一本关于苏州的英文小册子。杜步西1872年来华,经上海、杭州,再到苏州。杜步西曾在养育巷东侧购得荒地一块,并在此兴建教堂,即今日"使徒堂"前身。此外,有鉴于当时苏州民众吸食鸦片情况严重,杜步西还会同多位西方来华人士,成立了中国最早的禁烟会,杜步西任首任会长。杜步西在苏州工作、生活长达38年之久,其足迹遍布苏州大街小巷,与苏州结下了深厚情缘。《姑苏景志》1899年由上海别发印书馆(Kelly & Walsh, Limited)出版发行。全书共45页,从历史起源、历代名士、经济状况、风土人情、城市风貌、秀丽风光等多个方面较为详细地介绍了苏州这座千年古城,向世人展示了一幅美丽的姑苏全景图。

"Heaven above; below Soochow."

Antiquity

On the banks of the Grand Canal eighty miles west of Shanghai, twelve miles east of the Great Lake, and forty miles south of the Yangtse, stands a far-famed city, the silk metropolis of the Orient. Even in this hurried nineteenth century a crowd of admirers stand with reverent awe around the statue of antiquity, and gaze upon its towering heights, which seem to pierce the clouds. Let us go back two millenniums, and then along these same streets we now tread the father would lead his son and point to halls and palaces covered with the ivy of centuries. Twenty-four hundred years have these walls stood, and on these cobble-stone pavements eighty generations of men have trod to and fro. Founded B. C. 500, it was laid out only 250 years after Romulus traced the walls of the ancient mistress of the world, whose glory for fifteen centuries has consisted in the broken monuments of former grandeur, while during these same fifteen hundred years Soochow has been a literary and commercial centre. It was built during the lifetime of Confucius and synchronous with the completion of the second temple at Jerusalem under Ezra, which occurred shortly after the time of Nebuchadnezzar, whose reign marks an epoch in ancient history. It was in the days of Socrates the philosopher, Herodotus the historian, Phidias the sculptor, and Pericles the orator, that the fathers of a numerous and distinguished race first built their primitive residences in this city. There is a stone map in the Confucius temple nearly one thousand years old, and on it the streets and temple sites are almost identical with the present.

The Reign of Hoh Lü

China was not always the solid cube it is at this time. Before the warring states had amalgamated, Soochow was the capital of the "Kingdom of Wu", as the country south of the Yangtse was called. It included a portion of this and the two adjacent provinces, and was independent from the 12th to the 4th centuries (B. C.) inclusive. There is nothing in the history specially germane to our subject

"上有天堂,下有苏州。"

悠久历史

上海以西八十英里[1]、太湖以东十二英里、长江以南四十英里的大运河沿岸,矗立着一座远近闻名的城市,它就是东方丝绸之都。即便在这纷纷扰扰的十九世纪,还是有一群崇拜者怀着无比崇敬之情围绕在巍峨高耸的古老雕像前仰望。回首两千年前,一位父亲领着他的孩子正沿着我们现在走的这条街道漫步,并指给他看那些缠绕着数百年常春藤的走廊和宫殿。现在这些城墙已经矗立于此两千四百年之久,在这些由鹅卵石铺成的道路上先后走过了八十代人。苏州建于公元前五百年,仅仅比罗慕路斯建立罗马城晚二百五十年。然而,经历了十五个世纪之后,罗马城过往的荣耀只能在残垣断壁中找寻,而在此期间,苏州却一直是文化和商业中心。苏州城建于春秋时期,该时期也正是孔子生活的年代。与此同时,以斯拉则在尼布甲尼撒二世过世后不久建成了耶路撒冷的第二座神庙,尼布甲尼撒二世的统治可以说开创了古代历史的一个新纪元。这一时期也正是古希腊哲学家苏格拉底、历史学家希罗多德、雕刻家菲迪亚斯和演说家伯里克利等人活跃的年代,大批高门大族也开始在苏州建立起自己最初的家园。苏州文庙中存有一幅近千年历史的石刻地图,上面所刻街道和寺庙的位置与现在几乎完全相同。

阖闾的统治

春秋时期中国尚未统一。在被战国诸侯吞并前,苏州是吴国都城,当时以苏州为中心的长江下游以南地区称作"吴"。吴国疆域包括苏州及相邻两个省。自公元前十二世纪至公元前四世纪,吴国一直保持独立。吴

---

[1] 英美制长度单位,1英里等于1.609 3千米。

till the accession of Hoh Lü (阖闾)[1], who issued the decree that Soochow be laid out as the capital of his dominions. Hoh Lü was of royal decent, the grandson of a former sovereign, yet he ascended the throne not by succession but by assassinating the ruling monarch and seizing the reigns of government. His reign, however, was a successful one. "He did much to improve the general condition of the country, especially in opening up the water communications and draining the swampy lands that abounds. By his wise and just government he gained the confidence of the people and succeeded ere long in establishing himself firmly on the throne. He brought his army into a great state of efficiency, and none of the neighbouring states could cope with him, so that he was able to dictate his own terms on the conclusion of every one of the four or five wars in which he was engaged."

His pleasure parks must have been attractive resorts. On the hills beside the Great Lake, though the population in the thriving towns and villages is dense, yet deer are not unknown;—what splendid hunting grounds must these have been when the mountains were covered with their primeval forest! Form his rural palaces on the Mohdoh heights in the afternoon he could look westward upon the Great Lake, glistening as a sea of glass, and to the east behold thousands of workmen with their wooden pestles driving down the stone foundations of the great city just rising into sight.

Its Founder

The founder of Soochow was Wu Tsze Sü (伍子胥). To him, the Prime Minister, was entrusted the great task of building a capital. In many respects there is no people who have a more just appreciation of virtue than the Chinese. They are not blinded by the glamour of royalty, but give honor to the great statesmen who have wielded the destinies of the empire. King Hoh Lü is known by the literati only; Wu Tsze Sü by the people. There are no fabled accounts of his early years, for Asiatic history at that period is far more authentic than European. His father, the Primer of another state, was murdered by the monarch, and the son fled as a refugee to Wu. He became the friend of Hoh Lü, assisted him in obtaining the throne, and for twenty years was his trusted counselor. He advised the king, in order to strengthen his government "and secure the safety and prosperity of his people," to found "a large walled city where his subjects could dwell in time of

---

[1] 原文中括注为繁体字，编者收录时改为简体。

王阖闾登基之前，吴国的历史并没有太多与本书探讨主题相关的内容。阖闾登基后，颁布法令，将都城定在苏州。阖闾系吴国王室后裔，先吴王[1]之孙。然而，阖闾的王位并非通过继承，而是通过刺杀时任君主夺取政权而获得的。尽管如此，他的统治依然非常成功。"他采取措施提升国家整体实力，特别是开放水上交通，排干大量沼泽湿地。阖闾的睿智和公正管理为他赢得了民众信任，统治日趋稳固。他精兵强军，邻近诸国皆不能敌，因此，在其参加的四到五次战争中，他均能打败对手并按照自己的意愿与对方签订条约。"

阖闾的别苑想必定是度假胜地。尽管城镇和乡村人口稠密，但是生长在太湖之滨群山之中的鹿对苏州人而言，却并不陌生。群山之上覆盖着原始植被，这是多么壮观的狩猎场啊！午后，站在位于木渎镇上的行宫高处，阖闾西眺可见太湖，湖面波光粼粼，东望可见上千工匠举起手中木杵为新城打下地基。

建城者

苏州的建城者是伍子胥。作为吴国大夫，他被委以重任建造都城。在很多方面，没有人比中国人更懂得欣赏人的道德品质，他们不会被王权的光芒遮蔽双眼而有失公允，对于那些改变国家命运的伟大政治家们，他们给予赞赏。吴王阖闾仅为士大夫阶层所知，而伍子胥则为民众所知。伍子胥早年名不见经传，因为那时亚洲的历史记载远比欧洲来得真实。他的父亲是另一国（楚国）大夫，被国王谋害致死，伍子胥被迫逃亡至吴。他成为阖闾的朋友，并助其夺得王位。在随后的二十年里，伍子胥成为阖闾最为信任的谋士。他向阖闾建议，为加强统治，"保障百姓生命和财产安全"，应择地"建造城墙，可使臣民在危难之际得以庇护，国库免受长期威胁吴

---

[1] 指吴王寿梦。

danger and where his government stores could be protected from the enemies that constantly menaced his kingdom."The king was pleased, and directed Wu Tsze Sü "to select a site and proceed with the building of the city," whereupon, with the aid no doubt of geomancers and fung-shuy doctors, the history of the city tells us, he " prospected the ground, tasted the water, observed the heavens and planned the earth."

What a Herculean task to build a city! What an expenditure of money! What a witness to the civilization of those early ages! Wu Tsze Sü traced the foundations of the walls, laid out the streets, opened the canals, built the bridges, and, perhaps, according to the phraseology of western towns "sold the corner lots."By his own toil he erected the monument which perpetuates his memory. By the energy of Wu Tsze Sü the borders of the Kingdom of Wu were extended and the condition of the people so much improved, that it "became one of the strongest and most famous of the principalities into which China was divided at that time."

Hoh Lü was succeeded by his unworthy son Fu Ch'ai. With the resources which his father had collected, he erected magnificent palaces and the "Beautiful Soo Tower," so celebrated in ancient annals. His extravagance in building, his waste of the state revenues, and "the enforced labour of many thousands of his subjects in his building operations, caused widespread murmuring of dissatisfaction among the people."The faithful and honored statesman, the friend and counselor of his father, protested against the extravagance and dissipation of King Fu Ch'ai, and the latter used the short method of sending him a sword to take his own life. The noble citizens of the capital rescued his body from the canal, built two funeral temples, and called the south-west gate by his name.

We pass by the long line of kings when Soochow was the capital of an ancient state, and the four or five hundred governors since it became the seat of government of the central province along the coast line; —her statesmen and authors, warriors and poets, her men of fame and wealth can scarcely be alluded to, for our theme is the city as she is at present and not what she was in the historic past.

Its Situation

The capital of Kiangsu is situated in the vast plain between the Yangtse

国的敌国侵占"。阖闾非常赞同，遂令伍子胥"择地建造新城"。于是，据史书记载，伍子胥在风水师的帮助下，"相土尝水，象天法地"，建造苏州城。

建造一座城市是多么艰巨的一项任务啊！这又是多么大的一笔开支啊！这也是那些早期文明多么了不起的一个见证啊！伍子胥建造了城墙，铺设了街道，开凿了运河，修建了桥梁，也许，用西方城市建造术语来说，他还"出售了街角地段"。正是通过他的艰苦努力，伍子胥为自己树立起一座不朽的丰碑。在伍子胥的努力下，吴国的疆域不断扩大，百姓生活条件日益改善，吴国也"成为中国当时各诸侯国中最为强大的王国，显赫一时"。

继承阖闾王位的是其不肖之子夫差。夫差利用其父留下的丰富资源，建造了宏伟的宫殿及史书上记载的著名的"姑苏台"。夫差大兴土木，浪费大量国家税收，并且"迫使成千上万的民工为其修建各类工程，引发了民众广泛的不满与哀怨"。伍子胥，这位忠诚而又受人敬重的政治家、夫差父王的朋友与谋士，向夫差提出抗议，反对其铺张浪费、花天酒地。然而，夫差却很快命人送给伍子胥一把短剑，令其自刎。苏州城内的贵族从河中将伍子胥的尸体打捞上来，后为其建立两座祠堂，并用他的名字来命名苏州西南城门[1]。

作为古代王国的都城，苏州曾有多位君王在此执政；当苏州成为沿海中部大省的省会之后，也有四五百位行政长官历任于此——不过，这些历代政治家与作家、勇士与诗人、名士与富商在本书中将很少被提及，因为，本书关注的主题乃是苏州城市的现状而非其历史。

地理位置

苏州，江苏省首府，地处长江和杭州湾之间的广袤平原，被誉为远东

---

[1] 即胥门。

and the Hangchow Bay, the "garden spot" of Far Cathay. To the east the country is perfectly level and entirely bereft of trees, except a few at the hamlets. To the south-east are the lakes, nearly one hundred in number, each from one to three miles across, and this region is so much like an archipelago that we do not know whether it pertains to the domain of land or water. To the west is a range of the mountains, which from the parapets and towers of the city give a pleasing diversity to the eye. Beyond the mountains is the Great Lake, an inland sea sixty miles across, and in it there are mountain islands, twenty miles in length, covered with grove of yangmei and pepo, where the grapes of Eshcol and honey sipped from the *olea fragrans* are found, and with the perfume of flowers in the spring they seem, as compared with the dull rice fields of the plain, like the enchanted isles.

The Great Canal

Our city stands upon the great artificial highway of the Empire, the Great Canal, which is from fifty to one hundred yards wide and is spanned by magnificent stone arches—one of these bridges, near Soochow, has fifty-three arches, —and when on this great stream the white sails of the junks and small craft are spread to the winds, and the trackers along the path are towing in the opposite direction, it is a beautiful sight. In regard to inland navigation, Soochow is at the hub, and from it great and wide canals diverge as spokes in every direction, each of these, as the Chinese boatmen say, "a centipede," from the innumerable streams diverging to the right and left, as there is not a city or town or village or hamlet which can not be reached by boat in this "well-watered" plain, so inviting to the itinerant. Telegraph-poles, erected fifteen years ago, were the first mark of the approaching tread of western civilization. Last year to the north of the city was surveyed the new railway from Shanghai to Nanking, with a branch road running south, following the line of the Great Canal to Hangchow, unless diverted to the west via Nantsin.It is reported that the head office of this eastern railway system is to be in Soochow.

Its Renown

The Chinese have a proverb "Above is Heaven; below Soochow and

的"花园城市"。苏州东面地势平坦,除了一些小村庄内的树木之外,其余地方几乎没有植被。东南临湖,有近一百个湖泊,每个湖泊湖面宽约一到三英里不等,整个地区就如同一个群岛,很难分清水陆界线。西面群山连绵,从城内的护城墙和塔楼远眺,山势各异,令人赏心悦目。太湖位于群山之外,该湖为内陆湖,湖面宽约六十英里,湖中有山地岛屿,长二十英里,岛上果园种满杨梅、葡萄等瓜果,岛上还产桂花蜂蜜。每当春季来临,岛上花香弥漫,和单调的平原农田相比,更令人陶醉不已。

大运河

我们的城市坐落在大运河畔,该运河是人工开凿的一条交通要道。运河宽五十至一百码[1],众多壮观的石拱桥横跨河面——其中一座桥就在苏州附近,共有五十三个拱门——当风吹过河面,大小帆船上的白色风帆迎风扬起,岸边的纤夫拽着纤绳前行,这是多么美丽的景致啊!就内河航运而言,苏州位于中枢地段,多条宽阔的河流如同辐条一般,从这里向四面八方流淌出去,而每一条河流,又有数不清的支流分布在其左右两边,就像中国船民所说的"像蜈蚣一样",因此,在这片"水乡"之中,没有哪一个城镇村庄是小船去不了的,吸引着四方来客。十五年前竖起的电线杆可以说是西方文明进入中国的第一个标记。去年,因要修建从上海到南京的新铁路,相关人员已对苏州北部进行了测绘勘察,其中一条支线将会向南延伸,从运河至杭州,只在经过南浔时转向西部。据报道,这个东部铁路系统的总部将设在苏州。

名声

中国人有句谚语,"上有天堂,下有苏杭"。游客告诉我们,走遍中

---

[1] 英美制长度单位,1码等于3英尺,合0.914 4米。

Hangchow."Travellers tell us that throughout the eighteen provinces the Celestials speaks of Soochow as the terrestrial Paradise. The Buddhists point their votaries to the Western Heaven; the Taotists to the isles of the Immortals in the east; but this practical people consider it quite enough happiness to reside for three score and ten years in "Beautiful Soo."The gardens where flowers bloom through three and a half seasons, the brightly varnished pleasure-boats, the large tea-shops, the fine chairs borne on the shoulders of coolies, the streets thronged with men robed in silks and furs—for here it is men, not the gentler sex, who patronize fashion's bazaar— is all that the Chinaman's heart desires.

Literary Centre

The city was founded during the latter years of Confucius, "the throneless King," and though his foot never trod these street, nor his eyes beheld the mountain, lake and plain, yet he made Soochow his literary capital, the centre of his domain of letters, and so for twenty centuries to the four hundred millions it is what Athens was to the little peninsula on the Aegean. In this book-loving land it is "down hill in every direction" from Soochow. During the dark ages of Europe this city was as bright as England during Queen Anne's reign. Proud scholars have crowded the examination halls, authors have filled the shelves of the book stores, and poets have sung of the old landmarks so celebrated in history. Translations of these works do not do them full justice, for the thoughts of the Chinese mind appear best when clothed in their native language, and the freshness of the flowers of speech are gone when the ideas of the original are plucked and transferred into the western receptacle of thought. It is surprising, where aristocracy is not necessarily hereditary, and where it rests upon individual toil to climb the rugged heights of literature in order to obtain official preferment, how generation after generation are advanced to the highest position simply by personal effort."Wealth and luxury do not seem to enfeeble the mental vigor of the high gentry, but the son takes the father's place simply because he is worthy of the place."A noble succession. Oftener than any other city has the honor of the first literary graduate of the Empire—one in three years—been accorded to a Soochow aspirant. The late minister to Germany, Mr. Hung Kuin（洪钧）, whose coffin was brought from Peking in state, allowed to enter the city, and given a princely burial, was the "Senior Wrangler" in 1868. Another was Mr.

国十八个省份[1],苏州才是人间天堂。佛教徒指引信徒前往西方极乐世界,道教徒指引信徒奔向东方仙岛;但世人则认为能在美丽的苏州住上七十年则是人间最为快乐之事。苏州的园林一年有十个月鲜花盛开,苏州还有色彩艳丽的游船,有大型的茶室,有肩抬的轿子,苏州的街道上挤满了身着绸缎和皮衣的男士——在这里,是男士而非女士光顾时尚集市——这一切都让每一个中国人心生向往。

文化中心

苏州建城之时正值"素王"孔子的晚年。尽管孔子本人未曾踏足苏州,亦未曾亲眼见过这里的山、湖和平原,但他却认定苏州乃文化之都、文学中心。因此,两千年来,苏州之于四亿中国人就如同雅典之于爱琴海上的小岛一样。在苏州这块土地上,爱书尚学之风随处可见。当欧洲还处于"黑暗年代"之时,这座城市却如同安妮女王[2]统治的英格兰一样充满光明。考场里满是骄傲的士子,书店书架上摆满了各类作品,诗人们用诗歌赞颂着城中的名胜古迹。然而,这些中文作品的翻译却很难再现原作精髓,因为中国人的思维只有用汉语才能完美表达,一旦原作中的观点被孤立地转换成西方思想时,其原作语言之清新优美荡然无存。在这里,功名并非世袭罔替,个人只有依靠在科举这条崎岖坡道上不断攀登,才能在官场上获得晋升,一代又一代的人正是通过自身努力达到人生巅峰,其过程令人惊叹不已。"财富和奢侈似乎并未削弱上层人士的意志,子承父业是因为儿子的确有能力",这是一种高尚的传承。和其他城市相比,苏州学子在科举考试中——三年举办一次——高中状元的比例更多。已故驻德大使洪钧

---

[1] 清朝将原明朝汉人统治区中的十五个承宣布政使司中的湖广分为湖北、湖南,南直隶分为江苏、安徽,从陕西中分出甘肃,所设置的18个省份。

[2] 安妮女王,Queen Anne(1665—1714),斯图亚特王朝的英国及爱尔兰女王(1702—1714年在位)。

Loh Fung Zah（陆凤石）, and the day when his wife rode as a queen through the streets in 1874, and the whole populace turned out to do her honor, is well impressed upon our memories, as it was the innocent cause of a riot at one of our chapels.

In the Tang dynasty (A.D. 600-900)[1] there were two celebrated poets in Soochow, Pah Hiang Shan（白香山）whose ancestral hall is at the Level Bridge, and Loh K'wei Mung（陆龟蒙）, who went abroad as an official but returned to engage in literary pursuits.

In the Ming dynasty, Kou Ting Jen（顾鼎臣）became a minister to the Emperor Chen Teh（正德）and for three months as regent ruled "all under Heaven."His youth was legendary. The son of a concubine, he was cast by his father into a pig-sty and cared for by the four-footed animals. This marvelous protection marked him as a man of destiny, and soon his talents made him known.

T'ang Pah Hu（唐伯虎）lived on Peach Blossom Street and was a famous artist. His contemporary Chuh Chu Shan（祝芝山）was a celebrated penman. The pictures of the former and the manuscripts of the latter now command fabulous prices.

Hwang Ch'ong（况钟）, called Hwang Clear Heaven（况青天）, was a Prefect of Soochow. His monumental gateway "The People Can Never Forget Him," is at the official landing outside the West Gate.

Of the present dynasty, Kou Tan（顾炎）lived on the North Street. His life is given in the City History. Yih T'ieh Sze（叶天士）one hundred years ago was a celebrated physician and the author of several medical works. Ching Shen Tan（金圣叹）lived near the Twin Pagodas. His commentaries on, and prefaces to, works of general literature are highly valued at this time. During his day the Literary Chancellor was selling degrees, so to attract attention to the matter he took the image of God of Riches and placed it in the district Confucian Temple (thus defiling the scared shrine of letters) and brought Confucian's image to the idol temple. The Emperor decapitated the Chancellor and the perpetrator; and the coolie hong by assisting in the affair lost its charter.

A few years since, one of those who have recently acquired wealth, the late Kou Tsze Shan（顾子山）, returned from the Taotai's Yamen at Ningpo, built a palatial residence (according to Chinese ideas) and adorned the city with a pleasure garden. It is reported that many of the Mandarins in Soochow leave the city in moderate circumstances, but after a few years, with the spoils of office,

---

[1] 此处原作者对唐朝起止年份的括注有误，应为公元618—907年。

先生就是1868年的状元，其灵柩从北京运回苏州，并在苏州予以厚葬。另一位是陆凤石先生，1874年高中状元之后，其妻犹如女王一般骑马游街，所有民众聚集围观致敬，这一幕让我们印象深刻，因为这也引起了我们教堂前的骚乱。

在唐朝，苏州曾生活过两位著名的诗人。一位是白香山[1]，其祠堂位于平桥；另一位是陆龟蒙，他曾经外出做官，后归隐苏州从事文学研究。

在明朝，顾鼎臣成为正德皇帝[2]的内阁首辅，他曾作为摄政大臣监国三个月。顾鼎臣的青年时代颇具传奇色彩。顾鼎臣为小妾之子，其父将其赶进猪圈，由猪来照看他。正是这种不可思议的经历反而令其获得命运眷顾，很快他便因才华横溢而闻名于世。

家住桃花坞的唐伯虎是著名的艺术家。与其同时代的祝芝山[3]则是著名的书法家。如今，唐伯虎的画和祝芝山的字价值不菲。

况钟，人称"况青天"，曾任苏州知府。民众为纪念他而建的"民不能忘"[4]牌坊现坐落于西门外。

本朝的顾炎，住在北街。他的生平在史书上亦有记载。叶天士，一百年前的著名内科医生，著有多部医学著作。金圣叹，家住双塔附近。他对大众文学作品的点评以及所写的序言在当时非常具有影响力。金圣叹在世时，科举考试的主考官收受贿赂，为引起世人对此事的关注，金圣叹将财神像放到文庙之中（此举亵渎圣地），并将孔子像放到财神庙中。皇帝知晓此事之后将主考官与犯案者斩首，而协助搬运神像的苦力行也因此被取缔。

已故的顾子山，也是近年来获得巨额财富的官员之一。从宁绍道台衙门卸任返苏后几年，他便在苏州修建了一所富丽堂皇的花园式住宅[5]养老

---

[1] 即白居易。
[2] 应为嘉靖皇帝。
[3] 即祝枝山。
[4] "民不能忘"牌坊乃是苏州民众为康熙年间江苏巡抚汤斌所立，并非为况钟所立，此处杜步西有误。
[5] 即怡园。

return from distant provinces as semi-millionaires. The Book says, "Whatsoever a man soweth, that shall he also reap." We cannot expect the blessing of Heaven to rest upon the sons of those whose "inheritance has been gotten hastily " and whose official accounts have never been audited.

The present aristocracy of Kiangsu's capital, many of whom can prove a genealogical mandarinate of four or five centuries, is in itself an interesting field of inquiry, and to a wide-awake student who delights in the historic past, and with whom time is no special object, would richly reward enterprising research.

Soochow's Greatest Man

The most illustrious name in the annals of "Beautiful Soo" is Fan Wen Chen Kung (范文正公), who in the early part of the 11th century was the most renowned statesman of the Sung dynasty, an era remarkable in the classic history of this Ancient Empire for the high character of its officials and scholars. Born in Soochow A. D. 989, he became an L.L.D. at the early age of twenty-seven, and upon his appointment as State Historiographer at Kaifung, the capital, numbers of students flocked to his academy to hear his lectures on the classics, and from his private funds he was ever ready to assist poor young men in their efforts to obtain an education.

In 1032 there was a great drought in Southern Shantung and North Kiangsu. As no attention was paid to his first memorial, he sent a second to the Emperor in which he asked what he and the inmates of the palace would do if they were deprived of one-half day's rations? He was appointed to superintend the famine relief, and by remitting the taxes and opening the granaries he fed starving millions.

In 1038 he was sent to suppress a rebellion in the West. In the discipline of his army, the celerity of his movements and the vigor of his attacks, he exhibited the qualities of an able general, while his lenient treatment of the prisoners and the just government he established gained for him the goodwill of the tribes he conquered.

His outspoken opposition to injustice brought him frequently into collision with the Emperor, who would appoint him to a post in a distant province and then in a year or two recall him to the capital. The Prime Minister was as unscrupulous as he was powerful, and every one who desired to rise at court

（按照中国人的观念），为这座城市增色不少。据报道，很多苏州的官员离开苏州时身家尚属中流小富，然而混迹官场多年之后，从外地返苏之时已是身家显赫。正所谓"种瓜得瓜，种豆得豆"，我们不期望上帝保佑这些"仓促之间获得遗产"的子女或者"账目从未被审计过"的官员们。

苏州目前的贵族阶层，都能提供长达四五百年的家族官员谱系，这本身就非常有意思，是一个值得探究的领域，对那些喜欢研究历史的学生，以及时间充裕的学者而言，这样的研究必定会大有收获。

苏州最伟大的人物

苏州编年史上最杰出的人物非范文正公莫属，他是十一世纪初宋朝最为著名的政治家。在中国古代史中，宋朝以其官员和学者的高尚品德而著称。公元989年，范仲淹出生在苏州，二十七岁时高中进士，曾在首都开封担任史官一职，其间，大批学生蜂拥前往其所在书院听他关于古文经典的讲座，他还个人出资资助贫困青年就学读书。

1032年，山东南部和江苏北部大旱。由于第一次上书没有获得皇帝重视，范仲淹在第二次上书时质问皇帝：如果皇帝和宫内所有人都停食半日，那将会怎样？随后，范仲淹被任命负责监督赈灾事宜。通过降低税收以及开仓放粮，范仲淹拯救了数百万饥民。

1038年，范仲淹被派往西部平叛[1]。他率领的军队纪律严明，行动迅速，攻击有力，充分展示出他杰出的军事才能，而他随后对待战俘的宽容政策以及他所建立起的公正管理体制，为其在所征服的部落[2]中赢得了赞誉和尊敬。

范仲淹的秉公直言令其多次与皇帝产生冲突，皇帝将其贬至外省任职，一两年后又将其召回京师。时任宰相权势熏天，肆无忌惮，任何一位想要

---

[1] 此处原作者表述有误，应指西夏政权侵边，并非叛乱。
[2] 此处原作者表述有误，西夏是国家，而非部落。

must gain his favor by bribery. Fen Wen undertook to expose these abuses by describing graphically to the Emperor what Mandarins were in office by right and what ones were there by favouritism and corruption. His reward was temporary banishment, but soon invited to return as Vice-President of the Privy Council, where he became the principal counselor to the Emperor. He worked night and day in the discharge of his duties, dismissed unworthy and inefficient men, examined carefully into the details of the government, and required all officials to render a strict account of the expenditures. The changes he attempted in the administration were too sweeping and aroused such bitter opposition as to require his temporary withdraw from state affairs.

His literary works embraces some fifty volumes. He founded ancestral estates for the poor of the clan, drew up regulations for their management, and purchased the land for the Confucian temple at Soochow. His biographer says he was firm in his principles and mild in his manner. In the service of the king or dealing with his fellow men he always kept his words. He was honest in handling the public funds. Whether as a teacher meeting his classes, or as a Governor ruling a province, or as a General commanding an army, or as acting Prime Minister controlling an empire, he displayed both wisdom and genius. When he died at the age of sixty-three, the Emperor mourned his loss, the people felt that a prince had fallen, and even the barbarians on the frontier, whom he had brought under imperial sway, wept when they heard the tidings. In the ancestral temple in the center of Soochow, by Imperial authority, the Prefect and District Magistrate offer sacrifices twice a year in honor of Fan Wen Chen Kung and his four sons.

The Wealth and Poverty

Turning from Soochow's famous statesmen to its material progress, as might well be imagined, wealth has accumulated in this great emporium. The large wholesale houses, the pawnshops whose capital amounts to millions, the enormous value of real estate, the great trade which centres in the city, the variety of manufacturing interests, go to prove how vast is its wealth. Banks are numerous, and though the exterior of the building may be plain, the interior of the vaults displays the great deposits of silver. Through these banks money can be transmitted to any part of the eighteen provinces. The basis of the wealth is the

升职的官员都必须向其行贿。范仲淹上书皇帝揭露此事，他在奏章中言明哪些官员是凭借真才实学而任职，哪些官员是依靠偏袒腐败而任职。然而，他得到的回报却是被贬流放，不过，很快他又被请回京城担任枢密副使，也成为皇帝的股肱之臣。范仲淹夜以继日地工作，履职尽责，裁撤冗员，整顿吏治，要求所有官员详细说明开支情况。由于改革力度过大，引起强烈反对，导致他暂时被迫退出国家事务管理工作。

范仲淹的文学作品有五十余卷。他成立了范氏义庄，赡养族内穷困之人，并制定规章加以管理，此外他还购买土地在苏州设立文庙。史官在为其立传时写道，他性情温和但坚持原则。无论是在辅佐皇帝还是与同僚交际时，他总能信守承诺。在处理公款时，他廉洁奉公。无论是传道授业，还是治理地方；无论是统帅三军，还是监国处理政务，他都展示出睿智和才能。范仲淹在六十三岁[1]时去世，皇帝为其哀悼，民众痛其陨落，甚至是被其归化过来的远在边疆的蛮夷之众，听闻其逝世的消息时，亦痛哭流涕。为纪念范文正公及他的四个儿子，经皇帝批准，每年知府和地方长官均要在位于苏州市中心的祠堂内举行两次公祭仪式。

财富与贫穷

让我们将关注点从苏州著名的政治家转移到物质发展上来。可以想象，在这个商业繁荣的地方，财富得以快速累积。大型的批发商店、资金高达上百万的当铺、大量价格不菲的房产，市内大量的商贸活动，以及各式各样的手工行业，都证明了这座城市是多么富有。这里有很多钱庄，尽管从外部看，这些钱庄显得很普通，但其内部的金库里却存有大量白银。通过这些钱庄，资金可以从这里流通到中国十八个省份中的任何一个地方。苏州的财富基础，首先来自这一辖区种植的优质大米，每一平方英里的年产

---

[1] 范仲淹享年六十四岁。

fine white rice grown in this Prefecture, each square mile of which yields from twelve to fifteen thousand bushels annually. Next to this is the silk trade with its various ramifications. Then, besides the commercial interests, is the hoarded wealth of officialdom seeking secure investment. Also millionaires from other sections select Soochow as their place of residence. The land within a radius of twenty miles is mostly owned by those who dwell within the walls. These are the "happy families" who receive their "rent rice" and enjoy the fruits of other men's labors.

This is a land of contrasts—alone beside the money of the rich lies the penury of the poor. In the tenement houses from ten to thirty families are huddled together; some in two rooms, some in one room, and some whole families in one-half of a room. Tens of thousands live on the merest pittance, and some know not the pleasure of a hearty meal of food. With their board, the wages of book keepers is from $5 to $8 *per mensem*; of clerks from $2 to $5; of menservants, $1 with perquisites; and of women, fifty or seventy-five cents with meat once in two months. At embroidery, women usually earn from three to eight cents a day, unless a skilled hand is selected to embroider a robe for the princesses. Between the upper and lower class is the large middle class of teachers and of well-to-do shopmen and mechanics, over one-half of the population, whose wardrobes are liberally furnished with cotton cloth by the piece, and who eat a full allowance of rice, vegetables, fish and pork. All these things contribute a share to their abounding good nature as they smoke the pipe of peace and live happily from one year to another in the Paris of the Middle Kingdom.

The Expectant Mandarin

Besides those in office, the provincial capital is the home of the expectant Mandarin. Hard is the life of Chinese official, for out of office he is not permitted to engage in trade, and must live off the earnings or squeezes of his former term of years. He can not act as president of a company, or be placed in charge of important financial interests, or be the head of a law school or University. With the introduction of the civilization of the West, many of these may prove leaders in the line of national progress and not find it necessary to such a fabulous extent "to lay by in store" during the term of official tenure. The Mandarins of this class

量为一万两千至一万五千蒲式耳[1]。其次来自各类丝绸交易。除商业利益之外，还有来自官员的钱财，他们为自己积攒的财富寻找安全的投资。此外，来自其他地区的富翁们也纷纷选择在苏州安家落户。方圆二十英里以内的土地几乎都被这些生活在城内的人占有。这些都是"幸福的家庭"，因为他们靠收"米租"为生，享用着他人的劳动成果。

这是一个贫富差距对比强烈的地方——与有钱人的富裕相对的就是穷人的拮据。十到三十户人家挤在廉价的租住屋内。有的家庭住两间屋，有的家庭住一间屋，有的甚至全家就挤在半间屋内。成千上万的人仅依靠微薄的收入生活，很多人从未尝过一顿饱饭的滋味。一位账房先生每月的工资为5到8美元，包含伙食在内；职员每月2到5美元；男仆每月1美元外加些许津贴；妇女每月仅50到75美分，不过每两月可以领一次肉。在刺绣行业，除了因技艺精湛而被挑选出来专为皇室刺绣的人之外，通常一个普通女绣工每天可挣3到8美分。在上层和底层之间，还有一个庞大的中间阶层，主要有教书先生、生活富足的店主及技工，他们占这里人口总数的一半以上，他们家中衣橱里挂着一件件的棉布衣服，他们能够吃到大米、各式蔬菜、鱼和猪肉。这也养成了他们温和的性格，他们享受着生活的恬静，在这个如同巴黎一样的城市中年复一年地过着幸福生活。

等待任命的官员

除了那些在任的官员之外，苏州，作为省城，也是大批待任官员的聚集地。中国官员的生存是很困难的，因为离职之后，他不得从事商业经营，只能依靠前些年任期积攒下来的收入生活。他不能在商会里担任主席或与财务密切相关的职位，不能担任法学院或大学的校长。随着西方文明的传入，官员中许多人也许可以在关于国计民生的行业内发挥领导才能，而没

---

[1] 英美制容量单位（计量干散颗粒用），1蒲式耳等于8加仑。英制1蒲式耳合36.37升，美制1蒲式耳合35.24升。

are frequently sent as deputies to hold court in distant places or to settle local disputes and disturbances. There are over 2,500 "official residence" in Soochow, which includes all grades of officials, both civil and military, each with from ten to thirty retainers, or in round numbers 40,000, who form an idle portion of the population, as they simply buy and eat and enjoy themselves, all hoping for a vacancy in some distant Yamên. Patience is a cardinal virtue, for it may be two years and it may be five that the official must keep up the appearance of wealth and station, though he may be in desperate straits and living on borrowed capital, till a vacancy occurs, when, by a handsome contribution of some thousands to his superiors, he is again "set up in business." This vast number of Mandarins having their headquarters here gives weight and dignity to the city, and on the reception days of H. E. the Governor, the front of Yamên is crowded with the four-coolie chairs of those who come to bow and pass out without even the privilege of shaking hands.

Characteristics of the People

The people of Soochow occupy an intermediate position between the taller hardy race of the north and the short swarthy Cantonese. The "South of the River" people are not remarkable for their height or physical strength, for rice is not the food that furnishes muscle. The young scholars as a class are more like girls than men, and to look for the Grecian athlete, Soochow is not the place.

A marked characteristic of the people is their love of amusement. Though there is much bustle in the marts of trade and unceasing toil among the labouring classes, there is, on the other hand, an unfailing provision for the relaxation of tired workers and the gratification of the younger members of society. The theatres are not provided with "reserved seats," and the spectators, a compact mass, stand open-mouthed, gazing to their hearts' content and enjoying the sight of the masked actors stalking out on the stage in embroidered robes, and with wild antics and voices pitched to an unnatural key, representing imaginary characters of ancient days. One or two streets have several schools of harmony, and at weddings, funerals and the dedication of idols, choirs of boys and companies of musicians entrance their audiences with the celestial music of clashing cymbals, twanging guitars, and shrill flutes. Story-tellers

有必要在任期内空等"待命"。这一阶层官员经常会被派去边远地区担任副职，审理案件或处理当地纠纷与骚乱。苏州一共有超过2 500座官邸，包括了各级文武官员。每座官邸又有10到30位仆人，总计近40 000人，这些官员是苏州城内最为悠闲的人群，他们整日购物、吃喝，享受生活，希望有朝一日能在某个衙门内谋得一份差事。耐心是官员们最基本的素质，因为一个空缺有时需要等上两年，有时需要等上五年，哪怕是处境困难，需要靠借债度日，这些官员仍旧必须维持表面的风光，直到一个空缺出现，然后他再向上司送上一大笔贿赂，如此一来他就能够重新"开张营业"。如此众多的官员将苏州作为总部，这也增加了这座城市的分量。每逢巡抚接见日，衙门口车水马龙，挤满了四人抬的大轿，这些官员行色匆匆，相互点头致意，甚至连作揖的礼仪都顾不上了。

苏州人的特点

苏州人介于高大强壮的北方人与矮小黝黑的广东人之间。"江南人"并不以身高和力量著称，毕竟大米并不是适合肌肉生长的食物。年轻的学子看上去更像女子。要想在苏州找到像希腊运动员一样身材的人，恐怕没有那么容易。

苏州人的一个显著特征就是喜爱娱乐。尽管一方面集贸市场上一片忙碌，体力劳动者也有干不完的活儿，但另一方面，也有数不尽的娱乐活动，帮助疲惫的劳动者放松恢复，满足年轻人的需求。戏院内不"预留"座位，观众们挤成一团，站在台下，张大嘴巴，尽情地欣赏着一群戴着面具穿着绣袍的演员昂首阔步走上舞台，用滑稽的动作和夸张的声调演绎着古代人物。一两条街上就有好几家戏班，每当婚丧嫁娶及祭祀之时，戏班的男孩子们和乐队会用钹、二胡及笛子演奏出动听的音乐，让观众听得如痴如醉。说书人周围必定围着不少人，他们将历史上的逸闻趣事重新演绎，讲给听

are pretty sure to get a good crowd around, while interesting episodes in Chinese history are recounted to their listeners. "Punch and Judy" is the favourite of the youngsters and also their seniors in the open places along the streets.

The Women

There is comparatively more freedom allowed the gentler sex in this city than in other places. Those of the middle class go about the streets a great deal and visit the stores, and also at times the pleasure gardens. But the chivalry of the west, which has taken its tone from Christianity in the high place of honor it accords to woman, is utterly unknown in this country, as is seen by the men staring at a lady, and sometimes by the boisterous fun at her expense, as "she has to run the gauntlet of jeers from a crowd of rough men, all the worse to bear on account of her seclusion from all outdoor life, and as her small feet handicap her pace, her rude reception is reduced to a slow torture."It is generally estimated that five per cent of the women can read. Soochow is noted for its pretty ladies.

Another peculiar feature of the inland civilization of China, which boasts of its high church Confucianism, is seen in the fact that the gentlemen and ladies of aristocratic families will take an outing on the pleasure boats at the great festivals, and right beside them will be other boats whose occupants do not claim high respectability. Polygamy is common among the rich and noble. Suicide is a crime fearfully prevalent.

If the sky is clear and the sun past meridian—for this class do not agree with Benjamin Franklin "early to bed and early to rise"—the prominent object on the street is the Soochow dude, with his red bonnet, black satin jacket, blue silk robe, green trousers, embroidered slippers and loosely plaited queue; and his air of self-satisfaction is eminently pleasing to himself.

The number of wealthy and official families makes the feast a prominent feature of high life. The restaurants understand the art of preparing thoroughly cooked and highly seasoned dishes, and they present to the guests a variety that charms not only the celestial taste but is pleasing to the western palate; the only request the foreigner has to present is that he be allowed to take the dishes in sections during the next ten days.

众听。街上露天场所表演的木偶戏则是年轻人的最爱，同样也受到年长者的欢迎。

妇女

和其他地方相比，苏州的女性享有更大的自由。那些属于中产阶级的女性能够经常逛街，购物，有时还能游览园林。然而，这个国家的人对西方的"骑士精神"却一无所知，这种精神源自基督教，赋予了女性一种至高荣誉，但在这里，男人们会盯着一位女士看，有时会拿她开玩笑，"她不得不承受一群粗鲁男士们的嘲讽奚落，更为糟糕的是，她还要忍受与外界隔绝的生活，由于她缠的小脚令其步履维艰，她所遭受的无礼对待也就变成一种缓慢的折磨"。据估计，大约有百分之五的女性能够读书识字。苏州以出美女而著称。

中国内陆文明的另一个特征就是儒家思想所讲究的尊卑有别，下面的事实可以充分反映这一点。富贵之家的男女们会在盛大节日里乘坐游船出游，而在他们游船边上会有其他一些船只，相比之下，那些船上的乘客们的身份要低了很多。一夫多妻现象在贵族和富人中很普通。女性的自杀率相当高。

如果天气晴朗，日过三竿之后——这里的人并不认同本杰明·富兰克林所提倡的"早睡早起"——街上主要的人群就是一群游手好闲之辈，他们戴着红色包头软帽，穿着黑色绸缎的马褂，外披蓝色丝绸长袍，腿上套着绿色裤子，脚蹬绣花拖鞋，扎着松散的辫子，好一副怡然自得的模样。

苏州城内富贾和官宦人家数量众多，这也使得宴会成为他们奢华生活中的重要组成部分。饭店里的厨师们精通烹饪时令鲜蔬，他们给客人们呈上各式菜肴，不仅满足了中国人的口味，也让西方人为之拍案叫绝；外国人提出的唯一要求，就是希望能够用十天的时间慢慢品尝这些菜肴。

Profanity

Owning to the great wealth accumulated here, and to the numbers who are idle, we would naturally expect much voluptuousness and not a little looseness of morals among the gilded youth of China's Babylon, and in this respect we find the facts agree with the theory. Instead of running down the category of open sins we will single out one vice for which we think the Soochow wits are in a marked degree distinguished, and that is the ease with which they curse. Perhaps in the use of profane language they would, among all tribes and nationalities, be assigned the highest position. The most filthy, obscene, blasphemous language proceeds from their lips. They curse on the streets, in the tea-shops, and in their homes. Men curse and women curse, and the first words that infant lips pronounce are profane. Alas! For the last five-and-twenty years, foreigners have come in for their due share. In other places "foreign devil" is the style of address; here they have seven appellations which they have hurled at us seven times, as often with seven times the vehemence. Happily since the opening of the port this has improved. In other respects their conduct towards European has been in the main blameless. No placards against them have ever been posted on the walls.

There is, however, a bright side to the picture. Courteous! The inhabitants of this city are the soul of politeness! The Mandarins during the past years have done all in their power for the peace and security of the American citizens, their "foreign guests." Talented! Trained for these ages in the schools, their intellects flash as bright as a Damascus blade in the sunlight! Witty! Fond of the drama and quick at repartee, with a language capable of indefinite punning, their conversation sparkles with humor, and only one who admires a joke knows how to get on with them. In the large mercantile houses, except where it is a stranger or the uninitiated, there is scrupulous integrity to the amount of 90 per cent. In their business relations there is a marked courtesy, so that Chinese from other places say:"It is easy to transact business in Soochow."

The Language

Coming to the subject of the dialect, Mandarin is the language of China,

脏话

由于家财万贯,再加上无所事事,我们自然可以想象,在这座好比中国巴比伦的城市中,有钱的年轻人过着骄奢淫逸的生活,道德败坏,在这一点上,事实与猜想完全相符。在这里我们并不是要列出所有不当行为,而是选出其中一条,因为苏州人在这方面非常具有代表性,那就是毫不费力地说脏话。也许在说脏话方面,苏州人可以排在全世界所有部落和国家的第一位。他们的嘴里可以讲出最肮脏、最下流、最不敬的话。他们在街上骂,在茶馆里骂,在自己家里也骂。男人骂,女人也骂,婴儿开口讲的第一句话也是脏话。唉!在过去的二十五年内,外国人也成为他们咒骂的对象。在其他地方,外国人被称为"洋鬼子",但是在这里,他们却有七种方式来咒骂我们,而且咒骂的程度一次比一次过分。值得高兴的是,随着中国港口的开放,这种情况得以改善。在其他方面,他们对待欧洲人的行为总体而言并无可指责之处,墙上也从来没有贴过反对外国人的布告。

当然,苏州人也有好的一面。首先是彬彬有礼!苏州的居民就是礼貌的典范!在过去的几年里,官员们在他们职权范围内尽可能地保护美国公民——他们的"洋人朋友"——的安全。其次是才华横溢!由于在学校受过多年培训,他们的智慧就如同大马士革利剑一样,在阳光中闪耀着光芒!再次是机智幽默!他们喜欢戏剧,妙语连珠,他们的语言中富含双关,因此他们之间的对话充满了幽默的火花,只有真正喜欢幽默的人才知道如何与他们打交道。在大型商铺中,商家的诚信度高达百分之九十,除非这个老板不熟悉业务或是个门外汉。在商业合作中,他们非常注重礼仪,以至于从其他地方来这的人都说:"在苏州做生意很容易。"

语言

谈到方言,官话是中国的通用语,十八个省份中有十四个省讲官话及

as fourteen out of eighteen provinces speak it with its many variations. The exceptions are the four provinces on the coast South of the Yangtse. To the west of us is solid Mandarin. Also from Peking the Mandarin comes sweeping down to Chinkiang. At Changchow, sixty miles above here, it is a mixed dialect, but when we come to Soochow there is a complete change, —the hard speech of the north becomes as it were the soft language of the French capital. The voices of people are gentle, their notes musical, and the remarkable sweetness of the dialect may be specially noticed when the women speak. Instead of the measured tread of the Mandarin, the mellifluous Soochow is spoken with great rapidity; instead of striking at the tone of each character, the speaker has to catch the rhythm of the sentence. The Mandarin has but few particles or little words; here they are thrown in by the handful as in Xenophon's Anabasis, but the skill is in using them properly. If so, it goes far in securing an understanding of what is said, and in palliating other defects in talking. The Soochow dialect with its branches is spoken by about ten millions.

In respect to the number of its schools—for there are about 10,000, as each teacher has a half-dozen or a dozen pupils, and there are no high schools or colleges under native management with a number of preceptors — Soochow stands in the foremost rank. Some of the teachers make a comfortable support, but the rank and file, though highly appreciated, are poorly paid, or, as it is said, "They eat cold-plank bench rice." The school by its babel of sounds is heard long before it is seen; the pupil is taught that play is unscholarly and that he must talk and walk according to the rules of propriety; he studies for years in mental darkness, learning his task by memory; he says his lesson alone with his back to the teacher, and after he approaches man's height is taught to express his thoughts in this wonderful recondite literary style. A new era has recently dawned upon the youth, for the "rage for English" has taken the place of the "four books and five classics."

How the City Lies

Soochow is built in the form of a rectangle, and is about four miles from north to south, by two and a half to three in breadth, the wall being thirteen or fourteen miles in length. There are six gates. The arches are large and substantial,

其变体。长江以南的沿岸四省是例外。苏州的西面是纯正的官话区。官话从北京一路传到镇江。位于苏州北六十英里之外的常州,属于官话和方言混合区,但到了苏州,情况则完全不同了——硬邦邦的北方话变成了像法国首都巴黎式的软语。苏州人讲话声音柔和,声调富有音律,尤其是当女子讲话时,更让人感受到苏州方言的甜美。与节奏沉稳的官话不同,悦耳动听的苏州话节奏轻快;说话人要抓住整个句子的节奏,而不要求字字音调准确到位。官话中几乎没有小品词[1],然而这些词却经常出现在苏州方言中,就像出现在色诺芬的《远征记》中一样,问题在于是否能够正确使用它们。如果使用得当,将有助于理解说话内容,改善交流。目前苏州方言及其变体的使用者大约有一千万人。

就学校数量而言——苏州有近 10 000 所学校,排名第一。每位老师有 6 到 12 位学生,但这里却没有当地人管理的师资充足的高中和大学。一些老师的薪酬很高,但对普通老师而言,尽管他们受到别人尊重,然而薪酬却很低,正如人们所说,"他们吃的是'坐冷板凳'的饭"。学校的喧闹声远远就能听见;学校教导学生玩乐会影响学业,学生的言行举止必须符合礼仪规范。学生要在精神世界的黑暗中摸索多年,通过背诵来学习;他要背对着老师单独背诵他所学的内容,等他长大成人后,老师会教他用艰深的文体表达他的思想。最近,在年轻人中出现了一种新趋势,他们开始争先恐后地学习英语,取代之前的"四书五经"。

古城样貌

苏州城整体呈长方形,从北至南大约长四英里,东西宽二点五到三英里,城墙全长十三到十四英里。苏州城内共有六道城门。这些拱门高大结实,

---

[1] 小品词是语言中一种形似介词的副词。这是一类比较特殊的词,它既有副词的某些特征,又具有介词的词形。它往往与前面的动词形成修饰和补充说明的语义关系,本身不能单独充当句子成分。

and there is an outside wall enclosing a half acre, this also with its gate, so the entrance is doubly secure. The towers above may be seen at a distance, and remind one of Bible scenes in Palestine. The wall is over 30 feet high and faced with large brick $18 \times 8 \times 2$ inches, and has its bastions for cannon and port-holes for musketry. The interior is of dirt, like a railway embankment, and about fifteen feet thick on top. The walk on this parapet, with the hills, lakes, fields and city all in sight, is a splendid one. Outside of each gate there is a suburb; the largest, three miles in length, a city itself of 100,000, lying north-west of the Chang Men. The next in size outside the West Gate has 30,000 people. Many hongs are located in these sections, and a busy trade is carried on. By its proximity to the concession, the Pan Men suburb sprung up almost in a night.

The Streets

Within the gate we find ourselves in a Chinese street. What is a street? The European would answer: "A broad thoroughfare with rows of tall houses on either side, and rows of trees, —the side-walks for men, and the road for horses." How differently a native lexicographer would define the word. Wu Tsze Sü laid out the city with streets eight feet wide, but shopmen put their counters and railing forward, so on the main streets the space is narrowed to five or six feet. In the mornings the markets are along the streets, so that near the bridge rows of fish-tubs and vegetable baskets line the crowded alleys. Along those narrow defiles pass riders on horses, Mandarins in chairs with their official retinues, funeral processions a quarter of a mile long, workmen carrying the framework of a building, chair-bearers, burden-bearers, loads of straw, men with bundles and women with baskets, the aged tottering on a staff, and the blind feeling their way with a cane, the water-carrier with quick step, and the scholar with the snail's pace, —you wonder how you can thread your way through this tangled thicket of pedestrians. The streets are paved with small stones, raised in the centre, and in the rainy season are very slippery. A few are laid with flag-stones, as the Yang Yoh Hong, —this pavement being put down by a widow as a monument to her husband. The drains are eight or ten inches deep and are often filled with the mud

拱门外又有一道外墙围住半英亩[1]土地，外墙上同样也建有大门，如此一来入口就变得双倍安全。城墙上的塔楼远处可见，这不禁令人想起《圣经》中描写巴勒斯坦的场景。外墙高达30多英尺[2]，正对着由18英寸×8英寸×2英寸大砖建起的城门，墙上建有火炮炮垒及火枪枪眼。城墙内部为泥土结构，就像铁路护堤，顶部厚约十五英尺。走在护墙上，远处的山峦、湖泊、田地和城市尽收眼底，美不胜收。每道城门外边都是郊区；最大的一片长三英里，有100 000人，自成一城，位于阊门西北部。其次是在西门外，有30 000人。许多商行就位于这些地区，生意兴隆。由于靠近租界，盘门郊区几乎是在一夜之间兴起。

街道

走进城门，我们发现自己站在一条中国街道上。什么是街道？欧洲人会回答："一条宽阔的大道，两边高屋林立、树木成排——人行道供行人行走，道路供马匹奔跑。"然而，中国的词典编纂者对街道一词的定义却与之大相径庭。伍子胥建城之时将街道宽度设为八英尺，然而商铺的店主们却将自家柜台和围栏前移至街面，导致主街道的宽度缩减到五到六英尺。每日清晨，沿街都是集市，靠近桥边的一排排鱼缸和菜篮让小巷变得拥挤不堪。即便如此，骑马者、坐着轿子的官员及随从、蜿蜒四分之一英里长的送葬队伍、扛着建筑材料的工人、抬轿者、挑担者、推着一车车稻草的人、背着包袱的男人、拎着篮子的女人、拄着拐杖蹒跚而行的老人、摸索前行的盲人、疾行的挑水工，还有踱着四方步的文人也从这些拥挤的小巷中经过——你甚至怀疑他是怎么穿过如此拥挤的人群的。街道是用小碎石铺设而成，中间略微凸起，雨季路面会非常湿滑。也有一部分街道是用大石块

---

［1］ 英美制地积单位，1英亩合4 046.86平方米。
［2］ 英美制长度单位，1英尺等于12英寸，合0.304 8米。

swept from the shop doors. Piles of rubbish accumulate at the corners, but in the depth of winter they are comparatively free from unpleasant odors. As a stranger at the port remarked: "Oh! You live in Soochow. I have heard it is a fine city. It must be a nice place to live in." Visitors pronounce this a very clean Chinese city.

Houses

The magnificent churches, the stately edifices, the superb mansions with brown stone fronts, are all wanting in a native town, and in their stead we see row after row of shanty-like buildings. The houses are usually painted black, and are built upon stones driven down into the earth by huge wooden pestles, and upon these are laid large pieces of granite. Upon the side streets the stone-work reaches several feet above the ground. In building the better class of houses—and there are some which cost $100,000—large sums are expended on driving down piles before the granite slabs are laid upon them, yet on the street the mansions of the rich appear as humble as the homes of the shopkeeper. The houses consist of a series of rows of buildings with courts between for the sunshine and the rain. In front are small rooms for the entrance and porter's lodge, within is the reception hall, the front side consisting of long windows, and a very pretty system of king and queen posts has been contrived by which the weight of several beams is transmitted to the central pillars which sustain the heavy roof. In the rear are the sleeping apartments, mostly upstairs, as the ground floor is paved with tiles. The shops have the entire front open, the sign-boards hanging perpendicularly, and, as many of these are gilded, it gives the street an appearance highly ornamental. The street in front of the City Temple, with its fine display of embroidery, fans, rugs, ivory, silver-ware and foreign goods, is the handsomest in the city.

The quiet, peaceable dispositions of the people may be known by the fact that there are no police on the streets, whereas Chicago, which is one-third larger than Soochow, pays annually a million and a half dollars to her municipal force. Each of the five wards has a police-office, where a " Justice of the Peace " administers corporal punishment for minor offences—principally to the constables, the protectors of the peace, for allowing thefts in their precincts. A new-comer who

铺成，例如养育巷——这条街道是一位寡妇为纪念其亡夫而出资铺设的。下水道在地面八到十英寸以下，里面积满了从店铺门口冲下的污泥。垃圾堆积在角落里，但在隆冬季节并没有散发出难闻的气味。正如港口的一位路人所言："噢！你住在苏州。我听说那是一个不错的城市，那里一定非常适合居住。"游客们都认为苏州是一个非常干净的中国城市。

房屋

宏伟的教堂、壮观的建筑、带有褐色影壁的超级大厦都是中国本土城市所缺少的，代替它们的是一排排简陋的小木屋。这些屋子通常漆成黑色，建在石头上，这些石头被巨型木杵压入地下，上面还铺着一块块巨大的花岗岩。在小街道上，石雕高出地面好几英尺。在建造质量较好的房屋时——有些造价高达100 000美元——要先花一大笔钱打桩，然后再铺设花岗岩石板，不过，在街上，富商家的宅邸和店主的房子看上去一样简陋。这些宅邸由一排排的建筑物构成，这些建筑物中间有庭院，利于采光和走水。宅邸前面是入口和门房，往里是会客厅，厅的正面是一排长窗，厅内那些雕龙刻凤的柱子构成了一个精妙结构，通过它们，厅内横梁的重量被传递到中心支柱上，这些中心支柱撑起了沉重的屋顶。后面是卧室，大部分都在楼上，一楼的地面上铺着地砖。店铺整个正面都是敞开的，店牌悬垂高挂，由于许多招牌都是镀金的，这也让整条街看上去更具观赏性。玄妙观前的街道是苏州城内最漂亮的，这里随处可见精美的刺绣、扇子、地毯、象牙、银器和洋货。

苏州人性格平和、文静，大街上没有警察就充分印证了这一点。而在比苏州大三分之一的芝加哥，每年花在警力上的费用就高达一百五十万美元。在苏州每五个区有一个警察局，"治安法官"可以对轻微的渎职行为实施体罚——主要是对乡村治安官未能有效控制辖区内盗窃发生而实施体

did not like the behaviour of the throng in the afternoon at the City Temple asked, "What resource has a man in a crowd like this?" and was answered, "To get out of it."

No Ancient Ruins

There are no ancient ruins in the city. The local history tells us of many famous buildings which were the pride of the people in the centuries gone by, yet their walls were not built of hewn stone, as in Athens and Rome, so as to withstand the ravages of ages, but only of crumbling brick and of wood fancifully carved, which after a conflagration had swept away a block, or a destructive rebellion had drawn its ploughshare through the streets, preserve nothing to tell the tale of their former glory, save the decapitated and mutilated stone lions.

The Venice of the Orient

It has been said that there are more boats in China than in all the rest of the world put together, and truly Soochow claims her share of boats, long and short, large and small, broad and narrow, and here every facility is enjoyed for plying these crafts, which sit on the water like ducks. Around the city wall, within and without, there is a moat. The one outside is from fifty to a hundred yards wide and very deep, and in the recapture of the city from the T'aipings it formed a serious obstacle to storming the walls. Within the city there are, generally speaking, six canals from north to south, and six canals from east to west, intersecting one another at from a quarter to half a mile, or, all told, about thirty miles of canals within the city. There are a hundred and fifty or two hundred bridges at intervals of two or three hundred yards, some of these with arches, others with stone slabs thrown across, many of which are twenty feet in length. The canals are from ten to fifteen feet wide and faced with stone. In them are moored hundreds of quick pleasure boats, which, with their bright varnish, clear glass and fine carving, furnish little floating Pullmans to those who wish to go to the hills or the lakes. There are for hire thousands of uncovered boats which transport grain,

罚。一位新来者不喜欢玄妙观午后拥挤的人群,他问道:"面对如此拥挤的人群有什么办法?"得到的答案是:"自己离开。"

无古代遗迹

这座城市里没有古代遗迹。当地的历史告诉我们,在过去的几百年里,苏州有很多人们引以为豪的著名建筑。不过,这些建筑的墙体并不像雅典和罗马的城墙一样用巨型大石砌成,可以承受岁月的蹂躏。这些墙体只是用碎砖和精美雕刻的木头建成,当大火肆虐、战乱席卷过后,只剩下被砍了头和手脚的石狮子,再也没有什么留下来可以向后人讲述这座城市之前的辉煌。

东方威尼斯

据说中国的船要比世界其他地方的所有船都要多,的确,苏州船的数量不少,有长有短,有大有小,有宽有窄,在这里每一处设施都能让你方便使用这些船只,这些船就如同浮在水上的鸭子一样。城墙内外都有护城河。城墙外的护城河宽五十到一百码,河水很深。在从太平军手中夺回苏州城的激战中,这条护城河给攻击方攻占城门造成了很大障碍。苏州城内,总体而言,从北到南有六条河道,从西到东也有六条河道,在四分之一英里到半英里的范围内纵横交错,整个城市的河道大约有三十英里。苏州城内一共有一百五十到两百座桥,每座桥之间相隔两百码到三百码,有些桥带有拱门,有些桥则是用石板横跨两岸,很多桥只有二十英尺长。河道宽十到十五英尺,两边都是石头。河道内停泊着数百条快船,这些船色泽明亮,船上窗明几净,船身雕刻精美,为那些想上山下湖的游客提供了一间流动的豪华包厢。河道上还有数千条无篷船待租,这些船可以将粮食、商品、燃料、建筑材料、家具和水从城市的一头运送到另一头,也可以从一百英

goods, fuel, building materials, furniture, water, etc. from one end of the city to the other. Goods may be brought from one hundred miles and delivered at the door. Also the canals are a great convenience for laundry and culinary purposes, and favourite channels for Asiatic cholera. When the waters are high and fresh, boating is a pleasant mode of travelling for a family, but when the water turns green and then black, and melon rinds and garbage float on the surface, and the boats get jammed for a couple of hours amidst odors, not from "Araby the blest," the poor shut-in prisoner wishes he were ten thousand miles away from the Oriental Venice. Near the concession are several lakes whose peaceful waters will afford fine opportunities for the Rowing Club.

The Pagodas

The seven Pagodas in and around the city are the ornaments of Soochow. The Methuselah is the South Gate Pagoda, built A.D. 248, aged 1,650 years, nearly twice as old as the Antediluvian. We were once asked "How we knew this?" The reply was that "Fan Fen Chen Kung, the historian, who lived 900 years ago, said so, and it is supposable that he had access to trustworthy documents that gave this date." The Tiger Hill Pagoda stands second in rank among the Patriarchs; built A.D. 600 it is aged 1,300 years, or nearly one and one-half the age of Jared. The Twin Pagodas, Seth and Enos, were erected about A.D. 1000, and are 900 years old. The Great Pagoda, built A.D. 1160, has worn its crown for seven centuries. The Ink Pagoda is quite in its youth—it is only 300 years of age.

The venerable monument of antiquity at the South Gate, which bears upon its lofty head the weight of sixteen and one-half centuries, was much injured by the T'aipings. Twenty years ago Governor Wu headed a subscription with Tls. 10,000 for repairing the Pagoda. After about Tls. 50,000 had been expended, and its spiral crown blown down by a typhoon, the work was abandoned. The erection of the scaffolding is said to have cost $10,000.

里以外的地方购买货物然后将其运到家门口。同时，河道也为民众洗衣做饭提供了极大便利，不过，河道也是亚洲霍乱[1]传播的一个重要渠道。当水位很高，河水清澈之时，全家人坐船是一种愉快的旅行方式；但当河水变绿之后泛黑，河面上漂浮着瓜皮和垃圾，船只被堵在臭气熏天的河道里好几个钟头，坐在船舱中可怜的乘客是多么希望此刻他能远离这个"东方威尼斯"。靠近租界的几面湖水面平静，可以为划船俱乐部提供很好的活动场所。

塔

苏州城内和周边的七座塔点缀着这座城市。建成时间最久的是南门瑞光塔，建于公元248年，至今已有1 650年，其年代之古老几乎是《圣经》中所记载的大洪水之前的上古时代的两倍。有人曾问："我们是怎么知道的？"答案是："生活在900年前的范文正公这样说的，据说他是看到了确切的文件记载而给出了这个时间。"在这些塔中，虎丘塔排名第二，该塔建于公元600年，距今1 300年，几乎是雅列[2]年纪的1.5倍。双塔约建于公元1000年，已有900年历史。北寺塔，建于公元1160年，700年来被誉为苏州"塔中之冠"。相比之下，墨塔[3]显得较为年轻——仅有300年历史。

瑞光塔，这座位于南门的古塔，其高耸的塔顶已承载了1 650年的风雨，遭到了太平军的严重破坏。二十年前，吴巡抚带头集资10 000两白银用以重修瑞光塔。然而，在花费了50 000两白银之后，该塔的螺旋顶冠被台风吹倒，修复工程亦随之停工。据说，光搭建脚手架就花费了10 000美元。

---

[1] 此处应为"霍乱"，因此病长久以来，多见于亚洲印度等地，并经常向外扩散引起多次世界性大流行，故曾一度被西方人称为"亚洲霍乱"。2015年5月，世界卫生组织发布了《新人类传染病命名的最佳实践》，明确规定，在疾病名称中应当避免使用包括地理方位、人名、动物或食物种群，涉及文化、人口、工业或职业的内容，以及有可能引起过度恐慌的术语。

[2] 雅列，《圣经》中的人物。据《圣经·创世记》5章18—20节记载，雅列共活了962岁。

[3] 即文星阁，又称方塔，位于苏州大学校园内。

The Tiger Hill Pagoda is built near the grave of Hoh Lü, our first Soochow king. According to history, 600,000 men were employed to prepare his grave and attend the funeral. This Pagoda is the "leaning tower" of Soochow. It is much out of the perpendicular, and seems to have been so from time immemorial. From this knoll, which takes its name from the story that three days after Hoh Lü's death a white tiger was seen crouching near the grave, a fine view of the city is obtained, stretching as it does, including the suburbs, seven miles to the southeast. There is a pool on the hill, fifty feet long by twenty wide, called the "Sword Pool," where it is said Shi Hwangti whetted his sword when he attempted to slay the tiger and rob the grave of Hoh Lü. The flat rock beside the pool is called the "Thousand Men Rock," as it is supposed that number can stand on it at one time. Near by it is the "Nodding Rock." "It is related in the history that on one occasion, when a noted Buddhist missionary was expounding the law to the people, so eloquently did he preach that a stone in front of the temple nodded to the priest in recognition of the power of his oratory."

The Twin Pagodas, standing near the Examination Hall, and exerting a fine influence upon the aspiring genius of the candidates for literary honors, are models of architectural beauty, and seem, as a pair, to be unique among China's towers. The tradition is that some centuries ago it was found that the fung-shuy was not good. A professor, skilled in determining the influences of the wind and water, was called in. "Why," said he, "do you not see these Pagodas are like pencils (pens); of what use is a pen without ink?" and so the Ink Pagoda was built, — a large black tower about twenty-five feet square and 120 feet high.

The Great Pagoda

The glory of the capital is the Great Pagoda, the highest in China, and so the highest on terra firma. Stand near it and behold one of the great wonders of the world! Count the stories, note the verandahs, see the doors, as so many pigeon-holes, and men as pigmies on those giddy heights! Consider the foundation, and what a quarry of hewn stone supports that mighty pile of masonry, which, including its spiral crown, rises to nearly 250 feet in height. Walk around the base, which, with the shed room on the ground floor, is one hundred feet in

虎丘塔就建在吴国定都苏州后第一个国君阖闾的墓边上。据历史记载，共有60万民工被征调过来为阖闾造墓并参加了他的葬礼。这座塔是苏州的"斜塔"，它偏离中垂线很多，似乎从造好之日起就是如此。虎丘这个名字源自一个故事，据说在阖闾死后三日，有一只白虎伏在他的墓旁，故而得名。从虎丘上远眺，整座城市包括延伸至东南七英里的郊区一览无余，风光尽收眼底。虎丘山上有一个叫作剑池的水池，长五十英尺，宽二十英尺。据说秦始皇曾在这里磨剑，准备杀虎并挖掘阖闾之墓。剑池附近有一块扁平的大石，称为"千人石"，据说一次可同时站立一千人在上面。"千人石"附近是"点头石"。"这与一段历史有关。据说，一位著名的得道高僧曾在这讲经说法，这位高僧滔滔不绝，以至于寺庙前面的一块石头向他点头，认可其宣讲。"

双塔，是建筑史上精美作品的典范，作为成对的塔，双塔在中国的塔楼中也是独一无二的。双塔矗立在贡院附近，这给渴望金榜题名的考生们带来极为不利的影响。据传，几百年前，人们发现这里的风水不是很好，因此请来了一位善看风水的先生，"为什么，"他问，"你们没有发现这两座塔就像笔一样；有笔无墨则有何用？"因此，后来又造了一座墨塔——一座黑色高塔，大约占地二十五平方英尺，高一百二十英尺。

北寺塔

北寺塔是苏州的荣耀，它是中国最高的一座塔[1]，同时也是陆地上最高的一座塔。站在塔边，抬头仰望着这世上伟大的奇迹！数一数这塔上的楼层，看一看塔上的廊道，看到塔上的门就像许多鸽子洞，而站在塔里的人就像站在云端的小矮人。仔细看一下塔基，这是一块多么巨大的石头才能支撑住如此高大的建筑，塔顶呈螺旋状，高达近二百五十英尺。塔的

---

[1] 天宁宝塔为中国最高的佛塔。杜步西误。

diameter or one hundred yards around. Note the images in *basso relievo* among the clouds, carved on the stones, seated upon the roof, hiding in the niches, and sitting majestic upon the shrines; Buddhist gods inside and Brahman divinities without—two hundred in number,—it is a high temple of heathenism. The name of the Sir Christopher Wren who planned this tower has not come down to us, but we can admire the skill of the master hand which drew the lines. The walls are octagonal, one wall within and one without, or a pagoda within a pagoda, each wall ten feet thick, the steps rising between them by easy gradations with a walk around before the next flight is reached, the floors being paved with brick two feet square. There are eight doors to each of the nine stories, and, with the cross passages, the halls are full of light. And what wonderful proportions—sixty feet in diameter at the base, it tapers to forty-five feet on the upper floor; each story slightly lower as you ascend, each door smaller, each verandah narrower. Walk around these porches; see the city lying at your feet; the Dragon Street running south to the Confucian Temple; the busy north-west gate; the pile of buildings constituting the City Temple; the Great Lake to the west; the range of hills and the picturesque pagodas that crown the jutting eminences; the plain dotted every fourth mile with hamlets. See the pagoda to the south,—it marks the city of Wukiang. Follow the Shanghai canal glistening in the sunlight to the east till your eye rests on a hill,—that is Quensan. At the foot of that mountain, thirty miles to the north-east, is Changsoh, a city of 100,000 inhabitants. Look north-west up the Grand Canal, thirty miles—that is Mount Wei'tsien. There is Wusih, with a population of 150,000, and within this radius of thirty miles are one hundred market towns of from one thousand to fifty thousand inhabitants and probably 100,000 villages and hamlets——five millions within the range of vision!

The City Temple

The centre of pagan worship in the Kiangsu province is the Uön Miao Kwan or City Temple, which is under the control of the Taoists. The first building was

直径约一百英尺，绕着塔基走一圈，圆周约一百码，塔内底层有一间储藏室。留意浮雕上的云纹图案，有的刻在石头上，有的刻在屋顶上，有的隐藏在壁龛中，有的则在庄严的神龛上。塔内陈列佛教众神像，塔外供奉婆罗门教神灵——共有两百个——这是一个异教信仰的寺庙。尽管我们并不清楚该塔的设计者是谁，但我们却惊叹于这位大师在处理线条时所展现出的精湛技艺。塔身呈八边形，共有两层墙，一墙在内，一墙在外，形成塔内有塔，每道墙厚十英尺，尽管如此，在到达下一段楼梯之前，游客也可以轻松地绕着两墙之间的台阶走一圈，地面铺着二英尺见方的砖块。北寺塔共九层，每层塔上均有八扇门，这些交错的通道令整个厅内光线充足。整座塔的比例是多么奇妙啊——塔基直径六十英尺，每层逐级缩减，顶层直径为四十五英尺；当你每登上一层就会发现要比前一层略微矮一些，每扇门也小一些，每条廊道也窄一些。绕着塔上的门廊走一圈，可以看到整座城市都在你脚下，向南延伸至文庙的护龙街[1]、繁忙的西北城门、玄妙观内成排的建筑、西边的太湖、延绵的群山及立于山顶的古塔，每隔四英里就有一处村庄点缀在平原上。向南可以看见一座宝塔——它是吴江城的标志。顺着流向上海方向的河道往东远眺，河面在阳光照耀下波光粼粼，直到你的视线停留在一座山上——那就是昆山。在昆山的山脚下东北三十英里处就是常熟，一个拥有十万居民的城市。朝大运河西北方向看，三十英里处就是惠山。还有无锡，人口十五万，在半径为三十英里的范围内有一百个集镇。每个集镇人口从一千到五万不等，大约共有十万村民——整个视野范围内共有五百万人口。

玄妙观

江苏省异教徒[2]朝拜的中心是苏州的玄妙观，这是一个道观。玄妙观

---

[1] 今人民路。
[2] 此处指非基督教教徒。

erected about A. D. 300, so heathen ceremonies have been conducted on this spot for sixteen centuries. There are two main temples with thirteen other temples on the right, left and in the rear, a city of the gods, where five or six hundred are assembled to be worshipped. Among the larger groups are the sixty cycle gods, with cocks, squirrels, rats and snakes (Minerva like) rising from their craniums, "images of corruptible man, and of birds, and four-footed beasts and creeping things;" the seventy-two doctors or teachers, the fifty-six star deities and the thirty-six ministers of Heaven, these "sedate, hideous imbecilities which do duty as Chinese idols." From all parts of the country deputations come to engage in peace and thanksgiving services; besides, here is the gate of Tartarus, where the affair of the dead can best be transacted. The Soochowites often speak of Heaven as "just like the City Temple." The late Banker Hu, of Hangchow, gave $40,000 or $50,000 for its repair, but he went into bankruptcy before the work was completed. The temple to the "Three Pure Ones" has large pillars to support the massive roof, and the three gods, seated upon pedestals fifteen feet high, to add dignity to their appearance, were several years in construction. The bronze censer in the court is over twenty feet in height. The temple in the rear, three stories high, with its roof ornamented with green glazed tiles and twisting dragons, a tangled mass of Asiatic glory, has been pronounced the finest temple in mid-China. The central figure on the lower floor is the Pearly Empress, the Ruler of Earth and the wife of the King of Heaven, who, with her four female servants, is almost veiled from sight, for a mythology which includes " Juno," is rather too prosaic for the Confucianist. On the upper floor, where sits the ruler of gods and men, the gilded throne, the handsome shrines, the ornate decorations, and the rows of gods, are such as to impress the heathen imagination with ideas of the majestic.

  The temple grounds are the central attraction for pleasure-seekers. There are mat sheds for the hundreds who drink tea, toy shops and stands for the sale of porcelain, confectionery and trinkets of various kinds. Beggars frequent these sacred precincts, so do thieves and pickpockets and all the riff-raff of the city, as well as the "lewd fellows of the baser sort "—in actual fact it is "a den of thieves."There are peep-shows and puppet shows, bear shows and rope dancers, jugglers and sleight-of-hand performers,— truly a "Vanity Fair".

里的第一个建筑大约建于公元300年，因此，十六个世纪以来，异教徒的各种庆祝活动都在这里举行。玄妙观内有两个主殿，另有十三个配殿分布在左、右两边及后面。玄妙观也是一个众神之城，五六百位神仙聚集于此供世人朝拜。其中较大的几组神仙有六十花甲星宿，这些神仙的头顶上有公鸡、松鼠、老鼠及蛇（就像古罗马女神密涅瓦一样），"其形象有人，有鸟，有四足兽和爬行动物"；有七十二圣贤、五十六星君和三十六天罡，这些"神情肃穆、面目可憎、呆头呆脑的家伙们却在中国以偶像的身份获得百姓朝拜"。来自全国各地的代表团来玄妙观参加祈福和感恩活动；此外，这里是通往阴间之门，也是处理与死人相关事务的最佳场所。苏州人提到"天堂"时经常说"就像玄妙观一样"。杭州一位已故的姓胡的银行家，曾出资40 000到50 000美元，用以修复玄妙观，然而，在完工之前他却破产了。"三清殿"内立着很多高大的柱子支撑着整个屋顶。三尊神像端坐在高达十五英尺的神坛上，这也让神像显得更加威严。这三尊神像是很多年前建造的。殿内的青铜香炉高二十余英尺。位于"三清观"后面的弥罗宝阁有三层楼高，屋顶覆盖着绿色的琉璃瓦并配以代表亚洲荣耀的盘龙装饰，这个殿也被誉为华中地区最好的道观。弥罗宝阁底层中间安置的是王母娘娘神像，她是玉皇大帝的妻子，负责统管人间。她和四位侍女的面容几乎不为人所知，因为，包括娘娘在内的神话传说，对儒家学子而言过于平淡无奇。弥罗宝阁的顶层安放的是众神和人类的统治者，镀金的宝座、精美的神龛、华丽的装饰，以及一排排的神仙，这一切足以给人留下极为深刻的华美印象。

　　玄妙观殿外的场地是苏州城内的主要娱乐场所。这里有可供数百人喝茶的草棚，有玩具店，有卖瓷器、糖果和各类小装饰品的摊铺。乞丐经常出现在这片区域，此外还有窃贼、扒手、整个城里的混混及市井之徒——事实上，这里可是"窃贼的窝点"。在这里还可以看西洋镜、木偶剧、马戏、走钢丝表演、魔术和杂耍——是一个真正的"大千世界"。

Art Gallery

Around the large building in front is the famous picture gallery of the city, with pictures of gods and goddesses, mountain and trees, gardens and flowers, ladies and children, tigers and birds, some in gilt and all in bright colors, —"fine specimens," a fair young amateur pronounced them, "of decorative art." Height usually represents distance in a Chinese painting; that is to say, distant objects are put at the top of the picture and nearer objects below them, while but little difference is made in the size. Great attention is paid to painting the Mandarins' robes. With a Chinese artist, " the presentation of a living, feeling soul revealed in its index, the face, sinks into utter insignificance in comparison with the external advantages of rank and fortune." The pictures which seem to please the Chinese most are impossible mountains, chaotic masses of rock, and trees denuded of their foliage,—all dashed off with India ink. With the birds they are quite successful. They study carefully the attitudes and the passions of which attitudes are the signs, and thus represent the feathery tribe. With flowers they seem instinctively to know how to apply the colors, at once so delicate and so brilliant.

The Cheu Wang Miao (Jade Stone Temple) is near the northwest gate. Here are sold in the forenoon cat's-eyes and jade ornaments. With its noise and bustle and scores of importunate salesmen, the visitor finds it a regular pandemonium. The temple, where the punishments of the lower world are to be seen, is not far from the South Gate. There are, all told, from two hundred to three hundred temples and from fifty to one hundred nunneries in the city. The Taoist priests number about 2,000 and the Buddhist priests about 5,000. These religions are numerically well represented within the city walls.

Beamless Temple

Near the South Gate is the Wu Liang Dien, or Beamless Temple, so called because it is arched above and below, and has no woodwork. The walls are ten feet thick and made of very large and highly polished brick, and architects have pronounced the lines very fine. The central dome is quite handsome. The

美术馆

　　玄妙观前面不远处有一座著名的美术馆,里面陈设着男女神仙图、山水树木图、园林花卉图、妇孺人物图、飞禽走兽图,有些图还镶了金边,所有的图案都色彩明亮——"精美装饰艺术的典范",这是一位年轻的业余画家对这些作品的评价。在中国画中,高度通常代表了距离;换句话说,远处的物体应该位于画的上方,近处的物体则要置于画的底部,但远近物体的尺寸却没有太大区别。在画官员袍子时需要特别注意。对中国画家而言,"一个活生生的人物形象主要是通过其外在标志展现的,人物的脸,与其显露出的地位与财富相比,就显得一点也不重要了"。中国人最喜爱的画大多是群山、乱石和秃树——都可以用印度墨一蹴而就。在画鸟方面中国人是相当成功的。他们仔细研究鸟的姿态以及每个姿态所代表的情绪,他们的技法也代表了翎毛画派。在画花方面,他们似乎本能地知道如何配色,可以瞬间令整幅画变得精致亮丽。

　　周王庙(玉石庙)位于苏州西北城门附近。上午这里有卖猫眼和玉器装饰品的摊贩。嘈杂声、喧闹声再加上几十个纠缠不休的小贩,游客们会发现这里经常混乱不堪。庙离南城门并不远,据说在那里可以看到阴间的各种惩罚。苏州城内一共有庙宇、道观两百到三百间,尼姑庵五十至一百间。道教徒大约两千人,而佛教徒大约五千人。这两个宗教在苏州城内的发展从上述的数字中可以得到很好地体现。

无梁殿

　　无梁殿位于南城门附近。之所以叫无梁殿,是因为该殿上下拱门均不用木构梁柱。殿墙厚十英尺,由大块磨砖砌成,在建筑师看来线条精细美观。中央的穹顶相当漂亮。这座建筑物颇具异国风味,是一座具有防火

building has a foreign appearance and was designed as the fire-proof archives for the sacred books of Buddhism. All the cornices and ornamental work are of the most beautiful description, and as it is different from any Chinese building, it is probable the model was brought from the land of the "Heavenly Bamboo." As near as has been ascertained, it is about 800 years old; some of the neighbors say it was built by the celebrated artisan gods, Lu Pan and Chang Pan, and some of the priests think it might have been erected during the fabulous reign of the Five Emperors.

Confucian Temple

In the southern part of Soochow is the park, surrounded by a high wall, which contains the group of buildings called the Confucian Temple. This is the dragon's head; —the Dragon Street, running directly north is his body, and the great pagoda is his tail. In front is a grove of cedars ornamented with monumental slabs, each several tons in weight and sitting upon the backs of tortoises. To the west is a second avenue with buildings on either side which runs directly to the hall where the rehearsals are held on the days previous to the sacrifice.

The first large building opposite the gateway contains astronomical diagrams and mural tablets, placed there centuries ago, and in the long halls on either side of the courtyard are the tablets of the great men of the nation whose names are worthy to be enrolled in the Chinese Academy. In the temple in the rear five generations of Confucius' forefathers, who are honored with the title of "kings," are worshipped sacrificially.

The Sacrifice

The "Temple of Literature," 100 × 70 feet, with its massive double roof, is in appearance the most venerable building in Kiangsu. In front is a stone *dais* of about the same size as the temple, surrounded by a marble balustrade, and, at the spring and autumn sacrifices, over this is erected a large tent with a curving zinc roof. The Confucian Ritual gives a most minute account of how the services should be conducted. Every tap of bell or drum, or note of steel or string instrument, is prescribed most accurately, and any deviation would destroy the harmony which is an essential element in their "divine worship."Upon the large

功能的藏经阁，用来收藏佛教经书。所有的飞檐和装饰物均精美绝伦，因为其外表有别于中国建筑，很有可能是来自"天竺"的式样。据查，无梁殿距今已有大约八百年历史，周边一些邻居说该殿是由著名的工匠之祖鲁班和他的弟子张半所建，也有一些教徒认为该殿是在五帝统治的神话时代所建。

文庙

在苏州南部有一所庭院，高墙围绕，内有一群建筑，叫作文庙。文庙所处位置是龙头——朝北的卧龙街是龙的身躯，而北寺塔则是龙尾。文庙前方是一片雪松林和巨型石碑林，每块石碑都重达数吨，矗立在石龟身上。西面的第二条大道直通大厅，道路两边都有建筑，祭祀前几日的彩排都是在大厅内举行。

入口对面的第一座大厅内有天文图和壁画石碑，已有数百年历史。院子两边的长廊中立着不少名人的石碑，他们的名字都应该留存在中国的学术史上。在大殿的后方列着孔子五代祖先的牌位，他们也被尊称为"王"，接受奉祀。

祭祀

"大成殿"，面积约100英尺×70英尺，重檐飞宇，是江苏省内最为古朴庄重的建筑。殿前有一石台，尺寸大小几乎与大成殿一样，周围是大理石护栏。在春秋两季祭祀大典之际，主办方会在台上搭一个带有曲形锌制屋顶的大帐篷。儒家的礼仪对如何举行祭祀有着极为详细的描述。钟、鼓的每一次敲击，钢制乐器或弦乐器发出的每一个音都有严格精确的规定，任何一点偏差都会影响和谐，这也是整个"神圣祭拜"中最为重要

frames under the tent hang bells and triangle steel instruments, and upon the tablets lie the zithers. Long red candles burn in front of the shrines, and at the tap of the great drum, bonfires are kindled on the tripods, so that at dawn the grounds are lit up with the brilliancy of noonday. In front of the sage's royal tablet kneels a bull with his throat cut, his shaggy hair all besmeared with the mud which he brought from the fields, and close beside him crouch a sheep and a pig. Twenty-one pairs of sheep and pigs lie before the tablets of the sages.

At the appointed time, the Governor, who is called "The Sacrificial Lord," or "True Worshipper," with the high provincial magnates all in court dress, which consists of a red tasselled cover for the hat, a shoulder cape of gold thread, and a heavily embroidered skirt, takes his stand under the tent in front, and at the successive calls of the "Chief Praise Leader," five times enters the sacred temple. At the call "Worship," he kneels; "Prostrate the head," he bows; "Mount the incense," he raises his hands; "Return to your place," he follows the leader back to the tent. As he kneels before the shrine, sticks of lighted incense, fruits and viands, libations of wine in the sacrificial cups, and rolls of white silk with the government stamp, are passed by one attendant to the other. The whole service is intoned; the Musical Professor by a word directing his attendants in every sound of the instruments and tap of the bells, which are arranged in perfect order. The music is soft and sweet, and as the devout chant of the prayers is mingled with the gentle notes of the guitar, the effect is very solemn.

At the opening of the ceremonies, the presence of the divine spirit of the sage is invoked: " O, Confucius, how great art thou, first in prescience, first in knowledge, the peer of Heaven and earth, the teacher of ten thousand generations, the appearance of the unicorn foretold thy good fortune; with the harmony of music [we invite thee], the sun and moon so bright, and Heaven and earth clear and still." Afterwards the "Sacrificial Lord" takes his position in the centre of the hall, and the "prayer of blessing" is read, and at each return from the temple to the tents the civil and military officials make nine or twelve devout prostrations, adoring the Literary Prince of ages past and millenniums to come, by whose kind aid they have risen to posts both honorable and lucrative. At the close of the high service, the divine spirit is requested to return to its invisible and unknown resting-place.

的一个元素。帐篷内的架子上挂着编钟和三角形的钢制乐器，石碑上也放着弦琴。大红蜡烛在神龛前燃起，随着隆隆鼓声，堆在三角祭台上的篝火被点燃，清晨的地面被火光照得犹如正午般光亮。一头公牛跪在圣人的御碑前，它的喉咙已被割破，乱蓬蓬的毛发上沾满了田间的泥土，公牛边上还蜷伏着一只羊和一头猪。在众圣人石碑前一共供着二十一对猪羊。

到祭祀之时，巡抚，此时又称为"主祭"或"真正的朝拜者"，率领省内官员，身着由红色流苏帽、金线披肩和刺绣下摆组成的朝服，站在帐篷前，在"司仪"的不断召唤下，五次进入大殿。听到"敬拜"，祭祀者跪下；听到"俯首"，祭祀者弯腰鞠躬；听到"上香"，祭祀者举起双手；听到"归位"，祭祀者随着主祭退回帐篷。当祭祀者跪在神殿前，点燃的香、祭祀用的水果等食品、盛在祭祀杯中的酒，以及一卷卷盖有官府印章的白丝，从一个人手中传到另一个人手中。整个祭祀过程都是以吟诵的方式进行；祭祀的乐官通过给出一个字的指令来指挥他的乐队演奏出每一个音，敲打出每一记钟声，整个过程井井有条。音乐柔和甜美，虔诚的吟唱与柔和的琴声交织在一起，不禁令人肃穆起敬。

在祭祀活动之初，要召唤圣人神灵降临："唯吾先圣，斯世伟人，知者之先，智者之首，汝与天地同在，汝乃万世师表，麒麟兆瑞，琴瑟和谐（邀汝共听），日月同辉，天地清幽。"随后，"主祭"站在大殿中央，诵读祭文。每次当主祭从大殿返回帐篷时，文武官员都会行九拜或十二拜之礼，朝拜这位千古文学之王，保佑他们能够升官发财。在仪式的结尾，圣人的神灵被请回其安息之所。

Public Buildings

In Soochow there are ten principal Yamêns, all except two in the southwestern corner of the city. The Governor, the Provincial Treasurer, the Criminal Judge and the Superintendent of the Silk Looms reside here. They manage the affairs of 21,000,000. Besides these, the Prefect, the three County Governors, the Generals and the Chief of Police, have their respective Yamêns. If we consider the rank of the high officials and the lucrative positions they hold, their present Yamêns are better suited to the age of Arcadian simplicity than to the progressive spirit of the nineteenth century. The first step towards a high civilization must be the erection of public buildings that befit the station and honors of the great men of the capital. The courts, however, of H. E. the Governor's mansions are large, and the audience hall is spacious and imposing.

The Palace is a building of note in the central part of the city. Within it is a cage of unclean birds, but if external appearances are all right, the contented celestial asks no questions. It is a one-story hall, in a court of three or four acres, kept in fine repair; the walls are yellow, and a great amount of decoration has been expended on the massive roof, which is the chief feature of Chinese architecture. In front, the Mandarins kneel to receive an Imperial messenger, and on New Year's morning they repair to this place to present their compliments to His Majesty the Emperor.

The Examination Hall near the Twin Pagodas is about 250 yards long. The benches and tables are hard and narrow, and the Literary Chancellor can, from the rostrum, see the face of each competitor. Success in the Civil Service Examinations gains admission into the charmed circle of educated men, secures an elevation above the common people, makes the graduate conspicuous in his native place, and is a protection from corporal punishment. The applicants come by three or four, or half-a-dozen, from the country, bring a teacher who acts as security, and a servant as cook; they rent a room in an adjoining house and remain for a month. They seem quite clannish, and have little intercourse with those from other cities and towns. On the examination days they rise at 4 a.m.—not infrequently in the snow and rain—and sit all day in the hall writing their theses. As the successful candidates are limited in number, the larger part of the undergraduates return year after year to try their fortunes.

There are four camps in Soochow, each supposed to contain 500 soldiers,

公共建筑

在苏州共有十个主要衙门,除了两个,其余衙门都在苏州城西南一隅。巡抚、布政使、按察使和苏州织造的衙门均坐落于此。它们管理着两千一百万人口的事务。此外,知府、三位知县、提督及治安长官都有其各自的衙门。如果我们考虑到这些官员的级别和经济地位,他们所在衙门的建筑风格更符合田园派的素雅简单,而不似十九世纪所追求的革新精神。文明高度发展的第一步一定是建立起与省会管理者地位与荣誉相匹配的公共建筑。然而,巡抚官邸很大,会客厅也很宽敞壮观。

万寿宫是苏州城中心的一处知名建筑。尽管里面养了很多鸟,环境有些脏,但只要建筑外表尚可,中国人一般是不会提出什么问题的。这是一幢一层楼建筑,庭院占地三到四英亩[1],一直维护得不错;所有墙面为黄色,巨大的屋顶上有大量装饰,这也是中国建筑的主要特色。通常官员会在门前跪倒迎接钦差,而在新年的清晨,他们也在此举行朝贺大典。

贡院位于双塔附近,长约二百五十码。院内的桌椅板凳又硬又窄。考官可以在讲坛上看到每一位应试者的面容。科举考试的成功为考生获得了进入上层社会的机会,使他们地位高于普通人,令其光宗耀祖,也可使其免受肉体的惩罚。考生们三五结伴从家乡赶来,路上还带着一位老师和仆人,老师和仆人同时也分别担任保镖和厨师。考生们通常会在贡院附近租一间房住一个月。考生们似乎有派别之分,这一城镇的考生与从其他城镇来的考生几乎没有交流。在考试当日,他们凌晨四点起身——经常会碰上雨雪天气,坐在考场里,一整天都在写文章。由于中举考生人数有限,因此大部分考生不得不年复一年地回来再考。

苏州有四个兵营,每个兵营应该有士兵五百人,他们既有薪酬还可以

---

[1]　1英亩约为4 050平方米。

for whom pay and rations are drawn. One is outside the north-west gate, another near the Governor's residence, while a third is beautifully situated opposite the new Custom House. The most important one is on an open plateau in the central part of the city, formerly the palace grounds of the Kings of Wu. The soldiers are nominally trained according to western tactics, but under very inferior drill-masters, and their uniforms, loose and flowing, are of variegated colors, in which red predominates. Near the camp there is a monumental temple, with hundreds of funereal tablets for distinguished widows. The government printing office is one-half mile south of this, and the wooden stereotype plates are there stacked by the thousands.

Execution

Attached to each of the three District Magistrates' and the Prefect's Yamêns is a gaol. The principal one is that of the Criminal Judge, and is called the "earthly hell." From this place, the pirates, robbers and murderers that are collected from the sixty-four counties—one or two hundred a year——are taken to the execution ground near the pagoda and decapitated. As the criminals are borne rapidly along the streets the people from all parts of the city, both men and women, come in throngs to behold the spectacle, and as the head falls under one stroke of the executioner's sword, and the blood spouts, there is a general rush among the bystanders to redden a cash as a charm against evil spirits, or to dip bread into the flowing stream and eat it—a species of cannibalism—that the valor and prowess of the brave dead may be imparted to the living. The frequent witnessing of these executions is one of the potent causes for the wickedness of the Soochow people.

The Gardens

By way of contrast we will turn to happier themes. There are three noted gardens in Soochow, some of them being said to cost $200,000, not to mention higher estimates. The entrance fees to these pleasure resorts is five and seven cents. Besides, there is also the " Lion Forest," the largest rockery in Central China, but for want of custom it is not kept in repair. The Chinese deserve credit for their ability to provide a wonderful diversity of design within a limited space. Give a European a couple of acres and he has a grass lawn, a few select

领口粮。一个兵营位于西北城门之外，另一个靠近巡抚官邸，第三个就在新海关大楼对面。最为重要的一个位于城中开阔的高地上，此处原为吴王宫殿所在地。士兵名义上是按照西方战术进行训练，但教官教导无方，他们的制服松散，颜色杂乱，以红色为主。兵营附近有一座寺庙，内有数百块贞节寡妇的牌匾。政府的印刷所在此以南半英里处，里面堆放着上千块木质刻板。

行刑

三个知县衙门和知府衙门内都设有监狱。最主要的一个监狱隶属按察使衙门，又被称为"人间地狱"。来自六十四个县的海盗、抢劫犯和杀人犯——一年大约有一百到两百人——从这里被带到靠近塔边的刑场斩首。当犯人被快速押到街头时，全城男女都蜂拥而至观看行刑场面。随着刽子手一刀砍落人头，鲜血四溅，围观人群中产生一阵骚乱，有人用血去染红铜钱以对抗邪神恶灵，有人用馒头蘸血后吃掉——这是一种食人的行为——据说这样可以将死者的勇气和能力转移到活人身上。频繁围观行刑也是造成苏州人性格阴暗面的重要原因之一。

园林

让我们转到愉快的话题。苏州城内有三座著名的园林，据说造价达到 200 000 美元，还有更高的估价。进入这些休闲景点的门票为五到七美分。此外，还有一座狮子林，内有华中地区最大的假山，但是因为少有游客光顾，所以没有对其进行维护。在有限的空间内展示出设计的多样性，在这方面中国人是值得称赞的。假如给欧洲人几亩地，他会弄一块草坪，选种几棵树，搭一个由不同颜色和色度混合组成的漂亮花坛，种一棵乔木，再配一个温室。而让一个元代的风景园林师设计相同的空间，他会将之装

trees, beautiful beds of flowers with the grouping of colors and blending of shades, an arbor, and a conservatory. Let a Mongolian landscape gardener have the same space and he will furnish an Oriental Paradise. There is the lake with its winding bridges and the flower-beds on the water, for the still surface of the pond is embellished with the beauteous chalice-like flowers of the lotus, the emblem of Buddha's heaven, while under the large green leaves the gold-fish play hide and seek. The rockeries, made of lime rock cemented with lime and iron filings, with their labyrinthian caves and winding stairways, and surmounted with tall cavernous stones and petrified wood, in color like the fawn, standing as sentinels, are as surprising in their design as they are unique in their execution, and the pavilions, which cap their summits, give to the visitor a charming resting place. The halls and tea-houses, with chairs and tables made to suit the special apartments, face courts and hills and trees and lakes. The roads or covered galleries are all meandering, the object being to mystify the visitor, and the ornamental designs in the open-work walls are all of different patterns, while variety is also given by the octagonal, circular and pear-shaped doorways. "The literary tastes of the guests are met by the quotations from the classics hung up by the hundreds under the roofs of the sheltered walls," while students of the antique find delight in the old bronzes and stone inscriptions, and others may look at the peafowl, storks and deer in the cages and stalls. At every turn there are placed mirrors to reflect the changing scenery of the grounds, while views of the bamboo groves and flowering trees, and roses of varied hue climbing the walls, feast the eye.

One of these gardens, the *Liu Yuen*, is the property of the great railway magnate, Sheng Taotai. He has given Tls. 50,000 to run the "horse road" from the Chang Men to this already famous resort, and as the railway station will be in close proximity, it will command a patronage from far and near.

The Hills

It is quite natural to pass from the gardens within the city to the hills without. What mountain is that standing out alone on the plain, asks the traveller. It is the Lion Mountain, and if viewed from the north bears a striking resemblance to the king of beasts crouching on the ground. At its base, a lone missionary, the Rev. D. N. Lyon, resides and preaches in the country around.

饰成一个东方天堂。园林中，水塘上的小桥蜿蜒曲折，花坛浸在水中，象征着佛陀天堂、呈酒杯状的美丽莲花点缀着静谧的池塘，而金鱼则在宽大的荷叶下嬉戏追逐。假山是用石灰与铁屑黏合石灰岩构成，假山内的洞穴犹如迷宫，台阶盘旋而上。假山顶上立着高大多孔的太湖石和已经石化的木头。假山呈浅黄褐色，如同哨兵一样站立着，不光设计令人感到惊叹，制作工艺也是独一无二，而假山顶上的亭台楼阁也为游客们提供了一个休息的好场所。园林内的大厅和茶室都面向庭院、假山、树木和池塘，里面摆放着与之相配套的桌椅。园林内的道路或游廊迂回曲折，给游客增添了不少神秘感，墙面上的各种装饰设计形态各异，而八角形、圆形和梨形的出入口也体现出了设计的多样性。"亭台楼阁下悬挂着的数百句出自经典著作的名言佳句迎合了游客们的文学品位"，而研究古董的学生可以在园林里古老的青铜器和石刻碑文上找到乐趣，其他人则可以观赏养在笼子或庭院中的孔雀、鹤与鹿。园林的每一个拐角处都放置了一面镜子，映射出地面不断变化的景致，而竹林、开花的树木及爬上墙头的各色玫瑰亦让人大饱眼福。

在这些园林中，留园属于铁路大亨盛道台[1]的私家财产。他出资五万两白银修建了从阊门到留园的"马路"。如今，留园已成为著名的度假胜地。由于火车站就在留园附近，因此留园也吸引了来自四面八方的游客。

让我们穿过城中的园林来到城外的山边。那座独自矗立在平地上的山是什么山？一个游客问道。这是狮山，如果从北面望去，这座山在外形上就如同一只卧在地上的狮子一样。在狮山脚下，有一位名叫来恩赐的牧师，他孤身一人住在那里，向周边地区的民众传播基督福音。

---

[1] 即盛宣怀。

The Fan Wen Hill, the tomb of Soochow's great statesman and historian, is the prettiest picnic excursion from the city. A "quick boat" to the end of the canal, a walk or ride up the hill in a chair; through a tunnel and down again to a shady grove; then a climb up the precipitous mountain with the pretty temple nestling on its side; through the narrow passes between the overhanging boulders on to the flat rock, from which a fine view of the Great Lake is obtained, and then up to the summit.

The Witch's Hill, crowned with a pagoda, beside the Stone Lake to the south-west of the city, is another fine outing. The fish-ponds below mirror in the sunlight the willows which stand upon their banks. Here reside the " Five Holy Ones," or the gods the witches worship. And fearful gods they are! If a bride, with a pretty face, sickens and dies, the country people say, "The Five Holy Ones have taken her for their wife."

The history of Soochow puts the height of the Mohdoh Hill, where King Hoh Lü had his summer palace, at 3,600 feet, by measuring up the curving road. The pagoda has eight stories, is 150 feet high and 900 years old. There is not a rock or boulder or cave or eminence on its summit that is not historic, for the kings of many dynasties have visited this famous headland. The Arrow Creek, running direct to the Great Lake, was opened by Hoh Lü.

Mount Seven Sons, about 800 feet high, is another sacred hill, whither the pilgrims resort under the burning August suns. Just beyond is Mount Yao Fong, where the Emperor Shunche, the first of this dynasty, who ascended the throne 1644, spent the last ten years of his life in a monastery. Thus the conquering Tartar was led captive by the Buddhist monks.

Mount Kyiöng Lung, fourteen miles from Soochow, once had temples containing 5,040 rooms, and is yet a wealthy place under the Taoist directorship. The grove is a fine one and the view superb. Its height is 1,100 feet. The rich from the city and the poor from the country make semi-annual pilgrimages to this holy mountain. There is a tradition that, B.C. 2700, a rain priest resided here and sought for the elixir of immortality. The sides of all these hills are covered with

范坟山[1]是苏州著名的政治家和历史学家范仲淹的墓地所在地，也是苏州城外最美丽的远足野餐场所。你可以乘坐一艘快船到达运河尽头，然后徒步或坐上轿子上山；穿过一个隧道再向下来到一片阴凉的树林；随后爬上陡峭的山坡，一座小巧的寺庙就建在山边；钻过悬空巨石之间的狭窄通道来到一处平坦的石块上，在这里美丽的太湖风光尽收眼底，从此处就可直登山顶。

"女巫山"[2]位于苏州城西南方的石湖之畔，山顶有一座宝塔，此处是远足观光的另一个好去处。山下的鱼塘倒映出岸边沐浴在阳光中的柳树。据说这里住着"五通神"，即女巫所朝拜的神祇。这是令人感到害怕的神灵！如果一个漂亮的新娘生病去世，乡间的人就会说："是'五通神'要娶她为妻，所以带走了她。"

木渎山[3]在苏州历史上地位很高，吴王阖闾曾在这里修建行宫，通过测量弯曲的道路可知，此处高达三千六百英尺。山上宝塔有八层，高一百五十英尺，有九百年历史。山顶上一石、一砾、一洞、一丘无不具有历史意义，因为很多朝代的皇帝都曾造访此地。由阖闾开凿的箭泾河从此处直奔太湖。

七子山，高约八百英尺，是另一座圣山，朝圣者们顶着八月的烈日前往此处朝圣。在它的边上就是尧峰山，本朝第一位皇帝，1644年登基的顺治皇帝就是在那里的寺庙中度过了他最后十年[4]。这位曾经的征服者却最终皈依了佛教。

穹窿山，距苏州十四英里，山上曾有多座寺庙，共有房间5 040间，如今在道士的打理下，仍是一块富庶之地。这里有树林，风景甚好。山高一千一百英尺。无论是城里的有钱人，还是村里的穷人，每半年都要来这

---

[1] 即天平山。
[2] 即上方山。
[3] 即灵岩山。
[4] 这里原作者的理解有误，传说中顺治帝在五台山出家。

the sacred resting-places of by-gone generations. These are visited twice a year, and even the sombre worship at the graves, after the prescribed rites have been accomplished, is transformed into pleasant picnics and happy family reunions.

Kwangfoh, a town beyond Mohdoh, is the prettiest place on this plain. Near it on the shores of the lake is Uön Mo Shan, a celebrated monastery. Around these hills winds the Imperial Highway, twelve feet wide, paved with brick and faced with stone, now in fine order, which was built by the Emperor Kien Lung, who "sent his messengers before his face to prepare the way" when he visited Soochow a hundred years ago.

Benevolent Institutions

Returning from the hills we may visit the benevolent institutions, which, though only a small percentage of those in Protestant countries, yet constitute a distinct feature of Chinese civilization. Besides those which provide coffins for the dead there are five classes which care for the living: 1. Foundling asylums, one of which has 400 children let out to poor families, who are paid for their maintenance, and the orphans are generally kindly treated. 2. There are two homes for old women. 3. The old men's home, covering several acres, near the Tiger Pagoda. The veterans are supplied with one meal a day, and those who are able, go out and ask for alms. 4. The general distribution of clothing and food to the poor in the winter by wealthy families and benevolent societies. 5. Quite a number of free schools. One of these, on the Yang Yoh Hong, has six grades, and is a well-conducted native school. There are also reformatory institutions, as the "Prodigal Asylum," near the camp, for dissolute and rebellious sons, and the "Purifying Heart Institute" for those who desire a quiet retreat in which to "amend their ways."

Silk

When we come to the trade of Soochow, the principal article is silk. In the silk houses are found about one hundred varieties of satin and two hundred kinds of silks and gauzes, and as they are unrolled for the inspection of purchasers

座圣山朝圣。这里有一个传说,公元前2700年,赤松子曾居住于此寻找长生不老药。这里所有山的两侧都是历代去世之人的安息地。人们每年要来此两次,在进行完规定的仪式之后,在墓前的祭拜随后演变成了愉快的野餐和家庭团聚。

位于木渎边上的光福镇,是这块平原上最美丽的地方。玄墓山就位于光福附近的湖岸上,山上有座著名的寺庙。环山的御道,宽十二英尺,由砖块铺底,石块铺面,如今维护得很好,这条道路是乾隆皇帝修建的,一百年前来苏州游玩时,他"当场派人传令修缮道路"。

慈善机构

从山上归来,我们可以顺道参观一下这里的慈善机构。这些机构尽管在新教国家中只占很小比例,却构成了中华文明的一大显著特色。除了给死者提供棺木的慈善机构之外,还有五类这样的机构为生者提供帮助:(1)育婴堂,其中一家将近四百个儿童寄养在附近的穷人家,由机构承担这些孩子的生活费用,通常孤儿会得到很好的照顾。(2)有两所收养老年妇女的善堂。(3)在虎丘塔附近有一个专门收养老年男子的善堂,面积有好几亩地。这里每天免费为退伍老兵提供一顿饭,那些有活动能力的人可以外出寻求救济。(4)富裕家庭和慈善组织在冬天向穷人分发衣服和食物。(5)许多义学堂。其中一家位于养育巷内,有六个年级,是一所管理相当好的当地学校。此外,还有感化院,例如靠近兵营附近的"浪子收容所",收容那些浪荡子或逆子,以及"心灵净化所",收容那些希望"改邪归正"的人。

丝绸

谈到苏州的贸易,最主要的商品就是丝绸。在丝绸店中你可以看到近一百种缎子和两百种丝绸及纱布。当这些布匹在购买者眼前慢慢展开时,

the sight is a splendid one. Some of these hongs carry a capital of several hundred thousand dollars. Here merchants come to supply the markets of the great cities throughout the provinces. When a silk robe was considered too great a luxury for a Roman Emperor, the Soochow scholar wore his gown of this material. In plain Anglo-Saxon, there have been more fine clothes worn in this city than in any other place in the world. The weavers are divided into two guilds, the Nanking and the Soochow, and have together about 7,000 looms. One office owns fifty or a hundred looms and supplies thread to the weavers. As reeling the thread and preparing it for weaving takes many hands, there are probably a dozen or more men, women and girls employed to each loom, so these guilds feed several tens of thousands. The looms are in little houses of one story, and are worked by the feet treading on rickety bamboo rods; each loom has a hole in the ground, and underneath the chickens and the children play, but, *mirabile dictu*, from the very midst of all this dirt are turned out silks and satins with the most delicate colors of all descriptions. Great skill is displayed in weaving the figures. An artist lays off the warp and arranges certain perpendicular threads at which a little boy perched above pulls, while the weaver's shuttle flies to and fro, and here is finished a magnificent pattern of brocaded satin.

In and around the city embroidery employs 100,000 women, Mandarins' robes, ladies' dresses, and stage actors' apparel are all embroidered. The Superintendent of the Silk Looms twice a year sends on 1,000 trunks of embroidered clothing for the use of the Emperor's household. In this yamen 1,000 men, it is said, sublet the jobs to the women. The embroidery in gold or flowers is simply exquisite, and they will execute any design that is given them. This business makes the trade in silk thread a very extensive one, and as the shopkeeper unrolls a package he displays two dozen shades of one color. The women come to the shops to purchase one cent's worth of floss. At the first of the year, when the country women buy on credit, a popular shop may do a business of $1,500 in two week.

Pawnshops

The pawnshops have a capital of many millions; the clothing stores obtain

其场景之奢华令人叹为观止。有些丝绸行资产高达几十万美元。在这里，丝绸商为全国各省大城市的市场提供丝绸商品。罗马皇帝穿一件丝绸长袍被认为是极度奢华的事，而穿在苏州学子们身上的长袍就是用丝绸料子做的。在普通的盎格鲁-撒克逊人眼中，在苏州这个城市里，人们身上穿的漂亮衣服要比世界上任何一个地方都要多。织工分在两个织造局，一个在南京，另一个在苏州，共有织布机近7 000台。一间织房就有织机五十到一百台，并且为织工提供丝线。由于缫丝和准备环节需要很多人手，每台织机需要配备十二位或更多的男女工人和女孩，因此纺织行业养活了好几万人。织机就摆放在一层楼高的小房子内，织工的脚踩在摇摇晃晃的竹竿上；每一台织机地下都有一个坑，小鸡和儿童会在里面玩耍。但是，说也奇怪，从这些泥土中纺出来的却是最精细的丝绸和纱布。当织工在编织时，他上下滑动的手指展示出了高超技巧。他犹如一位艺术家先放下经线，然后安排一些纬线，由小男孩坐在上面拉动经线，而当织工手中的飞梭来回移动时，一个华丽的锦缎图案就完成了。

苏州城内外的绣纺一共雇用了十万名女工。官员的长袍、女士的礼服及舞台上演员的服饰上都有刺绣。苏州织造局的主管每年两次运送一千箱的刺绣服装供皇室使用。在苏州织造局这个衙门里，据说有一千名男工，他们将工作转包给绣娘。绣金或绣花的刺绣看上去很精美，这些绣娘可以绣出任何一种图案。刺绣生意也促成了大量的丝线交易，当店主打开一个丝绒包时，他展示了同一个颜色的二十四种色度。妇女们会来店里购买一美分的丝线。年初时，乡下妇女还要靠赊账购物，但一个生意不错的店两个星期内就可以做到一千五百美元的生意。

当铺

苏州的当铺有着数百万的资本，服装店可以从当铺这里买到库存商品。

their stock of goods from these. The Westerner must dismiss from his mind all preconceived ideas of the pawnshop, for in a country where there must be an annual and accurate settlement of accounts, goods have to be hypothecated for silver. These great hongs encourage the pernicious habit of temporarily disposing of valuables to realize ready money. The pawnshop is a safe repository for the gentlemen's and ladies' furs in summer, where they will be well taken care of and preserved from the destructive moth.

Hongs and Manufactures

Several streets are devoted to furniture. The wood is highly polished, and substantial tables and chairs, sofas and wardrobes, are on hand. The handsomely carved sets of furniture, inlaid with marble, where the princely bedstead includes bureau and sets of drawers, would do credit to any mansion. There is much fancy work done in the fine kinds of wood. Carving seems to be an art just designed for the patient persevering toil of a Chinaman, for no labor is too great to bestow on the most minute undertaking, and in a country where time enters so little into the essence of life, days and months are lavishly spent on what would be thought elsewhere to be unremunerative toil.

The north-west corner of the city is almost entirely given up to the manufacture of ornaments from jade, the emblem of virtue: hair-pins, six or eight inches in length, for ladies; large thumb rings, an inch broad, for gentlemen; bracelets for girls, and pen cups for the scholars, besides a great variety of trinkets.

On the central street, running from north to south, shops for antique wares and old curios are numerous. Bronze vases and other vessels, used in the most primitive of cults, which still have full sway over the Chinese mind, are for sale at every turn. The native drug-stores are extensive establishments. The book business is immense. There are large stores for the sale of moral and religious books only. Orders frequently come to Soochow for books of rare value. As in every part of China where such a large number are annually carried to their last resting-place, the coffin trade is prominent. Imported wood is on the hills cut the length of a dead man. Silversmiths have a prosperous business where the gentle sex is so fond of bracelets and head ornaments. "Your trade is a very extensive

西方人必须摒弃他们之前对当铺所有先入为主的观点,因为在一个每年都需要精确结算的国家,货物必须以白银作为抵押。这些当铺的存在,助长了暂时将有价值的物品典当以换得现金的不良风气。不过,当铺也是一个夏日安全存放男士和女士皮衣的好地方,因为在这里,这些皮衣会得到很好的保养,免遭飞蛾侵蚀。

商行和制造业

　　有几条街专做家具生意。木材都经过高度抛光,店铺里有大量的桌椅、沙发和衣柜。这些雕刻精美的成套家具,内嵌大理石,其中床架尤为豪华,包括了书桌和好几套抽屉,足以配得起任何一间豪宅。上好木材上的雕工都非常精致绚丽。雕刻似乎是专门为吃苦耐劳的中国人量身打造的一门艺术,因为极细微的一处雕刻都需要极大付出,在中国,时间效率这个概念尚未得到人们高度重视,因此,中国人可以很奢侈地花上几天甚至几个月时间从事一项在别人看来毫无回报的劳作上。

　　整个苏州城的西北角几乎都是生产玉器饰品的作坊,玉器是美德的象征:这里有女士用的发夹,六到八英寸长;有男士用的扳指,一英寸宽;有女孩用的手镯、学子用的笔筒,此外还有各式各样的小饰品。

　　在从北向南的中央大街上,古董店和古玩店数不胜数。青铜花瓶和其他器皿,这些在最原始的宗教仪式上经常使用的器物,如今对中国人依旧有很大吸引力,处处有售。本土药店的规模相当庞大。图书生意非常兴隆。一些大书店只出售道德和宗教方面的书籍。经常有订单到苏州求购珍贵的古籍。和中国其他地方一样,每年都有很多人要被送往最后的安息之地,因此棺材店生意相当好。做棺材的木材是从外地运来的,工人们根据逝者的身高在山上将木材砍下。银匠的生意也很兴旺,这里的女性非常喜欢手镯和头饰。"你的生意很不错。"我对其中一位银匠说。"但这交易是有

one," I said to one of this calling. "But it is a very sinful one," he replied. "Wherein consists the sin?" I inquired. " We adulterate with brass."

The traveller is struck with the number of eating-shops. The fruit stands so temptingly arranged, are loaded ten months in the year. Fish in endless variety—provided by a kind Providence for the hungry millions—are found in the market. In the meat shops are pork and mutton, tame fowls and " wild chickens" (pheasants), ducks and geese. The bakeries and travelling kitchens furnish bread and cakes, bean-curd and soups; and the restaurants, all the savoury dishes that please the Chinese connoisseur.

There are workers in iron, brass, pewter and the various other metals. Lime-kilns are found in the suburbs. The fur trade in winter, and the fan trade in summer, in this land where the lords of creation take the fan for the walking-cane (something to hold in the hand), and so gracefully use these feminine appendages with literary inscriptions or scenery in gilt on their faces, are both prominent in the marts. There are large establishments for the sale of pottery which is made west of the Great Lake, whence comes also the famous " Soochow bath tub." The city, up to the last few months, has had no large manufactures, with the smoke curling from the tall chimneys, but here in thousands of shops are made hats, shoes, drums, musical instruments, idols, paper goods for exportation to Hades, and the infinite variety of articles manufactured by the 360 trades into which the artisan class in this venerable country is divided.

As the newly established Imperial Customs will report quarterly on the market for foreign imports, no mention will be made of this trade in these pages, except to emphasize its rapid increase during the last decade.

Population

What is the population of Soochow? is a question constantly asked. Only an approximate answer can be given. The Pao K'ia Joh, or Tithing Office, which has charge of the police, taxes, public works, etc., does not take the census so much with a view of obtaining the number of inhabitants, as of accounting for everyman in the city. There are five wards within the city, and the two suburbs to the west constitute a sixth. A register is posted on each door and a duplicate kept in their book. The census is taken by families and not by individuals, so if

悖道德的。"他回答道。"哪里有悖道德？"我问道。"我们在银里面掺了黄铜。"

游客一定会对苏州城内的小吃店数量感到惊讶。水果摊上摆放的水果非常诱人，一年里有十个月摊头上都会摆满水果。市场上出售各式各样的鱼——这是仁慈的上帝赐给数百万饥民的食物。肉店中有猪肉和羊肉、家禽及"野味"（野鸡），还有鸭和鹅。面点店和流动摊贩提供馒头、蛋糕、豆腐和汤；饭馆里可以做出让中国美食家满意的各式佳肴。

也有不少工人从事铁、铜、锡及其他金属的加工。郊区还能看见石灰窑。冬季的皮毛生意以及夏季的扇子交易在集市上都很受欢迎。在这里，男士们将扇子当作手杖（拿在手里的东西），并且很优雅地摇着这些原本属于女性的物品，扇面上有的是题字，有的则是镀金的风景画。苏州还有销售陶器的大型场所，这些陶器出自西太湖，那里也盛产著名的"苏州浴盆"。整座城市，直到前几个月还没有大型的制造工厂，也看不到高耸的烟囱里冒出的袅袅烟雾，不过，这里却有上千家铺子生产帽子、鞋子、鼓、乐器、玩偶、冥间用的纸质商品，以及由三百六十个行业生产出的各类商品，这三百六十个行业是中国这个古老国家对工种的一种划分。

新成立的海关每个季度都要上报国外商品的进口情况，不过报告中不会提及具体交易情况，只是强调在过去的十年中，这类交易在快速增长。

人口

苏州人口有多少？这是个经常被问到的问题。只能给出一个大致数字。负责警务、税务及公共事务的保甲局并不重视人口普查，不清楚要获得居民人数需要将城内的每一个人都计算在内。苏州城内有五个区，而位于城西的两个郊区则构成第六区。每户门上都贴着名单，并且登记在册。人口普查是以家庭而非个人为单位的，因此，如果有两户人家，那么就算作二，

there are two doors, the family counts as two, but the tenement houses, where there are from fifteen to thirty families, often have only one register, so it is likely the numbers are much greater than represented. There are over 90,000 families, and as a family in China consists of "Noah and his wife, his three sons and their wives," and all the children and grandchildren (and the Soochow quivers are full), seven is not a high multiple, giving 630,000. But the 2,500 "official residences," with the Mandarin's family, servants and retainers, are not counted, and these contain about 40,000 people. Neither are the large boating population and the large floating population included,—probably 30,000 more. The whole population may be safely estimated at 700,000. Whether the opening of the port and the introduction of factories will add a further 300,000 remains to be seen.

A Bird's View

The fame of Soochow attracts many travellers. On leaving the Customs House the visitor can enter the Foo Men (south-east gate) and go first to the Ink Pagoda, and if the porter is at home, for a few cash the gate opens. Next, to the Twin Pagodas. Perhaps he may be able to get into the Examination Hall adjoining. Thence to the Palace, the entrance being on the west, and to the Temple of the Sun. It is well to visit the City Temple early in the morning to avoid the crowd. This is one of the principal objects of interest in the city. The street in front is perhaps the prettiest in mid-China. It is most convenient next to visit the Manchu Garden, and go from there to the Pagoda. The Great Street runs to the northwest gate, and here are the silk hongs and other large stores. Jade ornaments are found on the bridge outside the gate, and at the Jade-stone Temple. Fine furniture is on the Fan Ch'ong Tsien. This is well worth seeing. Old embroidery and bronze is on the Dragon Street. Here, too, is a fine garden. The tourist will go next to the Beamless Temple. The steps will be found in the east wall, and, though dark, one may ascend without fear. The only available entrance to the Confucian Temple is towards the western side, and through the kitchen, where a small fee may be left. The visitor must not fail to go to the Tiger Pagoda, and to the handsome garden (Liu Yuen)

但是如果是出租房内住着十五户到三十户人家，通常只能算作一，所以，真实的人口数字要比现在得到的数据大很多。苏州现有九万多户家庭，通常中国一个家庭由"丈夫、妻子还有他的三个孩子及他们的妻子"组成，如果再加上所有的儿女和孙辈（苏州基本上都是大家庭），七不是一个很高的倍数，这样算来，苏州应有人口 630 000。但是，苏州还有两千五百座官邸，这些官员的家庭、仆人和扈从并未计算在内，而这批人将近有 40 000。此外，大批船民和移动人口亦未包括在内——大约有 30 000 多。因此，苏州城内人口保守估计大约在 700 000。未来新开的港口及新建的工厂能否带来 300 000 新增人口还需拭目以待。

鸟瞰

　　苏州的名声吸引了大批游客。一走出海关大楼，游客就进入了葑门（东南城门），他可以先去墨塔，如果门卫在的话，只要花一点钱，门卫就会让他进去参观。随后，可以去双塔游览。也许他还能进入双塔附近的贡院参观。随后，再去万寿宫，宫殿入口就在西面，然后再去太阳宫。为了避开拥挤的人群，最好是一早就去玄妙观。这里是苏州城内最令人感兴趣的地方之一。玄妙观前的街道大概也是华中地区最漂亮的一条大街。从这去游览八旗会馆[1]最为方便，然后再从那里去北寺塔。中市大街直达苏州西北城门，这里到处都是丝绸行和其他大型商铺。城门外的桥上有人兜售玉器，而玉器庙[2]里也有很多玉器饰品。"范庄前"内有精美家具，非常值得一看。卧龙街上有不少老的刺绣品和青铜制品，这里还有一座不错的园林。游客下一站将会去无梁殿，台阶在东墙处，尽管楼道很黑，但游客还是可以无惊无险地爬上去。文庙的唯一进口在西面，需要穿过一间厨房，游客进文庙需要付一点费用。游客千万不能错过虎丘塔，然后可以再去附近的

---

[1] 即拙政园。
[2] 即周王庙。

near by.

Opium

No paper on Soochow would be complete without a reference to opium. Sixty years ago there were four or five opium-smokers in this city; now, probably, there are 60,000. The opium war was begun in Canton, but it is not a tithe as iniquitous as the opium peace continued in Soochow. The resident here is an eye-witness to the poverty entailed, the suffering accruing, the beggary produced, the bodies emaciated, the lives destroyed, the families ruined, the sons turned prodigal, the fathers becoming wretches, the husbands ingrates, the millions expended. The Chinese consider opium smoking as the ancestor of vices. They speak of its introduction as a crime of the first degree, and denounce all foreigners as the perpetrators of this iniquity. They say with bitterness: "You bring this evil upon the people and now hypocritically exhort us to virtue." When not one in twenty of the British residents in Far Cathay is interested financially in opium, and while outside of India the British nation receives not the most remote advantage from the trade, it is amazing that England, the bulwark of Protestantism and the acknowledged leader in the world's civilization, should tarnish her glory by even the touch of this nefarious traffic. Leaving out the rest of the 1,300 cities in the eighteen provinces, opium has brought enough suffering upon Soochow to cause the vials of Heaven's wrath to be poured out.

Let us now behold the silver lining to the dark cloud. For years there resided in this city the Provincial Treasurer and Acting-Governor, the late Futai of Yunnan, Governor T'an Kuin Pei (谭钧培), who stood a giant among the rank and file of Mandarins, and, as a great reformer, set himself as a stone wall against every form of evil. He sought to reform the manners and morals of the people, issuing his proclamations, the size of a counterpane, with forty prohibitions, and caused bad men to tremble. During four or five years he closed every opium den in Southern Kiangsu, except in the "model settlement" Shanghai, and had mounted on every door the number of opium-smokers who lived within. Fearfulness and trembling took hold of this pitiable class, and many broke off from the terrible habit. He demonstrated beyond the shadow of a doubt, were England to withdraw her

一座精致园林（留园）逛逛。

鸦片

任何一篇有关苏州的文章如果不提到鸦片都是不完整的。六十年前，苏州城内仅有四到五位鸦片吸食者；而如今，大约有60 000人吸食鸦片。虽然鸦片战争爆发于广州，但其造成的危害远不及和平时期鸦片带给苏州危害的十分之一。这里的居民目睹鸦片造成了吸食者生活贫困，痛苦加剧，沦为乞丐，身体衰弱，生命毁灭，家庭破碎；因为吸食鸦片，儿子挥霍家财，父亲成了无赖，丈夫变得忘恩负义，上百万金钱被浪费。因此，中国人将吸食鸦片看作万恶之源。他们将鸦片的输入称作是一级犯罪，并且谴责所有的外国人参与了这项罪行。他们痛苦地说道："你们先将鸦片这个恶魔带给我们，现在又来伪善地劝诫我们。"在中国，不到二十分之一的英国人对鸦片贸易感兴趣，然而，在印度以外，英国却在这项贸易中获得巨额利润。让人感到惊讶的是，英格兰，作为基督教新教的堡垒和公认的世界文明领袖，竟然会为了这种不道德的鸦片贸易而令自己蒙羞受辱。撇开中国十八个省内其他的1 300个城市不谈，鸦片光是带给苏州的灾难就足以让上天震怒。

现在还是让我们看看乌云中的一丝光亮吧。谭钧培曾在苏州任职多年，他先后担任过江苏布政使、代理江苏巡抚、云南巡抚和云南总督。和众多普通官员相比，他是一个伟人，一个伟大的改革家，以身作则，抵制各种邪恶与腐败。他努力提高民众的道德和礼仪，发布了一长串公告，共有四十条禁令，令坏人不寒而栗。在四到五年间，他关闭了除上海之外的苏南地区所有烟馆，并在每家每户门上标上该户家中吸食鸦片的人数，这也让那些可怜的吸食者内心充满恐惧，很多人因此而戒掉了吸食鸦片的恶习。他毫无疑问地证明了，只要英国撤除对鸦片的保护并允许中国禁止鸦片进

protectorate over the vile drug, and permit China to forbid its importation, the Middle Kingdom, with such a Martin Luther, could purge its coasts of the fields of poppy, and the nation, after a score of years of dreadful suffering to individuals, could again be free. All honor to the memory of Sinim's Great Hero!

Its Reverses

Situated as Soochow has been, centrally, near the east coast, as Washington in the United States, it has been much exposed to internal struggles. When the latter Kingdom of Wu was overthrown, A.D. 600, Soochow rebelled, and for forty years a new city was built near the hills. In A. D. 1300 the wall was destroyed and the moat filled. Five hundred and forty years ago the city was seriously injured by the insurrection of the "Red Turbaned Thieves." The words of the prophet, "Your cities shall be heaps"—that is, the rubbish of devastations piled up—have been fulfilled, and here and there are little hills to tell the sad tale.

The T'aipings

The last destruction by the T'aipings, who drove the ploughshare through these streets, is now around us and about us. In the year 1861 they came down the Grand Canal, capturing the city of Changchow, sixty miles north-west, on the 7th; the city of Wusih, on the 10th, reaching Soochow on the 14th of the 4th moon. ... The people of this city lifted up their eyes and beheld the smoke rising in the great suburb on its west side, which extended five miles, commanded an immense trade, and contained probably a half million people. In one night's conflagration it was entirely demolished. They knew that the horrors of Asiatic war were upon them. ... Many of the people crowded to Shanghai and perished in the pestilence. Many died of starvation. ... A number of the people who had money escaped to the hills and scattered through the country, and in that universal brotherhood of trial, where so much mutual kindness was shown, passed through the severe period ...

口,中国,有这样一位像马丁·路德一样的官员,就能够肃清沿海一带的罂粟,而这个国家,在民众经受了多年痛苦的折磨之后,定能再获自由。所有的荣誉都归于这位伟大的中华帝国英雄!

城市厄运

苏州和美国的华盛顿一样,地处东部沿海的中央地带,饱受内乱之苦。当吴国政权被推翻之后,公元600年,苏州抵抗隋军南下,花了四十年时间在苏州城外附近的山边建起一座新城。公元1300年,苏州城墙被毁,护城河也被填满。540年前,苏州城因"红巾军"暴乱[1]而遭到严重毁坏。"你们的城市将会变成一堆堆废墟"——即废弃物堆积如山——预言家的这句话,得到了验证,随处可见堆成小山状的废弃物,讲述着这个城市的悲惨故事。

太平军

我们周边所在之地最近一次破坏是太平军造成的。他们像犁地一般将这些街道破坏殆尽。

1861年,他们顺大运河而下,4月7日占领了苏州西北六十英里之外的常州;4月10日,他们攻占无锡;4月14日,他们抵达苏州。……苏州城内的老百姓们抬头就能看到城外西郊冒起的浓烟。西郊一带延绵五英里,商品贸易众多,人口大约有五十万。一夜之间,整个西郊被大火完全烧毁。老百姓清楚地知道战争的恐怖即将降临在他们身上。……很多人涌去上海,却死于瘟疫。很多人则死于饥饿。……不少有钱人逃到了山里,分散在全国各地,在这场兄弟情义的考验中,他们相互扶持,共同渡过了难关……

---

[1] 此处应指的是朱元璋与张士诚的战争。

Gordon

Then in 1863 came Chinese Gordon, leading the "Ever Victorious Army." The rebels were entrenched at Soochow and also at Quensan, twenty-four miles to the east. These cities were connected by a narrow causeway with lakes to the north and south of the canal, and along this causeway the rebel troops continually passed. From the south, in May, Gordon dispatched the little steamer "Hyson" with three guns on her decks, and her sides covered with sheet iron to protect against the rebel bullets, and with a bold attack the fort at Chen-ee was dismantled, communication between the two cities cut off, and the steamer, firing grape and cannister, followed the routed T'aipings, fleeing for their lives, almost to the gates of Soochow, and slaughtered them by the hundreds. At the same time Gordon captured Quensan, and made that city his headquarters, till in September he encamped at Nga-kwô-dong, five miles east of Soochow. At the first of October the force was conveyed on boats to the fifty-three arched bridge, called the Precious Girdle Bridge. The rebels, led by Burgovine with sixty foreigners, came out 200,000 strong (as the number was reported), and attacked them but were driven back. There was continual skirmishing. The "Hyson" had to be sent for reconnoitering to the west of Soochow, and as she could not pass under the bridge, the central arch had to be pulled down, and, when the keystone was removed, the arches to the north all fell in one after the other. Then followed the battle of Wukiang, at which Capt. Howard, one of the first of the Imperial Customs to be sent to Soochow in 1896, distinguished himself for his gallantry and was promoted to Brevet-Major by Gordon on the field.

The foreigners in the service of the T'aipings, seeing their cause hopeless, and tired of the wretched life of suffering they were leading under continual espionage, agreed with Gordon upon a plan of surrender, and, feigning an attack, they fled in a body and leaped upon the decks of the "Hyson," then standing in the Grand Canal. A part of Gordon's force was deceived by the pretence of surrendering the forts at the Wu Lung Giao, or Five Dragon Bridge, three miles south of the concession, and at night in the attack lost sixteen foreign officers, killed and wounded, and 280 men. A few days afterwards these fortifications

戈登

1863年，戈登率领他的"常胜军"来到苏州。太平军在苏州和苏州以东二十四英里之外的昆山都加固了壕沟。两地通过一条狭窄的堤道相连，这条堤道北连太湖，南接运河。沿着堤道，太平军的部队陆续通过。5月，戈登从南面调来一艘小蒸汽战舰"海生号"，该船甲板上装有三门炮，船两侧均有铁甲覆盖以抵御太平军的枪弹。在猛烈攻击下，太平军位于昆山正仪的堡垒被拆毁，昆山与苏州的交通亦被切断，"海生号"向太平军发射了葡萄弹和霰弹，一路追击溃败逃命的太平军几乎到了苏州城门口，此役共击毙太平军数百人。与此同时，戈登攻占了昆山，并在此设立他的指挥总部，直至9月，他才移扎到苏州以东五英里的外跨塘。10月1日，当运兵船行至五十三孔桥处（该桥又被称为"宝带桥"），太平军在白聚文[1]和六十位外国士兵的率领下，共出动了二十万之众（该数字是当时报道中所提）攻击运兵船，但最终被打退。双方一直冲突不断。"海生号"不得不前往苏州西面进行侦察，但它却无法从宝带桥下通过，因此只好将宝带桥的中央桥孔拆除。当基石被移除时，桥北面的拱门一个接一个倒塌了。接下来便是吴江战役。在此次战役中，霍华德上尉，作为1896年被派往苏州的最早的一批海关职员之一，因表现英勇而被戈登当场提拔为名誉少校。

帮助太平军的一帮外国人，一方面，觉得前途渺茫，另一方面，厌倦了这种长期以来被怀疑是间谍的压力，他们同意了戈登的投降计划。他们假装攻击，然后全体逃到正在运河上的"海生号"甲板上。太平军假意放弃了位于租界以南三英里处的"五龙桥"堡垒，戈登的一部分部队上当受骗。夜间，他们受到太平军攻击，有十六名外国军官被杀，士兵死伤二百八十人。数天后，这些防御工事被重新夺回。在苏州以北的蠡口和黄埭也有战

---

[1] 白聚文（H. A. Burgevine，或译白齐文，1836—1865年），美国人。白聚文曾加入常胜军，与太平天国作战。1863年，白聚文因被撤职而改投太平军。

were captured. There were also battles at Lik'eu and Wangtai, to the north of Soochow. Gordon, armed with his cane, his "magic wand of victory," as it was called, led his troops, always going in person into the thickest of the conflict. He did not command Forward!—he led. The forts at Shü-z-kwan, to the north-west of the city, were also captured and communications cut off from the beleaguered T'aipings. The "Ever Victorious Army" now attacked the fortifications on the east side of the city, but were much annoyed by two Dahlgreen guns, captured by the rebels the year before at Tatsong, when the force under Holland was defeated. These guns are now on the east wall, one on the bastion opposite the Custom House. While the pontoons were being prepared for storming the wall at its north-east corner, the Wongs, who had made Soochow their headquarters and selected the finest mansions for palaces, capitulated and surrendered the city; but one of these, the Mo Wong, objected, and there was heavy fighting among the rebels themselves within the city. The day following, when the Wongs came into the presence of Li Hung Chang, they refused to kneel, and were beheaded on a creek outside the north-east gate; a policy to the captured to whom Gordon had promised protection, in the face of western morality and the laws of nations; but when the treacherous character of the "kings" is considered, their haughty bearing in the Governor's presence, and the hopefulness of the T'aipings as long as their leaders lived, we must not be too rigid in our judgments, even though we cannot approve, for the traditional policy of the government is "To kill a snake you must cut off its head." Thus ended a great chapter in the city's history. Though there is yet waste ground within the walls, the city was rapidly rebuilt, and new houses are constantly erected on the former ruins.

Protestantism Missions

This brings us in point of time to the commencement of Protestantism in the city. For years the missionaries stationed at Shanghai looked upon Soochow as a great evangelistic centre, and longed for the time when its gates should be opened. Before the city was taken by the T'aipings, young Griffith John, now a veteran, and others visited the place with a view of securing a foothold. Rev. Wm. Muirhead came here in native dress, with a queue which was unfortunately

斗。戈登，拿着被称为"胜利魔杖"的手杖，率领他的部队前进。在战斗中，他总是亲自冲到战斗最激烈的地方。他从不下令前进！——因为他身先士卒，一马当先。戈登率军攻克了太平军位于苏州城西北浒墅关处的要塞，切断了此处与被围困在城中太平军的联系。"常胜军"在攻击位于城东的防御工事时，遭到两门达尔格伦炮的轰击，因而进攻受阻，这两门炮是太平军前年在太仓缴获的，在那里太平军曾大败奥伦率领的部队。这两门大炮就安置在东城墙上，其中一门正对着海关大楼。就在搭好浮桥准备进攻苏州城东北角之际，太平天国众王准备投降献城，这些王爷将苏州作为总部，并且选择最好的宅子作为他们的王府。但是，主将慕王反对投降，于是苏州城内的太平军自相残杀。第二天，当众王来到李鸿章面前，他们拒绝下跪，随后被押到东北门外的河边斩首。虽然戈登曾承诺保护被俘者的安全，但李鸿章对待战俘的政策却全然不顾西方道德和国家法律。不过，考虑到太平天国众王奸诈的性格，他们在巡抚面前表现的傲慢，以及只要他们领导人不死他们就仍对太平天国抱有一丝希望等因素，我们在对待战俘政策方面就不能太死板，虽然我们也不赞成中国政府传统的"斩草除根"的做法。这座城市历史上的一幕就这样落下了。尽管城墙内还有不少废弃之所，但这座城市被快速重建了起来，以前的废墟上不断建起新的房屋。

新教传教

让我们来看一下基督教新教在这座城市的开教时间。多年来，驻守在上海的传教士们将苏州看作是福音传播的中心，盼望着有一天其大门会被打开。在苏州被太平军占领之前，杨格非和其他几位传教士曾到访过苏州，希望能寻求一处落脚点，当年杨格非还很年轻稚嫩，如今他已变得非常老练了。牧师慕维廉曾穿着当地人的衣服，戴着假辫子来到这里，不幸的是，

too securely fastened. He was seized, dragged along the streets, and a heavy club on his head made him think the time was short.

The first foreigner to live in this city was Charles Schmidt, under the auspices of the American Presbyterians (North). He came in 1868. He had been an officer of the " Ever Victorious Army," and his extended acquaintance among the military Mandarins secured him an unmolested sojourn. He was a man of wonderful tact in dealing with the people, had a far-reaching acquaintance with Chinese affairs, was a fluent speaker, a gifted preacher, and wrote a most excellent tract. He afterwards withdrew from the mission service.

In 1867, Rev. J. W. Lambuth, D.D., obtained a room with a dirt floor near the Ink Pagoda, and on his regular visits to the city held religious services. He was afterwards aided by a native minister, Rev. C. K. Marshall, who had resided some years in America, in establishing the Southern Methodist Mission, which, now within a half mile of the mustard-seed chapel, has a church, six foreign residences, two large hospitals, a male college with 120 pupils, a female seminary and a Bible-woman's home. They have, besides these, near the city temple a large chapel with an English school of over 100 pupils; also a ladies' home in a native house.

During the occupation of Nanking by the rebels, Dr. Muirhead visited that place, and passing near the wall heard shrieks and groans. Going upon the wall he found a young lad wounded and ill, who was about to give up his life in despair. He was taken to Shanghai and kindly cared for. In 1872, when Dr. M. came to Soochow and tried to rent a place, a rice-merchant proffered his assistance and secured for him a chapel on the principal street of the city. It was the aforesaid lad, who in this way showed his gratitude. Thus Messrs Muirhead and Lambuth, *nomina nobilia et clarissima*, were the first regular preachers in this pagan city.

The American Presbyterians (North) have had for years their residences, with a church and high school annexed, in the " South Garden" —a euphonious title for the paddy fields— and also outside the Chang Men they have erected a large woman's hospital. The Southern Presbyterians began work in 1872 at the Yang Yoh Hong, and have now residences near the Great Pagoda and the Twin Pagoda, with a ladies' home at the Foo Men. The new hospital, with its capacious wards and physician's house, is outside the north gate. The Southern Baptist

假辫子没有戴好，他被抓了出来，拖到街上，他头顶挨的一棍让他一度觉得命不久矣。

第一个生活在苏州城内的外国人是查尔斯·施美德，他获得了美国（北）长老会的经济资助，于1868年来到这里，他曾是"常胜军"的一名军官，因此他与中国军官们相当熟悉，这也保障了其在苏州安居乐业。他在为人处世方面相当圆滑，对于中国事务了解广泛，他还是一个流利的演说家，富有天赋的宣教士，写了一本非常优秀的宣教手册。后来，他退出了宣教行列。

1867年，蓝柏牧师在方塔附近寻得一间民房。蓝柏定期来访苏州，并在屋内举行宗教仪式。后来，蓝柏在华人牧师曹子实的帮助下建立了南监理会传教基地，曹子实曾在美国待过数年时光。如今，在教堂方圆半英里内，有一个教会、六所外国人住宅、两家大型医院、一所有120位学生的男子书院、一所女子神学院和一所"《圣经》女子之家"。此外，他们在靠近玄妙观的地方还有一所大教堂，内设英语学校，有100多位学生，同时，在当地人家中还开设了"女子之家"。

在太平天国占领南京期间，慕维廉曾经参观过那里，在经过城墙附近时，他听到了尖叫和呻吟声。他登上城墙发现一个受伤生病的小男孩，在绝望中打算放弃自己的生命。这个小男孩后来被带到上海，得到了很好的照顾。1872年，当慕维廉来到苏州想要租场地时，一位米商提供帮助并为他在苏州的主街道上寻得一处开设小教堂。这位米商就是当年的小男孩，他通过这样的方式来表达他的感激之情。因此，慕维廉和蓝柏，这两位先生，成为这座异教城市里的首批常驻传教士。

多年来，美国（北）长老会在"南园"——对稻田的一种委婉叫法——建立了自己的住宅，并在内附设了一个教堂和一所书院，在阊门外还建了一所女子医院。南长老会于1872年在养育巷启动工作，如今在北寺塔和双塔附近建了住所，在葑门也有一所"女子之家"。新建的医院位于北门之

chapel and manse are in the north-eastern part of the city.

There are now twelve male missionaries and twenty-four female missionaries (including the wives) in Soochow: also six homes for the unmarried ladies. There are fifteen chapels; in several of these daily preaching. The large audiences and the attention they give to the speakers has made this a prominent feature of evangelistic work. There are twenty day-schools with about 500 pupils, and the instruction of these occupies the time of several of the ladies. Ready access is had to the women in their houses, and they come in numbers to the homes of the missionary families. Six or eight hundred thousand tracts or Scripture-portions have been sold in and around the city. There are one or two dispensaries, besides the four hospitals. The people entertain the kindliest feelings towards the American residents, who have lived so long among them and identified themselves with the city's interests.

The New Port

As a result of the Japanese-Chinese war, Soochow was opened as a foreign port in the beginning of 1896. The Japanese Consul-General was the first representative of a foreign power to come to the city. It was the desire of the officials that the settlement be located three miles to the south, at the Fifty-three Arch Bridge, mentioning "deep water" as one of the special attractions. The Consul assured them that " it was a fine place to plant rice and hunt pheasants." A site for the concession was agreed upon directly to the south of the city and opposite the wall. It has a frontage of one and one-third miles on the Grand Canal, which affords a commodious harbor for thousands of small craft. The autonomy of the western part of the settlement, with the exception of the Bund has been given to the conquering Japanese, while the eastern portion, facing on two sides the Grand Canal, is the general foreign concession.

The Custom House, opposite the south-east corner of the city, is a large and commanding structure, having more the appearance of a huge dwelling than of a public building. The Commissioner's Mansion, with its two-acre garden, is said to be the handsomest residence occupied by any Chief of Customs in Cathay. Next to this is the Police Station, containing a large and airy dwelling for the Captain-Superintendent, the "Municipal Hall," offices for the staff, and

外，病房和医生住所都很宽敞。南浸信会的教堂和牧师住宅位于苏州城的东北部。

目前苏州城内共有十二名男传教士和二十四名女传教士（包括男传教士的妻子），还有六所专为未婚女子所设的"女子之家"。苏州共有十五座教堂，其中不少教堂每天都有宣讲布道。大量的信众及其传教士们对宣讲者给予的关注也成为福音工作的一大特色。苏州有二十所走读学校，大约500名学生，教导这些学生占据了女传教士们很多时间。传教士们的家中随时欢迎女士，而她们也成群结队地前来参观。在苏州城内和周边地区，共出售了六十万到八十万本宣教小册子及部分《圣经》经文。除了四家医院之外，还有一两家诊所。当地人对这些美国人也怀有最亲切的感情，毕竟他们在当地生活了很久，感觉自己与这座城市的命运休戚相关。

新口岸

根据中日《马关条约》，1896年年初，苏州成为向外国开放的新口岸城市。日本总领事成为首个进入苏州的外国势力代表。领事馆官员希望将领事馆建在五十三孔桥以南三英里处，他们还特别提到那里"水很深"，非常具有吸引力。日本领事也向他们保证，"这里是种植水稻和捕猎野鸡的好地方"。租界的地点最终确定在苏州城南，正对城墙。租界里的大运河上有一又三分之一英里的临街地段，这也为上千条小船提供了宽敞的停靠码头。日本人拥有租界西部地区除河浜以外的自治权，而东部地区，面临运河，则属于公共租界。

位于苏州城东南角对面的海关大楼，是一幢高大威严的建筑，与其说是一幢公共建筑，不如说是一所庞大的公寓。海关关长的官邸内有两英亩花园，据说是中国所有海关关长住宅里最漂亮的一个。官邸边上就是警察局，内有宽敞通风的警长住所、"办事大厅"、职员办公室及关押犯人的牢房。

cells for the prisoners. These three buildings, with the Likin Club, constitute the eastern wing of foreign Soochow. The English and Japanese Consulates await appropriations from their respective governments.

The "Horse Road," when completed to the *Liu Yuen*, the celebrated garden of the famous rail way magnate, Sheng Taotai will be five miles in length. It will connect with the railway station.

The Chinese are an astute people. They succeeded in putting the concession in a quiet locality, then turned the line of progress to the native centre of trade, so that for years, it may be, the vacant territory allotted to Europeans and Japanese may afford fine pasturage. A little city has sprung up outside the P'an Men, which, with its cotton mill, filature and tug offices, presents the appearance of a busy mart, and the Chinese will probably unite it by a line of shops with the Ch'ang Men.

The Italians, however, are erecting a large silk filature on the eastern portion of the settlement, and as it is stated as a fact that on account of the fresh, soft water around Soochow, the silk brings a better price in the market than that from the filatures on the Hwangpoo, in a few years factories by the score may be built. The concession is laid out with great regularity, and with broad avenues shaded by the elm and poplar may in time become one of the most beautiful places occupied by foreigners.

The Imperial Post Office is in new quarters near the centre of the city. Fifty or sixty tugs, which tow native boats and also those specially built for canal traffic—all of these packed with Chinese—ply between this place and Shanghai, Hangchow and Chinkiang. The natives are fully alive to their opportunity. The immense hoards of silver within the walls seeking investment, the magic sound in a Chinese ear of the name Soochow, the widespread belief that now the provincial capital is to attain its former commercial importance, its position in the centre of the silk district, the influx of population from the surrounding country, the right given under the new treaty to foreign capital to open factories at the ports, and its prospects as the centre of the Shanghai, Hangchow and Nanking Railway system, give promise of a most successful future to the new city, which, with the wisdom of mature years, and the vigor of young manhood, commences its twenty-fifth century.

这三幢建筑，连同厘金局构成了外国势力在苏州的东翼。英国和日本的领事馆的建造还在等他们各自政府的拨款。

"马路"建成后将长达五英里，通向留园，该园是铁路大亨盛道台所拥有的著名园林。这条"马路"也将与火车站相连。

中国人是非常精明的。他们成功地先将租界设在一个偏僻之所，然后把此处发展成本土贸易中心。如此一来，也许数年之后，这些当初划给欧洲人和日本人的空地就能获得很高的回报。盘门外已经发展成了一座小城市，里面有棉纺厂、缫丝厂和拖船公司，呈现出一片喧闹的市集景象，将来中国人很可能用一排商店将这里和阊门连在一起。

意大利人在租界的东面修建了一所大型缫丝厂，据说由于苏州地区的水质清新、柔软，因此这里出产的丝绸价格在市场上要高于黄埔缫丝厂生产出的丝绸。在未来的几年中，这里将会建立起几十家工厂。租界内的整体布局规范，宽阔的道路两旁绿树成荫，假以时日，这里将会成为外国人居住的最美丽的地方之一。

帝国邮政局就在靠近市中心的新城区。五六十条拖船，拖着本地船只，以及那些专为在运河航行而造的船只——所有这些船只都载满了中国人——往返于苏州和上海、杭州以及镇江之间。当地人已经开始充分意识到他们面对的机遇。城内有大量寻求投资的储备资金，苏州这个名字对中国人的吸引力，对其即将恢复原先重要商业地位的普遍共识，在丝绸贸易区内的中心地位，周边地区不断涌入的人口，新条约赋予外国资本在口岸城市开设工厂的特权，以及未来有望成为上海、杭州、南京铁路系统中心的前景，这一切都让这座城市焕然一新，前途一片光明。凭借着岁月累积下的智慧和年轻人的活力，这座城市翻开了它第二十五个世纪的新篇章。

Some Notes from the History of Soochow [1]

苏州历史见闻

(哈登 著 孟祥德 译)

《苏州历史见闻》(*Some Notes from the History of Soochow*)作者是美国人罗伯特·艾伦·哈登(Robert Allen Haden)。哈登十九世纪九十年代初来华,后居苏州。

《苏州历史见闻》初为哈登1915年12月4日在苏州文学社(the Literary Society of Soochow)宣读的论文,后由上海文汇报馆以小册子形式印刷出版。该文主要内容涉及春秋战国时期吴国的兴亡,历史上苏州地区的宗教、战争,苏州历代名称沿革,苏州历史名人,以及总的评论等。该文文笔简洁,行文跳跃性大,亦有一些内容为原作者个人观点,或与史实不符,对阅读造成一定的挑战。

---

[1] Read before the Literary Society of Soochow, 4th December, 1915. (1915年12月4日,宣读于苏州文学社。)

When we take up the history of a place so ancient as the city of Soochow, a city where kings and ministers, courtiers and minions, nobles and peasants, princely merchants and humble artisans, beautiful women, charming maidens, and fair ladies, have come, played their little play and gone the way of all men, and women, little more in a paper of this kind can be done than give a few salient points.

At the same time it should be remembered that there is not now in the city a single very ancient building or monument. This is owing to the flimsy character of all the building material used by the chin.

When T'ien Shia（天下）[1] was divided by Ta Yu（大禹）, the Great Yue under Shen（舜）, into nine chou（九州）or Divisions, the region in which Soochow is now situated was known as Yang Chou（扬州）, and so continued to be designated through the Hsia（夏）, B. C. 2205-1766, The Shang（商）, B. C. 1766-1122, and a part of Chou（周）, 1122-255 B. C.

In this district or division there arose the state or Kingdom of Wu（吴国）which occupied a small portion of eastern Anhui and some portion of Chekiang and all of Kiangsu south of the Yangtsze River. This state or kingdom of Wu lasted from B. C. 1260 to 475 or 785 years. The most significant fact during this time was the building of Soochow city.

Tai Peh（泰伯）and Chung Yung（仲雍）were brothers, elder and second sons of Tan Fu（亶父）, the progenitor of Fu Wang（武王）who founded the Chou dynasty[2]. Tan Fu being partial to his youngest son Chi Lih（季历）desired him to succeed to his power. The two older brothers learning their father's desires, were determined to put no obstacle in the way of the young brother and quietly left home and travelled south. Passing the River they came to a place called Ching Man（荆蛮）and there settled. This was some where near the present city of Chang Chow（常州）. They taught the people the arts of civilization, agriculture, house building, and to make clothing for themselves. Thus they gained the confidence of the people, and Tai Peh was chosen their chief and established a state, more than a thousand families joining in this allegiance. The kingdom or Principality thus set up was called Kou Wu（句吴）in imitation of the local sound. Mai Li（梅里）was the capital of this principality. There is considerable uncertainty as to where Mai Li was. In the annals of Soochow Fu

---

［1］ 原文中括注为繁体字，编者收录时改为简体。
［2］ 原文中表示"朝代"时"dynasty""Dynasty"均有，为全书统一，收录时统一为"dynasty"。

提起像苏州这样一座古老的城市的历史，仅凭一篇文章，不过浮光掠影。在这里，帝王将相、近臣差役、贵族农夫、富商大贾、微工末匠、美妇娇娃，各自上演一段故事，你方唱罢我登场。

同时，需要注意的是，如今苏州城内非常古老的建筑或碑阙已荡然无存，这是由于中国建筑所用材料不结实导致。

舜帝手下的大禹将天下分为九州，今天的苏州即位于当时九州之一的扬州。而扬州这一称谓历经夏（公元前 2205 年至公元前 1766 年）、商（公元前 1766 年至公元前 1122 年），以及周（公元前 1122 年至公元前 255 年）部分时间。

在这一地区，或这一州内，吴国逐渐崛起，占据了今安徽东部一小片、浙江部分区域，以及长江以南的江苏全境。从公元前 1260 年至公元前 475 年，吴国存续了 785 年。其间，最重要的事件是苏州城的建造。

亶父是周朝建立者周武王的祖先，泰伯与仲雍分别是亶父长子、次子。但是，亶父偏爱幼子季历，意欲传位于他。两位兄长得知父王意愿后，决定悄悄离家，远涉南方，以便幼弟顺利即位。过江后，他们来到号称"荆蛮"的地方，安顿下来。这就是今天的常州。他们传授当地人农耕、造房、作衣等技艺，就此赢得他们的信赖。泰伯被推为首领，建立王国，上千户人家归顺。按当地口音，该王国或封地被称为"句吴"，都城梅里。今天

（苏州府志）, it is said to have been something over fifty li north of the city of Soochow. In the Lih Kue Chuen （东周列国传） it is placed west of the present city of Wu Kiang （吴江） while others say somewhere in the district of Wusih.

From the time of Tai Peh the histories jump over nineteen generations to the time of Prince Beautiful, Shou Mung （寿梦）. Aged Dream had four sons. He regarded Chi Cha （季札） as the most worthy and desired to leave him the throne, but Chi Cha refused to usurp the rights of his brother, Chu Fan, and accepted the fief of Yien Ling （延陵）the present Chang Chow, instead. Chu Fan ruled only a few years and was succeeded by the second son. In a short time he was succeeded by the third son, and on his death Chi Cha was again called to the throne but he refused again, this time giving his age as his reason for declining. He remained in his Fief, occupying his time (in retirement) with agriculture and study. His tomb is at Shen Kiang Chen （申江镇） in Kiangyin Magistracy, where is also his temple. Near the grave is a large lime stone tablet, claimed locally to have been written by the hand of Confucius. Because of his high virtues, and eminent services his name has been entered by compilers of the History among the Noted Sages.

When Chi Cha had definitely declined the throne, Prince Beautiful （遼王）, son of the last ruler, was chosen to the throne. From this time we can speak of the History of Soochow with confidence, and Prince Beautiful can be looked on as a reliable historical character.

Up to his time practically nothing is said about the progress of the country, nothing of the inhabitants as to number and condition; no records of products or manufacture of any kind. Seeing the weakness from a literary standpoint revealed in this lack of essential facts the explanation is given that the records were destroyed during the "Burning of the Books" by Shih Huang Ti （始皇帝）, the First Emperor. But it should be remembered that the Imperial edict directed every subject, under pain of branding and banishment to work four years on the Great wall, to send all their literature except works on Agriculture, Medicine, and Divination to the nearest office to be destroyed by fire. And further that all Libraries belonging to the government and the books belonging to the officials of the rank of Po shih or Learned Men were excepted. And not nearly such destruction of books took place as later scholars claim.

The Chou dynasty was already in decadence, for the encroachments by the Dukes of the Feudal states had been more and more aggressive. The smaller

已很难确定当时梅里所在。《苏州府志》称其位于苏州城北五十多里，《东周列国传》称其位于今天的吴江西部，也有称其位于无锡某处。

自泰伯始，十九代后，"姬寿梦"即位。寿梦育有四子，最宠季札，欲传王位于他。季札不愿攫取兄长诸樊的王位，于是接受延陵（今常州）封地。诸樊即王位仅几年后，便传位于寿梦次子。又不久，次子再传位于三子。三子去世后，季札又被召回即位。季札借口年事已高，再次婉拒。季札一直待在他的封地。从自己的位子退下来后，他勤于耕读，死后葬在江阴的申江镇，季子庙也在那里。墓边有一石碑。当地流传其碑文为孔子所书。季札因德高业勤，被史官列为圣贤。

当初，季札坚辞王位后，寿梦第三子之子僚[1]即位。此后的苏州历史比较明晰。僚可以看作一个可信的历史人物。

在此之前，几乎没有关于吴国历史进程、人口多少与状况如何的记载，没有任何物产、手工的记录。由于缺乏对基本史实的记载，可见历史文献的不足。这主要是秦始皇"焚书"造成的破坏。但是需要记住的是，秦的臣民，被黥面、流放，饱受四年修筑长城之苦，又被勒令就近上缴除农业、医药、占卜之外的书籍至官府，尽行焚毁。官府藏书，以及具有博士职位的官员藏书除外，以致此后学者断言，如此毁书，后无来者。

诸侯国强盛后，鲸吞蚕食，导致周王室式微。小的诸侯国被征服后，封地被大的诸侯国吞并，直到最后形成群雄争霸的局面。吴国位列其中，

---

[1] 即吴王僚。

powers were conquered and the territory appropriated by the stronger states, until there had grown up independent and powerful states. One of these was Wu which soon began to make such progress that it was the most powerful and resourceful of all. For the first and one of the greatest of all the men who shaped the affairs of Wu now makes his appearance—Wu Yuen （伍员）or Wu Tzu-shu（伍子胥）. His father was minister of Tsu （楚）. Having fallen in disfavour, being falsely accused by a flittering minion, the Prince of Tsu, The Pacificator（平王）, ordered the minister to be imprisoned and forced him to write to his two sons to come to court. The plot being known the two brothers agreed that the elder should return to captivity in order to fill the commands of his father and made evident his filial regard while Tzu-shu should escape for the purpose, in due time, of avenging the death of father and brother, in case they were put to death. The whole family to the number of three hundred and forty souls was exterminated. Only Wu Yuen escaped. He fled southward. Strict orders were given and a large reward offered for his apprehension. Arriving near Chao Kwan（昭关）he took refuge in the secluded home of an old physician who promised to help him pass the barriers. After seven days of anxious waiting his beard, which was a foot broad, and his hair, became quite white. This fact led to his escape. Being hotly pursued, and descriptions of him having been put out over all the land, he only escaped by another assuming his dress and allowing himself to be arrested, while Wu Tzu-shu, in the garb of a peasant passed unobserved, in the confusion of the arrest. One of China's most famous Dramas is founded on this incident in the life of Wu Tzu-shu.

  That Wu Yuen was able to powerfully influence those he came in close contact with was twice proven during his flight. Arriving at the banks of the Yangstze, with soldiers in close pursuit, he persuaded a fisherman, to ferry him over the river. Comment on his unusual appearance and bearing, by the fisherman, led him to reveal his identity and suffering together with his undying purpose of revenge. The fisherman gave him food, and having nothing but his trusty sword Wu Tzu-shu offered this in payment. The offer was positively refused. Tzu-shu then asked for the utmost secrecy. The man of net and hooks assured Tzu-shu of his faithfulness. "But," said he, "Lest you should doubt me, I will disappear," with which speech he pushed off from the shore, plunged into the water and disappeared. Wu Yuen then followed the banks of the river until he came into the region of Lai Yang（溧阳）. There hungry and weary he met

最终成为国势最为强大、物力最为充足的诸侯国。在奠定吴国国政的众多了不起的人物中，首推伍员，即伍子胥。伍子胥父亲是楚国大夫，失宠后，为佞臣诬陷。楚平王命他写信，召二子回朝。兄弟二人识破楚王阴谋，兄长决定遵从父命，自投罗网，以表孝心。伍子胥则选择逃亡。万一父兄被杀，他将来可以报仇雪恨。之后，伍子胥一家三百四十口被杀害，只有他一人南逃，幸免于难。楚王巨额悬赏，严令捉拿伍子胥。行近昭关时，伍子胥躲进一位行医老翁僻静的家里。老人答应帮他过关。经过七天焦急的等待，他足有一尺长的长髯，连同头发全变白了。这一变化倒有助于他逃脱。由于官府到处画影图形，追拿甚紧，只好由他人装扮成伍子胥模样，自投罗网，而伍子胥身着农夫衣衫，无人注意，趁乱逃出关口。中国一传统剧目即根据伍子胥这一故事编排的。

　　凡是接触到伍子胥的人，都会受到他的影响，这一点在他逃亡路上有两次得到验证。到达长江岸边时，后有追兵迫近，他求一渔夫渡他过江。渔夫称赞他相貌举止不俗，他于是将自己的身世、家仇及复仇决心如实相告。渔夫给他食物。伍子胥无以为报，解佩剑相赠，渔夫坚辞不受。伍子胥于是央求渔夫千万保密。终日与渔网、鱼钩打交道的渔夫向伍子胥保证不会出卖他。"但是，"他说，"我还是消失吧，免得你疑心。"说完，他撑船离岸，跳入江中，不见踪影。伍子胥沿岸边潜逃，最后来到溧阳地界。他又累又饿，碰巧遇到一位女子挎着一篮子食物。他向前称饿乞食。

a young woman carrying a basket of food. He asked for food, stating that he was starving. This she gave and partook with him. Then when he promised to return and reward her she told him she had been living in seclusion for thirty years, never having spoken to a man, but now having broken her vows, she was too full of shame to live. She immediately drowned herself. Taking an oath by high and azure heaven to return and reward such sacrifice he made his way to the court of Prince Beautiful. Arriving there he made his flute pour forth his tale of woe and at the same time gained a pittance of food. His flute playing was heard by Duke Brightness（公子光）, the cousin and senior in order of birth to the reigning prince. Through the influence of the Duke, Tzu-shu was taken into the service of Prince Beautiful but remained in this service for only a short time. For his worth and ability were recognized by Duke Brightness, who desired to have Wu in his own service. Being son of the eldest son of Aged Dream the Duke considered that since Chi Cha had refused the throne he, the duke, was rightful heir. Consequently he had long since determined on the destruction of Prince Beautiful. But an opportunity did not offer until the coming of Wu Tzu-shu. Being in the service of the Duke, Wu Yuen now had a commanding position at the court. The plans and purpose of the Duke having been made known to him Tzu-shu soon proposed a plan for the destruction of the Prince.

  Prince Beautiful was very fond of broiled fish and this fact was to be made use of for his undoing. On arrival in the borders of Wu Kingdom, Wu Tzu-shu had met and formed a blood covenant with Chuan Chu（专诸）, a man of great prowess and strength, and of an unscrupulous character. Chuan Chu readily entered into the plans against the Prince. In order to learn all the best methods of broiling fish Chuan Chu went to the Great Lake and for three months studied the art. Prince Beautiful having returned from a successful predatory raid on a neighboring state was invited by Duke Brightness to a feast of broiled fish, prepared by a man who had just returned from the Great Lake and was an expert in preparing the delicacy. The Prince was suspicious, and was advised by his mother not to accept the invitation. But fearing that his non-appearance at the feast would be taken as an exhibition of weakness he went surrounded by his body guard. Duke Brightness had secreted three hundred men in an adjoining room, and warned Wu Tzu-shu to be ready without with more men. When the first dish was handed up, some disguised soldiers quietly slipped into the room. The Duke at this time said that his leg was cramped, and, excusing himself,

女子分食于他。伍子胥许诺日后回来报答。女子告诉他自己独居已三十年，未尝与男子交谈。如今失节，无颜再活世上，随即自溺而亡。伍子胥向苍天起誓，日后定当回报，然后径往僚统治的吴国。到达吴国后，他一腔冤屈无处诉说，只好吹箫乞食于吴市。箫声恰好被公子光听到。他是当时吴国国君的堂兄。在公子光的举荐下，伍子胥辅佐了僚，但是时间不长。公子光赏识伍子胥的才干，便将他招到自己的麾下。作为诸樊的儿子，公子光认为，既然季札让位，自己才是王位的合法继承人。因此，他一直暗下决心除掉僚。但是遇到伍子胥之前，一直苦于没有机会。这时，效忠于公子光的伍子胥在王宫里有了指挥权。公子光将计划和预谋告知伍子胥，伍子胥马上提出了除掉僚的计谋。

僚酷爱炙鱼，伍子胥提出可以利用这一点干掉他。当初伍子胥进入吴国边界时，巧遇专诸，并与之歃血为盟。专诸武艺高超，力大无穷，但为人鲁莽。他欣然参与到刺杀僚的谋划中。为了学习最为精湛的炙鱼技艺，专诸专门跑到太湖边，潜心学习了三个月。一日，僚掳掠邻国，凯旋。公子光趁机邀请他赴宴，称一人刚从太湖来，尤擅炙鱼。僚狐疑，其母劝阻。但是，僚担心缺席宴会是示弱的表现，于是在侍卫的簇拥下赴宴。公子光在隔壁房间预先埋伏士兵三百名，并叮嘱伍子胥务必在外准备更多人手。第一道菜呈上来后，部分伪装好的士兵悄悄潜入房内。此时，公子光借口腿部痉挛，告退片刻。专诸预先将一柄短剑藏于鱼腹，在将炙烤好的鱼献

stepped out for a moment. Chuan Chu had concealed a short knife in the main dish of broiled fish. In the act of presenting this dish to Prince Beautiful, Chuan Chu seized the knife and plunged it into the breast of the prince. Chuan Chu was immediately attacked by the body guard, but owing to his great strength he was able to stab the prince a second time, who with a great cry fell over dead. The body guard made mince meat of Chuan Chu. But Duke Kwang led in his minions and half the guard were put to the sword, while the fleeing half were met by Wu Tzu-shu and dispatched. Duke Brightness seized the throne, and proclaimed himself king under the title of Ho Lu（阖闾）. This man in the history of Soochow is one of the most famous, for it was during his reign and under his direction that Wu Tzu-shu built the city.

Ho Lu reigned B. C. 514-496. He was noted for his simplicity of life and when on his numerous campaigns shared alike the fare of his soldiers. As soon as he was secure in the throne he made Wu Tzu-shu minister of state, and set about putting his country in order. The defences were strengthened, the finances reformed, the army reorganized, and agriculture had due consideration. All this was with the sole purpose of being able to defend his country and overcome the old enemies of his state—Yueh, on the South, Ch'i and F'u on the north. For during the time of the feudal states the normal condition of the whole country seems to have been that of war. The smaller states were overcome and appropriated by the stronger, and might was right in fact, though the theory was never acknowledged. The desire for leadership and pre-eminence was the cause of many a war between the rival states. Tsu was the most powerful, and to defeat her was the first step to pre-eminence（霸业）. At the same time Wu Yuen lived for no other purpose than vengeance on the bloody house of his Enemy. Ho Lu spoke quite freely with his minister about his ambitions and desired of him a plan for their accomplishment. But Wu would do nothing to further his schemes until he received a solemn oath that Ho Lu would help him to avenge himself on Tsu. On receiving this promise he at once set about conserving the forces of the country. By his diligence, skill and general ability, Wu Tzu-shu soon brought the Kingdom to a high state of prosperity and efficiency. At this time the capital of Wu was still at Mai Li which was not sufficiently strong nor large enough for a flourishing state. So Ho Lu was dissatisfied and said to Tzu-shu "My kingdom is secluded, being on the south east (of China) and is surrounded by the difficulties of low marshes (this would seem to point to the country south and west of the

给僚时，专诸抽出利剑，一下刺入僚的前胸。侍卫当即拔刀砍向专诸，但是由于专诸力大，他再次刺向僚，僚应声倒地而亡。侍卫将专诸剁成肉酱。公子光急召护卫入内，僚侍卫当场半数死于刀剑之下，逃出的另一半被伍子胥截杀。公子光于是夺取了王位，改名阖闾。在他统治期间，命伍子胥修建苏州城，阖闾因而成为苏州历史上最为著名的人物之一。

公元前514至公元前496年阖闾在位。他素以生活俭朴而著称。在数次征战中，甚至与士兵同食。坐稳王位后，他任命伍子胥为大夫，着手治理吴国：加强防御，改革赋税，重组军队，重视农业。所有这些只为一个目的，就是能够保卫吴国，征服宿敌——南面的越国，北面的齐国、鲁国。因为，春秋时期，战争乃国之常态。那时小国经常被大国征服、吞并，强权成为公理，尽管没有人承认这一论断。争夺领导权，成就霸业，成为各诸侯国之间战争不断的原因。当时，楚国最为强大。其他诸侯国要想成为霸主，就必须先打败楚国。同时，伍子胥一心只想灭掉嗜血残忍的楚王王室。阖闾与他的大夫随意谈起自己的抱负，希望伍子胥出谋划策，帮助自己实现这些抱负。但是，伍子胥不为所动，直到阖闾郑重发誓帮他复仇。得到阖闾的许诺后，他立即着手推行富国强兵之策。凭借勤奋和才干，伍子胥很快使吴国强盛起来。那时，吴国的国都还在梅里。但是对于日益崛起的吴国来说，梅里的城池不够坚固，地域不够广阔。因此，阖闾不甚满意，对伍子胥说："吴国闭塞，地处东南，地势低洼，沼泽成片（这个主要是指今天的苏州城南部与西部地区），海水、潮汐泛滥，困难重重。加之粮仓、

present city) and subjected to the inundations of sea and tides. The granaries and the treasury are empty, the arable land is not cultivated; the kingdom has no safeguards against depredations; the people have no constant ambition; I have no means of overawing the neighboring states. What can be done about it?"Wu then quoted precedent from the instruction of ancient statesmen. For precedent ruled then, does now, and from present appearances ever shall rule the lives, of high and low, among the sons of Han. He laid out a plan for establishing granaries, equipping and training an army to preserve order in the kingdom, and for protection against out-side enemies. Full authority was given to Wu Yuen for carrying out his purposes. So successful were they that Ho Lu was able to throw off his allegiance to the house of Chou, which had from the beginning of the Wu Kingdom, been acknowledged as the Proper Government（正统）. Part of Wu Tzu-shu's plan was the building of a great city.

  He surveyed the land as to height, tasted the waters as to salt or sweetness, observed the celestial signs, laid out the plan and built a city 47 li in circumference. What a stupendous task! Build a city and such a city. Twelve to thirteen miles around. What thousands of workmen, stone masons, brick kilns, lime kilns, hod carriers, diggers, carpenters, and smiths. Such an undertaking would cause any people of this time to sit down and reckon the cost. Wu Tzu-shu built the wall, laid out the streets, and dug the canals and built the bridges. While probably no part of the wall remains as it was originally built, and no bridge that has not been reconstructed, yet it is equally probable that the place of the outer wall has not been materially changed, though the inner wall, has long since disappeared. That this city did not grow along watercourses or by pathes is proved from evidences of design on every hand, in the lay or direction of streets and canal through the whole city.

  Wu built eight land and eight water gates. He built eight land gates to resemble the eight winds of heaven, and eight water gates to resemble the eight diagrams of earth. On the west were (1) The Ch'ang Gate（阊门）, the Gate of Heaven. It was so called that the winds of heaven might find entrance to the city. Another reason for the name was that Ho Lu desired the downfall of Tsu and that state would not be able to stand before a city whose gate was the gate of heaven. It may be of interest to note that the keeper of the gate of heaven, in these later years, is Kwanti, the god of war, and that the main gate to the palace of an emperor was called Chang or gate of heaven. From the description of the gate

国库空虚,农田待垦。国无御敌之屏障,民无长久之谋划,寡人无威慑邻邦之手段。计将安出?"伍子胥援引古代政治家之成法以应对。因为祖宗成法在过去、现在和将来都主导着汉家子孙的生活,无论贵贱。他建粮仓,修武备,内安其邦,外御其敌。阖闾全面授权伍子胥施展抱负。他们大获成功,阖闾不再拥戴周王室。在吴国建立之前,周王室一直被奉为正统。伍子胥计划之一就是兴建一座大城。

他相土尝水,象天法地,建周长四十七里大城。建一城如斯,这是多么艰巨的任务!阖闾大城周围十二三英里。征调的石匠、砖窑工、石灰窑工、脚夫、挖掘工、木匠、铁匠等不可胜数。这样巨大的工程,换了任何人都会坐下来,盘算一下成本。伍子胥指挥工匠建城墙,通街道,挖运河,架桥梁,终于建成阖闾大城。时至今日,当时的城墙恐怕早已荡然无存,如今的桥梁都是重建的。不过同样可能的是,外城墙所在的地方没有实质性的改变,而内城墙早已不见踪迹。在设计时,对贯穿全城的街道与水路的布局、走向考虑得面面俱到。这足以证明此城并非循水道或傍陆路而生。

伍子胥建陆门八,以象天之八风;水门八,以法地之八聪。西门为阊门,乃天之门,因天风从此穿过。之所以叫阊门,还有一个原因:阖闾欲伐楚国,而楚国无法立于有天之门的城下。有意思的是,后来守卫天之门的是战神关帝。王宫主门称作闾,即天之门。从当时对胥门(即"胥吏"之门)以及其顶部结构的描述来看,与今天胥门的建筑外观颇为相似。之所以称为"胥

and its superstructure it must have resembled the present structure in appearance, (2) The Shu (胥门) or Clerks Gate. So called because just inside this gate was the palace or enclosure of Wu Tzu-shu. Another explanation is that the name came from Shu San (胥山) which is directly west of the gate. The place of the gate was fixed by Ho Lu who desired a convenient exit to his summer palace on Ling Yienshan (灵岩山), Spirit Peak Hill. According to the *Annals of Wu and Yueh*, Fu Ch'ai had the head of Tzu-shu hung on this gate to frighten the soldiers of Yueh away.

On the south was (1) The Dish Gate (盘门). Of old it was called the Coiled Gate (蟠门) because a coiled dragon was carved over the gate to overawe the tribes of Yueh (越). In this controversy about names we are in the condition of Confucius when he heard two boys hotly discussing the sun. One said: "When the sun rises he is as big as a wheel, but at noon the size of a plate and therefore further off." The other said: "In the morning he is quite cool, but at noon be is like hot water, and therefore nearer to us." Confucius was unable to decide which was correct. And (2) The Snake Gate (蛇门). Tzu-shu built the Snake Gate to resemble the Door of the earth, and further on account of Yueh, for this kingdom was to the South East, and the gate was built to signify the restraint of Yueh. This gate has long since been done away with.

On the east was (1) The Artisans Gate (匠门), which was now known as the Kan Chiang gate (干将门). So called in honor of the famous sword-maker who had his shop just inside this gate. Kan Chiang had great difficulty in producing a good sword and consulted his wife Mo Yeh (莫邪). She told him the metal would not run properly without the essence of man in the flux. Again the furnace was prepared, and the two cut off their hair and nail and threw them in the furnace. As a result there came two swords from that one heating of the furnace of such high excellence as to be worthy to present to the prince. Mo Kan Shan (莫干山) takes its name from these two sword-makers. There is considerable controversy as to whether this gate was finally done away with or the name changed to Boundry Gate (喋门). (2) Tethered Gate (娄门) which was at first known as Liu (嘹) for to the east there was a city with a mud wall built by Aged Dream of this name now known as Kuen Shan. The name was changed in the latter Han to Lou. Another authority says the name Lou came from the name of a river Lou Kiang which flowed past Sung Kiang and entered the sea. This is probably the correct explanation. On the north was (1) The

门",是因为该门正对伍子胥官邸。另一种说法是,该门正对西边的"姑胥山",因而得名。后来,阖闾为方便出城前往灵岩山的避暑别馆,将城门位置改动。据《吴越春秋》记载,夫差曾将伍子胥人头悬于该城门,以吓阻越国军队。

南门为盘门("杯盘"之"盘")。古称"蟠门",因城门雕刻一蟠龙以威慑越国而得名。这些名称的由来众说纷纭,一如孔子听"两小儿辩日"。一个说:"太阳初升的时候,大得像车轮。但是到了正午,就变成盘子大小。所以到了正午,太阳就离我们远了。"另一个说:"早上太阳给人感觉是凉的,但是到了正午时分,太阳如热水一样,因此距离我们更近了。"孔子听了也不能确定谁对谁错。[1]另有蛇门。伍子胥效法地之门而建蛇门,以约束地处东南的越国。该门很早前就被拆。

东门原为匠门,今称干将门。为纪念铸剑名匠——干将而取名。相传他的匠铺即位于该城门内。干将欲铸宝剑一把而不得,遂向其妻莫邪求教。莫邪告诉他,融化的金属缺少人的精气,就无法顺利地流动。二人再次点燃匠炉,断发剪甲,投入炉中。于是,一塘炉火铸就宝剑两口,献与吴王。莫干山亦取名自干将、莫邪。至于后来该门被拆掉还是改名为"𨂿门",亦有争议。娄("拴""系"之义)门初为"𨂿门",因寿梦用土墙建城,名曰"𨂿"。此城即如今昆山。其后,汉朝改称"娄门"。另有专家说该名称取自娄江。娄江流经淞江入海。这个解释或许是正确的。北门为齐门。

---

[1] 一儿曰:"日初出大如车盖,及日中则如盘盂,此不为远者小而近者大乎?"一儿曰:"日初出沧沧凉凉,及其日中如探汤,此不为近者热而远者凉乎?"孔子不能决也。

Ch'i Gate（齐门）. According to the Annals of Wu and Yuen, in the tenth year of Ho Lu, Wu made war on Ch'i, and that kingdom having been conquered, the prince of Ch'i, as one of the conditions of peace, was forced to give his only daughter in marriage to the crown prince of Wu. The princess being young and home-sick came often to the north wall to look out towards her home, Ch'i, at the north. So the name of the gate was given in memory of the maiden who died of homesickness, for she was never married to the prince. (2) The Level Gate（平门）. So called because it was from this gate that Tzu-shu as General-in-Chief led the armies of Wu, to the leveling of Ch'i, and so the gate had its name. It has long since been done away with.

While Wu Tzu-shu was building the city and thus making his name known to all succeeding generations, Ho Lu was no less busy building his summer palace and pleasure gardens on Spirit Peak Hill. In many respects, the Chinese are a people that appreciate real worth. Ho Lu is known to the learned but Wu Tzu-shu is known to the people. By the energy of Tzu-shu the borders of the country were extended and the condition of the people so improved that Wu became one of the most powerful of all the states into which China was divided at that time. So that it was with confidence that Ho Lu and Wu Yuen gathered their army to attack Tsu. A great victory was gained, the capital of Tsu was taken, the city given up to loot, and Ho Lu made his head quarters in the palace. Wu Tzu-shu found the burial place of The Pacificator, disentombed the corpse, gave it a beating of three hundred lashes, cut off the head, and scattered the remains, to be devoured by wild beasts. Some years after this Ho Lu lost his life in battle and was succeeded by his unworthy son Fu Ch'ai, B.C. 495, who held the throne until 473. Ho Lu was buried by his son on the advice of necromancers outside of the Destroying Ch'u Gate, on what was known as Sea Wall Hill. Workmen were sent to dig a cave in the hill for the reception of the catafalque. The knife which Chuan Chu took from the dish of broiled fish, the personal sword of Ho Lu, together with a thousand suits of armor and swords, besides gold and jade bowls, were buried with him. The burial ceremonies having been completed all the workmen employed in the construction of the tomb were killed and buried in the cave along with Ho Lu. Three days after this a white tiger was seen crouching on the grave mound, and from that time the hill has been called Hu Chu Shan（虎邱山, Tiger Mound Hill）.

Fu Ch'ai kept Wu Yuen as his minister and for a long time maintained the struggle against the state of Yueh, which was under the rule of Kou Ch'ien（勾

根据《吴越春秋》记载，阖闾统治第十年，吴国与齐国开战，齐国战败。作为停战条件之一，齐王被迫将自己唯一的女儿许配给吴国太子以和亲。齐国公主年幼思乡，常常伫立北门，向北遥望齐国。后来，终因眷恋故土，尚未成婚便郁郁而终。为纪念这位女子而取名齐门。另有平门。因吴王任命伍子胥为将，率军平齐，从此门而出，故而得名。如今，齐门早已被毁。

伍子胥建城，名垂千秋万代。阖闾则忙于大兴土木，在灵岩山建离宫别苑。在很多方面，中国人尚实，因此，阖闾之名闻于学者，伍子胥之名闻于百姓。凭借伍子胥之力，吴国开疆拓土，百姓生活也得以改善。当时的中国，诸侯并起，吴国成为最强盛的诸侯国之一。阖闾与伍子胥因此有底气集结军队讨伐楚国。吴国大胜，攻占楚国都城，然后纵兵掳掠。阖闾进驻楚宫。伍子胥找到楚平王埋葬之处，掘墓曝尸，鞭三百下，枭首肢解，任凭野兽分食。几年后，阖闾死于战场。公元前495年，阖闾之子不肖夫差即位。夫差在位时间至公元前473年。夫差听从巫师建议，葬阖闾于"破楚门"（即阊门）之外，"海涌山"（即虎丘）之上，并命民夫山顶挖墓穴存放棺椁。阖闾的佩剑——专诸行刺用的鱼肠剑——连同一千套铠甲兵刃、黄金玉碗与阖闾一同下葬。葬礼结束后，所有造墓的民夫被杀，为阖闾殉葬。三天后，人们见一白虎卧于墓堆上。之后，人们称之为虎丘山。

夫差继续任用伍子胥为大夫，吴国与勾践统治下的越国常年争斗。夫践). He defeated his enemy at the great battle of Fu Chiao (夫 椒). Kou Ch'ien, his wife, concubines and immediate attendants were put in captivity, and forced to do the most degraded services for the court of Wu. Peace was made with Yueh in spite of the earnest protest of Tzu-shu. For, said he, if Wu does not obliterate Yueh then Yueh will exterminate Wu. After three years of captivity Kou Ch'ien was liberated by the advice of corrupt officials, though Wu Yuen solemnly protested against the rash act.

Kou Ch'ien was appointed feudal Lord of Wu and restored to his principality, and this was the beginning of the downfall of the Wu Kingdom. For though the prince of Yueh was in prison the affairs of state were conducted by faithful ministers and the prince returned to a prosperous country. Kou Ch'ien assumed the greatest simplicity of life. He slept on fire wood, refusing a bed or a quilt, his drink was mingled with gall, he instituted sumptuary laws of the most rigid but benevolent character, lightened the taxes of the people; meeting some by the way he asked their name and occupation; at the time of plowing he went personally to encourage the people; his wife wove her own cloth; he suffered with the people, and ate no meat as an example of economy; his clothing was without adornment. So that all became passionately devoted to him. He lived only for revenge, and every month called a conference of his ministers to ask about methods for action against their common enemy. His minister Wen Chung on one of these occasions proposed Seven Plans for the subversion of Wu.

All of the plans were based on the known dissolute character of Fu Ch'ai, and his corrupt officials, and they all succeeded. The execution of these plans was committed to Fan Li and it is probably owing to this fact that foreign writers on the history of the Wu Kingdom have credited him with their authorship.

1. Make voluntary offerings of valuable goods and silks to prince and ministers in order to gain their favour. This was entirely successful.

2. Make special stores of millet and grain in abundant years, in order to cause it to be unnecessary for Wu to make provision. This succeeded so well that Wu was brought to famine.

3. Send presents of beautiful women for the purpose of bringing into error the hearts and minds of Wu.

4. Send skilled workmen and excellent material for the building of palaces and dwellings that they might waste their treasures.

5. Dispatch able ministers to the court of Wu to defeat their plans.

椒之战，夫差大败敌军。勾践及夫人、姬妾、近侍都成了俘虏，被迫为吴王宫室做最为下贱的活计。吴王不顾伍子胥直谏，跟越国讲和。伍子胥曾警告，非吴灭越，即越灭吴。勾践被俘三年后，夫差听信佞臣谗言，不顾伍子胥极力反对，贸然将勾践释放。

勾践被封为吴国封邑的领主，恢复爵位，吴国之亡初见端倪。当初越王被囚禁时，国家事务由几位忠臣掌管。越王被放归时，越国已然欣欣向荣。此后，勾践生活起居极为简朴。就寝时，他撤去床榻被褥，但卧柴薪之上；就餐时，他和胆汁而饮。他修订法度，禁止奢侈，其法律宽严相济。他减轻赋税，礼贤下士，农耕时节，亲往民间劝农。他的夫人亲自动手织布。他与民共患难，用素餐，着素衣，以为表率。上下皆心悦诚服。他一心想着复仇，每月召集群臣，共商伐敌之策。大夫文种献破吴七术。

夫差荒淫无度，群臣腐败不堪，越国的所有计划都是根据这一情况制订的，并一一奏效。范蠡专门负责实施这些计划。或许正因为这一点，国外研究吴国历史的学者将范蠡看成他们研究写作绕不开的人物。

　　1. 进献奇珍异宝、绫罗绸缎，以取悦吴国君臣。[1]（此计完全奏效。）

　　2. 丰年专储粟谷，使吴国放弃积谷防饥，不备不时之需、不备饥荒。[2]（此计得逞，后吴国饥荒。）

　　3. 进献美女，以蛊惑吴国君臣心神。[3]

　　4. 进献能工巧匠，珍料良材，怂恿吴国大兴土木，建造宫殿住所，使其国库空虚。[4]

　　5. 派遣能臣出仕吴国，以挫败他们的计谋。[5]

----

[1]　一曰捐货币，以悦其君臣。
[2]　二曰贵籴粟槁，以虚其积聚。
[3]　三曰遗美女，以惑其心志。
[4]　四曰遗之巧工良材，使作宫室，以罄其财。
[5]　五曰遗之谀臣，以乱其谋。

6. Use secret violence against his admonishing ministers (Censors), cause them to commit suicide, and thus make inefficient their assistance.

7. Accumulate treasure and train soldiers, to take advantage of the corruptions that will arise, and invade the country.

The plans were joyfully received and their execution immediately put into action.

Three thousand workmen were sent to Fu Ch'ai, with a great quantity of building material. These were gladly received. For Fu Ch'ai had conceived the plan of building the Ancient Su Tower. He now entered on extravagant building plans. Enforced labour was laid on the people. Palaces and gardens, parks and pleasure resorts were built. The revenues were wasted. Public affairs were neglected. His Chief Minister of State found great difficulty in gaining admittance to the reckless prince. The execution of the third plan had the most baneful effect. Wu Tzu-shu warned Fu Ch'ai that the house of Hsia was ruined because of Mo His（妹喜）. The house of Shang was destroyed by Ta Chi（妲己）; Chou came to ruin because of Pao Ssu（褒姒）[1]. Almost always beautiful women had been the cause of the downfall of state. The King should not receive them. At this time 300 women were sent to the prince, and 30 to his ministers; his answer was: "Kou Ch'ien has not retained these beautiful women for himself, but has sent them to us. This is evidence of his loyalty to Wu. Let the minister pat doubt out of his mind."

Not however until the coming of Hsi Tzi（西子）or Hsi Shih（西施）was Fu Ch'ai completely fascinated. When Fu Ch'ai first saw her the effect was magical. He thought he witnessed a divine being or fairy come to earth. His soul and spirit became drunk.

Hsi Shih was born of humble parents at Chu Lo Shan in Chekiang. There were at this mountain two villages east and west all of the people being named Shih. Hsi Tzi belonged to the west village and hence her name. She gained her living by washing silk, for we have the phrase "a girl of Yueh washing silk in the morning, concubine of the king of Wu in the evening"（朝为越溪女，暮作吴王姬）. Kou Ch'ien hearing of her unusual beauty had her brought to his court and trained in deportment and dancing, and the accomplishments of a court lady, for three years. She was dressed in gorgeous apparel and sent to Fu Ch'ai. A palace was built for her on the hills west of Soochow. Fu Ch'ai now abandoned himself

---

［1］　此处应为"褒姒"。

6. 暗中陷害直言劝谏的大臣，逼他们自杀，以此来削弱他们对吴王的辅佐。[1]

7. 积累财富，训练士兵，趁吴国腐败渐起之机，进犯吴国。[2]

勾践欣然接受这些计划，并立即实施。

勾践给吴王送去三千名工匠及大量的土木建材，夫差欣然接受。夫差早就有意修建姑苏台。现在他可以大兴土木了。接着，他强征民夫，修建了宫殿园林、离宫别馆。耗费国家收入，弃民生于不顾。吴王任意妄为，他的大夫却觐见无门。破吴第三术的实施产生了最为恶劣的效果。伍子胥告诫夫差，夏亡于妹喜，殷亡于妲己，西周亡于褒姒。自古红颜祸水。吴王不该接受她们。此时，已有三百名女子被送至吴王身边，另有三十名被送给大臣。夫差辩称："勾践不敢私藏美女，而进献给我们。这足以证明他对吴国的忠诚。大夫还是不要疑神疑鬼了吧。"

不过，西施到来之前夫差并未完全沉迷美色之中。但是，一见西施，如同着魔，以为亲眼所见仙女下凡，神魂为之迷醉。

西施出生于浙江苎萝山一小户人家。山之东西各有一村落，村民皆姓施。西子因住西村，故名西施。西施浣纱为生，我们可以从"朝为越溪女，暮作吴王姬"词句得知。勾践听闻其美貌非同寻常，命人带到王宫，教习礼仪舞蹈，各色才艺，如宫廷贵妇故，三年乃成。西施穿上华美的衣衫，被献给夫差。夫差为西施建一别宫，位于苏州城西山上。从此，夫差开始纵情声色。

---

[1] 六曰强其谏臣使自杀，以弱其辅。
[2] 七曰积财练兵，以承其弊。（以上见冯梦龙：《东周列国志》，北京：华夏出版社，2013，第601页。）

completely to dalliance and pleasure.

Hsi Tzi was one of the most famous of the beautiful women of China. For she has been the text for philosophers cogitation. Chuang Tze（庄子）wrote of her: "When Shi Shih was distressed in mind she knitted her brows. An ugly woman of the village seeing how beautiful she looked, went home, and having worked herself into a fit frame of mind, knitted her brows. The result was that the rich people barred up their doors and would not come out, while the poor people took their wives and children and departed elsewhere. That woman saw the beauty of knitted brows, but he did not see wherein the beauty of knitted brows lay." (Giles.)

Every possible luxury was provided for her, and Fu Ch'ai spent his whole time in attendance at her palace on Spirit Peak Hill. He even went so far in his enfatuation that he personally assisted in the doing of her hair. Her end is not known though it is said she died early and was buried with great ceremony by Fu Ch'ai at Huang Ya Shan who ordered the sacrifices to the dead. The record says there is now at the foot of the mountain an ancestral hall called The Beloved Beauty.

Another account says that when Kou Ch'ien returned to Yueh he carried her back with him. His wife dispatched men secretly, had her taken to the river, a heavy stone tied around her neck, and she was thrown in the river, saying: "That is a piece of ruined kingdom baggage. Why should it be preserved?"

The continued remonstrances of Wu Tzu-shu became more and more irksome to the debauched, who failed to consider that the wealth and freedom of his kingdom were due to the efforts of his faithful minister. Finally after a violent altercation, when Tzu-shu predicted dire calamity to the state, Fu Ch'ai sent him a sword. Receiving this he went to the throne hall and taking his stand below the throne called heaven to witness that Fu Ch'ai did not desire him to witness his power, "but it was by my influence that you were made heir. For you I have subjugated Chu Tsai and put to rout Yueh, and brought in subjection the powerful duke. Now you not only refuse to heed my words but desire my death. I die today, but the soldiers of Yueh will be here tomorrow and will destroy your state." He then cut his throat and died at the foot of the throne he had labored so many years for and with such signal success to establish. Fu Ch'ai had his head taken off and hung outside the Tea Dish Gate, his body sewn up in a leathern bag and cast in the canal at Shu Kon. But the grateful people rescued the body, and

西子是中国最为著名的美女之一，甚至被写进了思想家的文章。庄子写道：“西施病心而颦其里。其里之丑人见而美之。归，亦捧心而颦其里。其里之富人见之，坚闭门而不出；贫人见之，挈妻子而去之走。彼知颦美，而不知颦之所以美。”（翟理斯语）

灵岩山馆娃宫内，西施起居极尽奢华。夫差陪伴，不离左右，甚至亲自服侍西施梳妆，足见其着迷程度。西施结局已无人知晓，尽管传说她芳龄早夭，夫差举行隆重仪式，将她葬在黄茅山[1]，并下令为西施殉葬。有记载称，如今山脚下依然有"爱姬祠"。

另有记载称，当初勾践返越，携西施而归。勾践夫人暗中派人将她带到河边，拴巨石于其脖项，推入河中，称："此祸国之物，留之何为？"

伍子胥反复劝谏，令那位昏君不胜其烦。夫差忘记了这位忠臣为吴国的富足安逸付出的辛劳。最终，一次君臣激辩后，伍子胥预言吴国将大祸临头，夫差派人给伍子胥送去一口利剑。接到剑后，他来到王宫大殿，立于阶下，高呼苍天做证，夫差不用其计，"非吾之力，王何以即位？非吾之力，王何以破楚陷越，使越人臣服？今王不纳良言，唯欲吾死。吾今日即死，但恐越国甲兵明日即来，王社稷不保。"然后，割喉自尽，死于夫差脚下。他曾积年为夫差奔走辛劳，其功绩有目共睹。夫差命人将伍子胥头颅割下，悬于盘门，密封尸体于皮袋，抛至胥口运河中。但是，人们感念伍子胥恩德，将他的尸体打捞上来。夫差死后，人们为伍子胥立祠祭祀。

---

[1] 此处应为郑旦，早逝，葬于黄茅山。

after the death of Ch'ai built a temple to his memory.

In the meantime Kou Ch'ien of Yueh had been diligently putting into practice the seventh plan of Wen Chung, viz. laying up treasure and drilling an army. The devotion of his people was complete, so that when he called out his army the only difficulty he had was to choose from the great multitude of men offering for the invasion of Wu. Fu Ch'ai was taken completely by surprise, his soldiers were unable to stand before the onrush of Kou Ch'ien. They were totally routed at Sungkiang. Fu Ch'ai took refuge in the city of Soochow. The city was besieged for only a short time when it fell. Kou Ch'ien forced Fu Ch'ai to kill himself in order to rid the world of a worthless prince. The Kingdom of Wu came to an end by being added to Yueh which kingdom was soon declared fief of the house of Chou, and Kou Ch'ien was appointed Duke of the Eastern Regions. The Kingdom of Wu came to an end in 475 B. C.

RELIGION

We have been mainly concerned with a period in which Confucius was making his pilgrimages and attempting to find a prince worthy of his teaching. But Confucius never taught a religion. He only attempted to inculcate principles of morality for private and public life. Charity of heart, duty to one's neighbors, justice and truth was the burden of his teaching. These had not yet been put in writing and so his teaching could not have been broadly known or followed. In fact his teaching did not find extensive following until long years after his death. The hearts of men were not ready for such principles.

I have been unable in the time at hand to find any references, as such, to the religious beliefs of the time. But there are a number of incidental references from which we may make just inferences. I consider the statements, scanty though they be, in the annals of Soochow, too vague and indeterminate to accept, though I have been unable to search the whole of the eighty one volumes.

Faber's *China in the Light of History* tells us: "In early days three groups of divinities were recognised—those of heaven, the earth, and man. Besides these, ancestral worship was largely practiced. Various kinds of sacrifices were offered according to strictly enforced rituals at stated times. Oracles were consulted even before the smallest undertakings."

Contrary to general belief, the worship of idols was not at all prevalent in

与此同时，勾践加紧施行文种提出的第七术："积财练兵"。此时，越国臣民已经全身心投入备战中。勾践只需从众多将士中费心挑选攻取吴国的人选即可。结果，一交战，夫差就被打得措手不及，吴国士兵没能抵挡住勾践的突袭，大败于松江。夫差只好躲进姑苏城内。城池被困不久即陷落。勾践逼夫差自杀以除此昏君。越国吞并吴国。周王室分封越国，勾践为东伯侯。公元前475年，吴国灭亡。

我们主要关注的是孔子周游列国，欲择明君而事的时期。不过孔子所传授的并非宗教，而是做人为政之道，以仁爱、友邻、信义为重。孔子述而不作，所以其学说当时不为众人所知，亦少有追随者。事实上，直到孔子去世后很久，他的学说才被广泛接纳。而彼时人心不为所动。

我手头一直缺乏有关当时宗教信仰的材料可做参考。不过，还是有一些附带的资料可以帮助我们做出恰当的推断。虽然我没能详细翻阅《苏州府志》八十一卷，但我还是认为这些资料尽管内容含糊不清，难下定论。

花之安[1]所著《从历史角度看中国》告诉我们："（中国）古时三神并尊，即天神、地神、人神。此外，中国人普遍供奉祖先。封建时代，各色祭品严格按照祭祀礼仪上供。即便是无关紧要的小事情，也要求神问卜。"

与一般信仰相反，周朝神像崇拜并未盛行。中国最早关于神像的记载

---

[1] 花之安（1839—1899），德国人，汉学家。

China in the Chou dynasty. The earliest record of an image or an idol in China was in B. C. 1198, made by Wu I, a prince of Yin. He called this image Tien Shen (天神) but seems to have kept it for strange purposes. When defeated in battle he whipped this image. Before going into battle he put the image in a skin sack filled with blood and shot arrows into the sack. When the blood began to flow he said he had killed the god and of course could kill his enemies.

Astrology, fortune telling (a very old practice) and the interpretation of dreams were universally practiced and shaped the practices of men.

The mysticism of Laot'zu seems to have found congenial soil in the Chinese mind or condition of mind at that time. His teaching was carried on by his enthusiastic and able pupil Chuang Tzu. But Taoism did not become broadly accepted until after the appearance of the famous forgery, the *Tao teh king*, which probably took place some time in the Early Han. It is impossible to think that there was such a work in existence at the time of Chuang Tzu and that work not be mentioned by him.

Buddhism had not yet made its appearance in China. That only came about the time of the birth of our Lord. The Han historians make no mention of the cult even down to the 2nd Century. Thus by exclusion we may get some idea of the religious practices of the people of Wu. But did they even have those practices that were known to pertain to China proper—Shantung and Honan? The arts of civilization were brought to Ching Man—by Tai Peh and Chung Yung. The religious practices of their own people must have been known to them.

Religious practice and belief occupies too large a place in the lives of leaders of men to be neglected or concealed. Therefore Tai Peh and Chung Yang taught the people to whom they had come what they knew.

When Wu Tzu-shu was fleeing for his life he more than once called High Heaven to witness his integrity and suffering; and he declared his life to be in the hands of heaven. Thus he recognised a higher power. When he came to plan the city of Soochow he cast the horoscope of the place, and laid off the city according to the diagram of the heavens, and to conform to the necromantic principles of earth. Our inference is that astrological teaching was known to the early civilized inhabitants of the country.

We know that it was the custom of the people to build ancestral temples and the inference is that worship of the departed took place in these temples, though we have no direct statements as to methods or ritual by the people of Wu. But it

是公元前 1198 年，神像由殷商王武乙所造，称为"天神"，但是用途似乎怪异，逢战败则鞭笞神像。开战前，武乙将神像置于皮囊中，鲜血、箭镞一并放入。血流出时，他说他已杀死天神，自然也能杀死敌人。

那时，占天卜卦、算命（非常古老的做法）、解梦司空见惯。人们的很多做法都受此影响。

其时，老子的玄妙学说似乎已经与中国人的心智、心态相契合。庄子才学过人，习老子所教，习之不倦。但是，在《道德经》被伪造出来之前，道家思想并非广为人知。伪造时间大概在西汉早年。否则，庄子在世时，不大可能不提及该书。

当时佛教在中国尚未出现。佛教出现的时间跟耶稣诞生的时间大致相当。甚至直到公元二世纪，汉代史学家都未提及时人对佛教的崇拜，这样一来，佛教的影响排除了。我们可以一窥吴人的宗教活动，当时地处中原的山东、河南所习以为常的一些宗教活动，不知道吴人是否也有？当初，泰伯和仲雍将农耕技艺带到荆蛮之地，中原的宗教活动想必也为吴人所知。

宗教活动和信仰在那些首领日常生活中占据重要地位，无法忽略，亦无须遮掩。因此，泰伯、仲雍将自己所知道的宗教知识传授给了当地人。

昔年，伍子胥逃命途中，曾不止一次大声疾呼，其忠诚、其冤屈苍天可鉴，并声称其命由天。这说明他认识到众生之上存在更强大的力量。苏州城筹建之初，他勘察风水，按照天象地卦谋划布局。我们据此推断，开化的中国先民早已熟悉占卜。

我们知道中国先民有建宗祠的习俗，因此我们推断祠堂是他们祭拜先人的地方，尽管我们并未掌握有关吴地先民祭拜方法或礼仪的直接证据。

is evident on every hand that morals were low. Murder was common. Polygamy was universal, by those able to meet the expense. There was no recognised system of religion either of state or among the people.

WARFARE

The History tells us: All the princes of Wu and Yueh were brave soldiers so that their people to the present time were good swordsmen, who looked lightly on death and quickly revived from calamities.

The wealth of a state was reckoned by the number of soldiers that could be put into the field. Cavalry had not yet come into use in China. But the war chariot was used in Wu as well as throughout China at this time. We have evidence that boats were extensively used in Wu. The offensive weapons used were the two edged sword （剑）; the knife, one edged, long or short （刀）; the Lance （戈）; the halberd with crescent shaped blade （钺）; the spear （矛）; the lance with two points （戟）; the battle axe （斧）; the bow and arrow （弓箭）(That the latter was made of bamboo is proved by the formation of the character, and was the piece of bamboo sent on before).

Their defensive armor was the shield （牌）; the curras （甲）, made of skin; the helmet （盔）made of metal or of skin. The present long list of offensive and defensive weapons, besides the above, were of later invention.

The ministers of state were not only administers of justice under the sovereign in times of peace, but were also commander in time of war. The soldiers went into battle to the sound of drums, which had been smeared with the blood of a victim! The left ears of the killed were taken instead of the scalp, to shew the number of the slain.

There was little or no peace in Wu or any of the Feudal States, because the time had not come, in the words of Yu Fei (12 century A. D.) "When civil officials are no longer greedy of money, and the military of officials no longer fear death." And it has not come yet.

ADVANCEMENT OF CIVILIZATION

That culture had reached any high stage can not be supposed; nor is there any historical evidence for the supposition. That large building operations of a

但是，从各方面来看，很明显，当时的道德水平不高，杀戮司空见惯；能者多妻，十分常见。官方、民间均未有认可的宗教信仰体系。

战争

历史告诉我们，吴越国君作战勇敢，吴越人民因而擅长铸剑。他们看淡生死，即便遭受大灾大难，也能很快恢复生机。

投入战场的兵力可以衡量一国之财力。当时的中国还没有骑兵。但是兵车在整个中国已经投入使用，吴国也不例外。有证据表明，吴国大量使用战船。兵刃有双刃的剑、单刃的长刀或短刀、戈、其刃状如月牙的钺、矛、戟（两个尖儿的戈）、战斧、弓箭（由汉字"箭"可见，其为"竹"片，且置于"前"）。

防护用的铠甲有盾牌、皮制甲胄、金属或皮制的盔。今天，用于进攻或防守的武器，可以列一长串的清单。不过，除上述外，多是后来发明。

当时，一国的大夫和平时期主持政务，战争期间指挥军队。士兵闻战鼓而进击。战鼓涂以人血。士兵杀敌后削敌左耳，而非剥其头皮，以计算杀敌人数。

春秋时期，吴国，乃至各封建诸侯国，常常国无宁日。岳飞（公元十二世纪）所言"文臣不爱钱，武臣不惜死"而"天下太平矣"的时代尚未到来。

文明进程

很难推测当时文化发展程度有多高，也没有历史记载可以佐证。就我们所知，这些专制君主，发号施令，驱赶民力，营造公众建筑。富者寥寥，

public character were undertaken and executed we know. This was done under the behest of an absolute monarch by enforced labour. The rich were few indeed, and the poverty very real and universal. Writing material in no single form as we have it now had been invented.

BOOK REFERENCES

1. *Annals of Soochow*（苏州府志）. This work is in 81 vols., compiled originally by Lu Hsung of the Ming dynasty. There have been a number of revisions of the work. It may be taken as reliable in the main, though the early history is in many respects unreliable and is partial to Soochow, often twisting history in order to make a good show for her sons.

2. *Narratives of the Contending States*(东周列国传) in 108 chapters. 12 vols. It begins with the establishment of the Chou dynasty and gives a fairly full history of the whole time down to the beginning of Tsing.

3. *History Made Easy(* 纲鉴易知录) in 16 volumes from the earliest times through the Ming dynasty. This is a condensation of the great work （通鉴目 ）compiled under the direction of （朱熹）.The *History Made Easy* should be in the library of all students of Chinese.

4. Of English books on the Chinese language the following three are indispensable to the student: (1) Giles' *Chinese English Dictionary*. (2) Giles' *A Biographical Dictionary*, a store house of information treating with the most famous characters in Chinese History. (3) A. Wylie's *Chinese Literature*, the best of its kind and invaluable.

5. Du Bose' *Beautiful Soo* is the most complete hand book on Soochow. Kelly and Walsh have issued an illustrated edition of this little book that is very attractive.

6. Dr. A. P. Parker has several papers in old issues of the "Chinese Recorder," which are of the excellence to be expected from so accomplished a scholar. I have made use of these papers to verify some of the facts of my paper.

7. There has this year been issued "Outlines of Chinese History" by Li Un Bing, edited by Prof. Joseph Whiteside. This is a work of high excellence and readable style, and is the best attempt at an outline of Chinese History in existence, being a great improvement on the Chinese Chronicles. I have made free use of this work.

而贫者实属常见。用来书写的材料已然发明出来，但种类不一而足，与我们今天不同。

参考书籍

1. 《苏州府志》。该书计有八十一卷，初为明代卢熊纂修。后经多次修订。书中所涉苏州早期历史疑点重重，因编者偏爱苏州，又期望给苏州后世子孙留下苏州好的印象，故而常常歪曲历史。除此以外，人们认为该书大体可靠。

2. 《东周列国志》。该书计有十二卷，一百零八回。记载了从周朝建立伊始，直到秦代初年比较完整的一段历史。

3. 《纲鉴易知录》。十六卷，从盘古开天辟地，直至明代。由朱熹[1]主持编纂的纲目体通史。中国国内图书馆应该都藏有该书。

4. 下述三本有关汉语学习的英语读本，不可或缺。（1）翟理斯的《华英字典》。（2）翟理斯的《古今姓氏族谱》是中国历代名人生平事迹的宝库。（3）亚历山大·伟烈亚力的《中国文学》是同类书籍中的佼佼者，弥足珍贵。

5. 杜步西的《姑苏景志》是关于苏州的一本内容很全的手册。上海别发洋行发行为插图版的小册子，读来引人入胜。

6. 潘慎文发表在旧版《教务杂志》上的几篇短文，甚为精彩，足见其大家风范。拙文所叙几处史实，皆引之为证。

7. 今年（1915年），李文彬著，约瑟夫·怀特塞德教授编《中国历史纲要》出版。该书内容精彩，可读性强，为现存中国历史概要著作之最佳尝试，在《中国编年史》基础上大有改进。我置于手头，随时翻阅。

---

[1] 应为清代吴乘权等编辑，朱熹的《通鉴纲目》是其参考书目之一。

The world has no parallel to the Chinese as chroniclers, but she has no historians. Dr. Martin says: "Their chronicles are composed with studied elegance and abound in astute criticisms of character and events, but the whole range of their literature contains nothing that can be called a Philosophy of History. They have no Hegel, who after reconstructing the universe, applies his principles to explain the laws of human progress; no Gibbon or Montesquieu to trace the decay of an old civilization; no Guizot or Lecky to sketch the rise of a new one. They have not even a Thucidides or a Tacitus who can follow effects to their causes, and paint the panorama of an epoch," and history "is little more than the register of the crimes, follies and misfortunes of mankind". —Gibbon.

No more faulty historian can be found than the father of Chinese history, Confucius. His famous *Spring and Autumn Annals* is not even a book of annals. Events great and small are strung like beads on a string (after Martin).

China has never produced the scholar with broad enough views to break away from this method and "The Annals History of Soochow" is no exception. But this work is further faulty in that there is not even this string of beads, or at most a very short one, viz. from the founding of the city by Ho Lu and the disastrous reign of his profligate son Fu Ch'ai. A feeble attempt is made under military affairs to relate the rebellions that have raged in and around the city, and even this is under the form of biographies of the principle actors.

Dr. Du Bose said: "In this book loving nation it is down hill in all directions from Soochow. Proud scholars have crowded the examination halls; authors have filled the shelves of the book stores, and poets have sung of old land marks so celebrated in history." But with all her wealth, learning, preeminence and culture, she has never had and has not now, a library of any importance, public or private. Hence great difficulty has attended every effort to find anything at all worthwhile to present to this august and learned body of missionaries, on the subject of The History of Soochow; The great work, "The Annals of Soo chow" is more a series of biographies and topographical descriptions than a history. And while this is extensive enough, there being eighty one good size volumes in the work, yet the great bulk of it is almost worthless. Thus it was necessary to read many pages to find one tit-bit, and review whole volumes only to reject all the contents. Any attempt at a connected chronological account of the events of the history of Soochow has been impossible with the time at my disposal.

说起编年体史家，中国人独占鳌头。但是，中国无史学家。马丁博士说："他们所著编年体历史，文辞典雅，不乏对人物、事件敏锐的评判。但是，其文献所涉无一可称之为历史哲学者。他们既没有重构世界，以自创理论来解释人类进步规律的黑格尔，也没有追溯古代文明衰亡的爱德华·吉本或孟德斯鸠，更没有能概述新帝国崛起的基佐、莱基。他们甚至没有可以循果溯因，描绘一个时代全景图的修昔底德、塔西佗之类的历史学家。"吉本认为，历史"所记者，不外乎人类之罪，之蠢，之难"（吉本语）。

孔子虽为中国历史之父，其谬误颇多。孔子所作《春秋》甚至不能称为编年史书。不过将大小事件，连缀如珠串，如此而已。（从马丁所言）

中国史学家从未有足够宽广的视野，以打破此陈规者。《苏州府志》的撰写也不例外。但是，该书甚至连这样的珠串都没有，或者即便有，也不过是短短的一串，即从阖闾建城至夫差荒淫误国，所以其谬误尤甚。至于爆发在苏州城内或周边的民间反抗斗争，少有记载，淹没在你争我战的历史中。即便有，也不过以帝王将相传记的形式呈现出来而已。

杜步西博士曾言："中国人素好读书，但是仅从苏州来看，国势渐弱。曾几何时，赶考举子，意气风发，挤满贡院；著书立说者，汗牛充栋；骚客诗人，歌咏怀古。"但是，苏州虽属富庶之地，文脉绵长，文化昌盛，出类拔萃，却无一家像样的私人或公共图书馆，古今亦然。因此，即便踏破铁鞋也难以寻觅到任何有关苏州历史的、有价值的东西，来呈现给尊贵而博学的诸位。《苏州府志》与其说是历史，倒不如说是传记与地志。虽然记载广泛，足有八十一卷，然而大部分几乎没有价值。因而，为一趣闻逸事，常常翻阅数页；回顾整卷，尽弃所读。就我的时间而言，想要通读彼此相关、前后相继的苏州历史事件，几无可能。

THE NAMES OF SOOCHOW

The city and district has had many names in the course of its two thousand four hundred years of existence. The district was known as Yangchow in the time of Ta Yu. When *The Spring and Autumn Annals* were compiled it was the Wu Kingdom Division. But when civilization was brought south by Tai Pao(泰伯)and his brothers, the country was called Kao Wu（句吴）by the aborigines (the thistle barbarians（荆蛮）of the country. First called Wu Kingdom （吴国）at the time of the founding of the city, when that kingdom was conquered by Yueh（越）it became known as Wu Ti（吴地）. But under the reconstruction of the empire by Tsing Shih Hwang Ti the territory south of the river including Kiang Su, Chekiang, and part of Anhui, was known as Kuei Chi Prefecture （会稽郡）and so continued throughout the dynasty. Much of this time the seat of government was at Soochow. But in the time of the Three Kingdoms our territory was called Wu Prefecture（吴郡）, having five magistracies. The old name Wu Kingdom was restored during the short time of the Sui dynasty. But during the Sung, Ch'i, Liang, Chen, and Wei dynasties the city was called Wuchow（吴州）and the territory Wu Prefecture（吴郡）. The name Soochow was used for the first time in the ninth year Sui Kai Huang, the district still being Wu Prefecture. During the Tang dynasty the city and district became Soochow. But when the Five Dynasties were contending for power, 苏州 was the name of the city, and the district was made a military division called 苏州节度. Later the name was Ping Kiang Fu; and Pin Kiang Lu by the Yuan or Mongol rule. The Name Soochow Fu was restored by the Mings and has so continued ever since.

Being the center of wealth, culture and influence of so large a district, it is not surprising that Soochow has been in the course of her long history subjected to rebellions and ravages. After the fall of the kingdom of Wu under the descendants of Ho Lu the centre of power for this part of China shifted to Kuei Chi, in Chekiang, the whole being known as the Kingdom of Yueh. This was brought about by the king of Wu rejecting the advice of Wu Tzu-shu, and giving heed to the council of the corrupt minister Tai Tsai P'i(太宰嚭). The Yueh was exterminated by Tsu in combination with Ch'i, and Soochow with its territory was subjected to Tsu, and for the time being the spirit of the people seems to have been broken. But rebellions and counter rebellions have been too numerous to attempt anything like a complete account, and I have selected only a few of the

历代苏州名称

在长达两千四百年的历史进程中，苏州城及周边区域几易其名。大禹时期，这里是扬州的一部分。《春秋》编纂时，此地为诸侯国吴。泰伯众兄弟南下开化时，当地人（荆蛮）称之为句吴。阖闾大城建成后，此地始称吴国。越灭吴后，人称吴地。但是，秦始皇帝一统天下后，长江以南设会稽郡，含江苏、浙江，以及安徽部分区域，终秦一朝该名称未变，其治所多在苏州。但是三国时期，此地称为吴郡，下设五个地方长官。隋朝短暂，其间沿用"吴国"旧称。在宋、齐、梁、陈、魏时期，苏州城改称吴州，隶属吴郡。隋开皇九年[1]，首称苏州，其周边区域仍隶属吴郡。唐代，该城及周边称苏州。五代争雄时，其城名为"苏州中"，其周边为"苏州节度"。元朝，称平江府、平江路。明代复称苏州府，此后沿用至今。

作为财富、文化与权力中心，且地域广阔，苏州在漫长的历史进程中，难免饱受叛乱、蹂躏之苦。阖闾后代统治下的吴国衰落后，中国这一区域的权力中心转移至浙江会稽，即越国。这一切皆因吴王不听伍子胥劝谏，而一味听信佞臣太宰嚭所致。后楚联齐灭越，苏州及周边臣服于楚。吴人精神似乎暂时受挫。但是叛乱与平叛不胜枚举，难以详述。所以我仅选取几件大事略一叙述。诚如雨果所言："微末细节，显然无足轻重，却可谓大事件之枝叶，常埋没于久远的历史中。"

---

[1] 公元589年。

most significant. For, says Victor Hugo, "Small details, apparently unimportant, are, so to speak, the foliage of great events and are lost in the distance of history."

One of the earliest rebellions occurred in the Han dynasty. The city was taken by one Kwan Yin, and put to the sword and looted.

Sun En(孙恩). In the year 340 A. D.Sun En was a small military official at Soochow. He started a rebellion, assisted by his uncle, who was a man of strong magnetism, and soon gained a great following of the people, but was captured and put to death. Sun En collected the desperate among the people and attempted to avenge his uncle. The people were sorely oppressed by the rulers and he soon found a ready following. The city was taken and Sun assumed the title of Generalissimo of The East （征东将军）and called his followers "The Immortals." He murdered, without discrimination, all who were opposed to him, and added to his infamy by killing a great number of children. His rebellion and success was the signal for extensive uprisings throughout the country. By this time the martial spirit of the Soochow people had been lost. Long peace had brought complacent indifference to the conditions of the outside world.

Having neither martial spirit, nor implements of war, they were an easy prey to the invaders who met almost no opposition. The granaries, together with practically the whole city, were burned. Soochow was made the headquarters of the rebels and here the spoils of the surrounding country were collected. Hearing that relief from the north, under Liu Tsai-tsi（刘宰之）was approaching, Sun En collected several tens of thousands of men and women and withdrew to the east in an orderly manner. He attacked Yinpu, near the present Shanghai, and put to death the local officials. Three other generals with supplies and a great number of soldiers were sent against him. One of these, Yuan Shan-sung（袁山松）,built a mud fort at Hu Tu （沪渎）(402 A. D. and this was the beginning of Shanghai) against the ravages of this robber chief. Sun En forces were routed at Tsa Kon(浃口) on the Yangstze, Sun succeeded in taking Hu Tu, and put its builder to death. After a long struggle in which infinite calamity was wrought to the country, finding himself abandoned by his followers, and without resources he drowned himself in the sea (river?).

The city was taken and looted more than once in each of the Ch'i and Liang dynasties. That in the Liang under Yu Tzu-yueh, which extended over several years, was marked by the extraordinary extent and severity of the ravages on women. The people caught as between two contending forces suffered the apprehensions of unknown terror, and the frightfulness of starvation and violent

早期叛乱，汉代有一。瓜田仪曾攻破苏州城，肆意杀戮、劫掠。

公元340年，孙恩不过是苏州一低级军官。在叔父协助下，孙恩发动叛乱。其叔父习学秘术，一时从之者众。后其叔父被俘处死。孙恩召集死士，伺机报仇。当时百姓饱受统治者压迫之苦，一呼即应。攻占苏州城后，孙恩自封"征东将军"，称呼其党众为"长生人"。孙不问青红皂白，诛杀异己，连大量孩童也不放过，愈加恶贯满盈。孙叛乱得逞，预示着举国暴动即将风起云涌。其时，苏州民众尚武精神尽失。百姓承平日久，安逸自得，对外界发生的情况漠不关心。

既无士气，又无战备，苏州官府、百姓只能任人宰割，叛军几乎没有遭遇任何抵抗。叛军烧毁粮仓，城内四处纵火。苏州城沦为叛军大本营，从周边地方劫掠所获，堆积城内。听闻刘宰之[1]率朝廷援军从北迫近，孙恩纠集男女数万民众，有序撤退至城东方向。他袭击靠近今天上海的邢浦，处死当地官员。朝廷另派三位将军，调拨给养、士兵，对阵孙恩。其中袁山松将军在沪渎建土垒一座（公元402年，此为上海之开端），以抵御叛军的劫掠。孙恩率部取道长江岸边的浃口，成功夺取沪渎，处死袁松山。之后，战争持续了很久，给整个国家带来无尽灾难。最终，孙恩眼见众叛亲离，大势已去，跳海（或河？）自杀。

齐、梁两代，苏州城不止一次被攻占、掳掠。梁朝年间，叛军于子悦领兵攻取苏州城。苏州城因此数年遭劫，尤以妇女饱受蹂躏之苦为甚。攻守双方几经鏖战，百姓深陷其中，忧惧、饥馑、暴死，苦不堪言。

---

[1] 应为"刘牢之"。

death.

In the Sui dynasty the people of Soochow, driven to desperation by oppression and want, started a rebellion led by Shen Yuanchen（沈元会）. The city was besieged for eighty days by the imperial soldiers. It was taken and given over to the sword.

That this was a time of great unrest is proven by the fact that another rebellion was soon started under the Liu Yuan-chin（刘元庆）, who took Soochow, and assumed the imperial title. The sorrows and sufferings brought on the people by this were beyond expression. This suffering drove the people to side with, as they thought, the lesser of two evils, and they threw themselves on the side of the usurper, and went out in thousands to welcome him to the city. But this was only to add to their woe, for the Imperial soldiers soon surrounded the rebels and they were exterminated. Passing over many rebellions and internal and external disturbances we come to a time when the city was subjected to a series of the greatest calamities in the whole of its history.

("Wars and the administration of public affairs are the principle subject of history."—Gibbon.)

In the Sung dynasty, Emperor Kao Tsung, 1127 A.D., the city was taken by Chin Yuanshu（金兀术）, who made his attack from Huchow. The Pan Men was taken at night, and the soldiers entered the city which was given over to fire and sword. The light of the burning city could be seen two hundred li distant. It burned for five days and nights and only about twenty per cent of the people escaped with their lives. The enormity of this calamity was added to owing to the fact that while the storm was gathering the emperor Kao Tsung, with his court, was in the city, and for that reason the people felt secure and took no precautionary measures. But just before the attack on the city was started the emperor with his court and following fled to Hangchow. With his flight the people lost all hope. But every effort was made to protect the city and the surrounding country. As so often happened, the soldiers who were sent to protect the people only subjected them to greater hardships. As the attacking forces drew nearer the people from the country took refuge in the city, which thus became overcrowded. The officers who were placed in charge for the protection of the city fled and the soldiers, seeing their leaders gone, gave loose rein to greed and lust. A great number of prominent buildings were burned by them. This explains the ease with which Chin was able to take the city. The civil government having fled, and the military control gone, there was almost no defence made. The whole city

隋朝，苏州百姓饱受压迫，民不聊生，在沈元会[1]带领下，揭竿而起。朝廷派军困城八十日，城破，双方刀兵相向。

之后不久，刘元庆[2]再起叛乱，夺取苏州，自立为王。彼时动荡可见一斑。生灵涂炭，苦不堪言。两害相权取其轻，他们被迫选择支持叛军，于是成千上万人开城迎接刘元进。然而，这只能让他们雪上加霜。因为朝廷军队很快就将叛军围困，剿灭。几经叛乱，内外动荡后，苏州城遭受有史以来一系列最为严重的灾难。

"战争与公共事务管理是历史主题。"（吉本语）

公元1127年，宋高宗时期，金兀术从湖州起兵，攻取苏州城。金军夜袭盘门，入城后，烧杀抢掠。城中火光冲天，两百里外可见。大火持续五天五夜，逃生者仅十分之二左右。当初，金军兵临城下，战云密布之际，高宗与群臣尚驻守城内，百姓因此感到安全，并未采取防范措施，这加重了灾难。但是，当金军开始攻城的时候，宋高宗、群臣及追随者逃往杭州。高宗出逃令百姓尽失所望。尽管如此，人们还是各尽所能保卫城池及周边乡镇。但是，官府派士兵去保护百姓，结果士兵令百姓更加遭殃，这已司空见惯。于是，乡下百姓眼见军队开拨而来，纷纷进城避难，结果令城内格外拥挤。被派去守城的将领逃之夭夭，士兵失去长官约束，肆意掳掠。城内大量著名建筑被付之一炬。这也解释了为什么金军如此轻而易举地攻占了苏州城。官府逃遁，官兵失控，城内几无防备，满城狼藉。金

苏州历史见闻

---

[1] 应为吴人沈元桧。
[2] 应为刘元进，隋末江南农民起义领袖。

was destroyed and then the rebels retired. The cowardly officials now returned victorious, not a single battle having been fought by them. What was left of the people and their possessions were again looted by the imperial soldiers. Such suffering and sorrow was never seen.

At the end of the Yuan dynasty when the whole country was in confusion, in 1349, Chang Shih-chen（张士诚）, a Taichow（泰州）salt merchant, raised the standard of revolt, and took Taichow. He was a man of little education, given to good deeds, and was driven to revolt by the impositions of those in power. A soldier grossly insulted him in public. He killed the soldier, and started the revolt with only eighteen followers, three of whom were his brothers. They looted the rich and burned their property, this being their practice wherever they went. Success attended his efforts and he proclaimed himself Prince Chen（诚王）of the great Chow（大周）. He sent a brother against Tungchow which he took. From there he crossed the river and took Fushan（福山）and then Ghangshu（常熟）. This opened the way for the main forces, which were now coming up, and Chang Shih-chen led the attack on Pin Kiang Fu (Soochow) which was taken. The people were carefully protected. This was so novel an experience in their history that the whole movement met with enthusiastic support by the people. He made the Shan Tien Monastery（承天寺）his palace. Changchow was taken and Chinkiang was attacked. Imperial forces coming south in numbers. Chang Shih-chen sent his brother Sinchen to attack and take Ishing. But Sinchen was himself captured after a valiant resistance. He advised Shih-chen to make his allegiance to Shen Ti of Yuan, and send in the demanded taxes in rice and treasure. This he did and was made Tai Wai（太尉）, general of a province, by the emperor. But his allegiance was of a very weak character, for he held the power without the name of king. Pressure was brought on him by the people to assume the royal title. Pride having found place in his heart, and Liu Fu-tung, the most able leader of the Yuan cause, being dead, he threw off allegiance and proclaimed himself Prince of Wu（吴王）, and gave his mother the title of Dowager Princess.

He built his palace at Wong Ru Chi（王废基）and appointed his brother Shih Sin（士信）Prefect of Hangchow. He now refused to pay tribute any further. His principality to the south included Hsiao Hsing Fu; north the whole of north Kiangsu; on the west the eastern half of Anhui, and the sea constituting the eastern boundary. He maintained a standing army of several tens of thousands of soldiers in armor. His rule was mild and benevolent. He had the appearance of great ability, but was in reality a man of few resources.

兵撤离之后，之前畏刀避剑的官员又俨然凯旋。事实上，他们不曾打过一仗。城内所余百姓，百姓所余财物，又被官军洗劫一遍。如此苦难，何曾见也！

元末，天下大乱。1349年，泰州盐商张士诚揭竿而起，攻占泰州。张读书不多，乐善好施。因不满当权者欺压，奋起反抗。当时，一官兵当众羞辱他，被他杀死。起义之初，追随者仅十八人，其中三人为其兄弟。他们劫掠富人，焚其家产，所到之处，莫不如此。伴随着他的努力，成功接踵而至。他自封大周诚王。夺取通州后，张留一兄弟守城。他则自通州渡江，夺取福山、常熟，为后续部队主力扫清道路。张士诚亲自指挥攻取平江府（苏州）的战役。城破后，他对百姓保护有加。这一做法在中国人的历史中很少见，因此整个行动得到老百姓热情拥戴。他将承天寺设为行宫。之后，张士诚攻陷常州，袭取镇江。朝廷大军向南扑来，张士诚派弟弟张士德攻取宜兴。随后，张士德顽强抵抗朝廷大军，战败后被俘。他建议张士诚向元顺帝称臣纳贡，上缴钱粮赋税。张士诚照做，被封太尉，即一省之军队统领。不过，他的臣服名不副实，因为他依然掌握政权，是个无冕之王。手下人纷纷劝他称帝。此时，张士诚心生骄纵，加上反元大业第一领袖刘福通去世，于是他将效忠元朝一事抛在脑后，自立为吴王，尊其母为王太后。

他在王废基建造宫殿，任命其弟张士信为杭州知府。此时张士诚不再向元朝廷纳贡。他占领的地盘，往南含绍兴府，往北含江苏全境，向西含安徽东部大半，向东直至大海。此时，他拥有将士数万人。他的统治温和仁慈。张士诚表面上看起来很有能力，但缺乏实际才干。

But he was surrounded by a cortege of sycophants. After many years of peace, when happiness and prosperity had come to the people, he gave himself up to ease and pleasure—public affairs being neglected. This gave opportunity for oppression of the people by his underlings, while revelry was abroad among them. Military officials neglected their duties; the camps were the resorts of dancing girls and gambling was rife. This was continued until he was attacked by the terrible Chu Yuan Chang, the founder of the Ming dynasty, whose power was coming more and more in the ascendancy. Forces of 200,000 men were sent into the Principality, and for seven years pillaging, looting, and burning with all the attendant horrors of oriental warfare continued. The whole country was brought to the very edge of ruin. Hangchow, Kashing, Huchow, Changchow, Taichow, with the magisterial cities, had fallen, and when Soochow was besieged, Chang Shih-chen was urged to give in his allegiance. But, as with many men of limited ability, he could not see the issue and refused. Starvation and disease decimated the people who crowded into the city. It was, during this time that the local names Three Family Village and Six Family Threshing-floor（三家村、六家场）grew up. The one is just inside the Fu Men, the other near the Tsang Men. The extreme significance of these names is shewn in that they tell a tale of horror and suffering such as has come to few cities that have ultimately survived.

With the last store of rice Chang had pots of congee cooked and poured over the wall of the city at the Chi'men to demonstrate to the besiegers the bountiful supply of food in the city. But the besiegers were not deceived. Chi'men was broken in and Chang Shih-chen made his last stand at the Imperial Temple. Being there defeated, he retired to his palace and hung himself. But respect was paid to his corpse and he was buried by Imperial order. His princess, who had promised that she would not disgrace him, collected a pile of fuel in the court of the palace, and she, together with the ladies of the palace, burned themselves to death. Sad commentary on the civilization of any people when such a desperate act could be preferable to the life that must ensue should they fall into the hands of the enemy! This happened in the early days of the Ming dynasty—say five hundred and forty years ago. But the same thing happened here at Soochow, when the city was taken by the Tai Pings, and that on a scale so large as to be staggering in its proportions. The same thing would happen today should the city be taken by a revolutionary force.

Chang Shih-chen's two sons disappeared in the confusion of the fall of the

张士诚身边簇拥着一群阿谀奉承之徒。数年太平岁月之后，百姓安乐富足。张渐渐安逸享乐，不理政事。这给了他手下人可乘之机，他们鱼肉百姓，到处寻欢作乐。将领武备松弛，军营里歌舞升平，赌博盛行。这一情况一直持续到他们可怕的敌人朱元璋打过来。朱元璋是大明王朝的建立者。他当时的军力越来越强大。朱元璋率领二十万军队杀向张士诚的领地，烧杀掳掠，伴随东方式战争产生的可怕情景，七年间不曾间断。整个区域处于毁灭的边缘。杭州、嘉兴、湖州、常州、泰州及其所辖城市，全部陷落。苏州城被围困之时，朱元璋招降张士诚。但是，由于张士诚身边缺乏辅佐的人才，他未能看清形势，予以拒绝。涌入城中的百姓饿死、病死者甚多。正是这一时期，当地才有了"三家村""六家场"的地名。一个位于葑门内，一个靠近相门。这些名称有着极为重要的意义，它们本身即讲述了一段恐怖、凄楚的故事。罕有城池陷落后而幸免于难者。

张士诚用所剩无几的大米，煮了几锅粥，从齐门城头泼下，向困城者宣告城内食物充足。但是这一把戏并未得逞。齐门被攻破。张士诚退守最后据点万寿寺，战败后，他退王宫，上吊自杀。他的尸体被按照君王礼仪厚葬。他的王后此前曾发誓为其殉节。张死后，她于王宫庭院内堆积柴草，与众嫔妃自焚而死。因为，在这种情况下，一旦落入敌手，他们将生不如死。如此文明，令人唏嘘！这是大明王朝前期，即五百四十年前，发生的事情。然而，后来太平军攻陷苏州时，这一幕再次上演。并且，其惨烈程度有过之而无不及。今天，假如革命军队攻打进来，同样的事情还会发生。

张士诚的两个儿子趁城池陷落，满城慌乱之际逃脱，后不知所终。正

city, and were never heard of afterwards. It is owing to this fact that on Tsingming when sacrifices are offered to the spirits of those without descendants, officials and people have ever since made sacrifices to the Chang Shih-chen, the resolute rebel and compassionate Prince of Wu.

The captain An Wan-nien（安万年）, a Soochow man who defended the Ch'i Men with such valour at this time, has been deified and worshipped as Tu Ti Shen（土地神）of that section of the city. Because of the strenuous opposition of Soochow and the surrounding country the district was penalized by Chu Yan Chang by having the taxes trebled above that of other places. This penalty has been maintained to the present time.

FAMOUS MEN

Fan Chungyen（范仲淹）, commonly known as Van Ven Chen Kong, A.D. 989-1052. There is no more worthy name than Van Ven Chen Kong among the long list of worthies of Soochow. His ancestor Fan Lipin was minister of the Tang dynasty. Left an orphan at two years of age, his mother married into the Chu family of Nanking, a merchant doing business in Soochow and Manchuria. Under this name he grew to manhood. As a child he was wise and self restrained. Arriving at manhood he came to know his origin, left his mother with tears, and went to the capital（天府）, where he lived with relatives and fellow students. He gave himself day and night to study. In winter, when wearied with application he used cold water to wash his face and revive his flagging energies. So bitter was his poverty that ordinary mortals could not have endured the suffering, but his poverty made no impression on him.

About 1012 A. D. he graduated as Chin Shih M.A. and entered upon his public career as a military official at Kuangteh in Honan. At this time he took his mother to his home and ever after protected her with solicitous care. He was rapidly advanced in positions of responsibility, and about this time reverted to his own name. Having filled the post of Director of Salt Revenue at Taichow, in Kiangsu, successfully, he was sent to Hupeh as Governor of Taxes.

On the death of his mother he retired from office for the period of mourning but gave his time to the study of civil affairs, and sent in several recommendations that attracted the attention of the authorities at the capital. At the end of his period of mourning he was appointed secretary of the Hanlin

因为如此，自那以后，每逢清明时节，人们准备祭品，祭奠亡灵之际，苏州官员百姓都会为张士诚献祭，纪念这位勇于抗争，富有同情心的吴王。

当时死守齐门的将领安万年，为苏州人，如今被尊为苏州城该区域的土地神。由于苏州及周边的顽抗，朱元璋后来将该区域赋税增至三倍，作为惩罚。这一惩罚保留至今。

苏州名人

范仲淹（谥文正），世称范文正公，公元989年生，1052年卒。虽然苏州才俊辈出，不胜枚举，但无出范文正公之右者。范先祖为唐朝宰相范履冰。范仲淹两岁时父亲去世，母亲改嫁南京朱氏。朱氏从商，往来苏州与满洲之间。仲淹从朱姓，直至成年。他幼年聪慧自律，成年后，渐知身世，遂泣别母亲，奔天府[1]读书，与亲友同学共居。他日夜苦读。寒冬，用功疲倦时，他以冷水浇面，抖擞精神。贫寒之苦，非常人可以忍受，但是丝毫没有影响到他的刻苦努力。

大约1012年[2]，范仲淹中进士，出任河南[3]广德军司理参军。此时，他奉母还家，关怀备至。他旋即数度升迁，之后恢复范姓。离任江苏泰州盐仓监后，监楚州[4]粮料院。

母丧辞官守孝期间，他钻研政务，屡次上书谏言，引起朝中官员注意。范守孝期满，出任翰林学士、皇帝御用谏议官。因此，通过皇帝，他一度

---

[1] 即应天府，位于今河南商丘。
[2] 应为1015年。
[3] 应为安徽宣州府。
[4] 今江苏淮安。

College and private advisor to the Emperor, over whom, for a time, he wielded great influence.

He was an elegant scholar and voluminous writer; conversant with the six classics, he was especially learned on the *Canon of Changes*. He became an authority on these subjects, consulted by the scholars of the empire. He imparted not only learning, but distributed his private income to help needy scholars, and took every opportunity to consult learned men on the difficult questions of the day as well as on abstruse questions in the philosophy of the ancients. Not considering his own ease there was no limit to his labours. Thus his character, example, and instructions brought about universal reforms.

However his unswerving integrity and fearless denunciations of corruption were the cause of many difficulties to himself and others. He would send in a denunciation that thundered with the power of righteous indignation, and bristled with historic references to substantiate his contention. Receiving no reply, he returned to the question with renewed vigor. He never knew when he was beaten, nor would he acknowledge defeat. He would fall into disfavor at court, be sent to an inferior post, do the work better than it had ever been done before, be recalled to the capital, and advanced in authority and to a higher position than ever. While a member of the Board of Censors, a severe scourge of locusts occurred over most of the country, but was especially severe in Kiangsu. Fan Chun Yen (he was not yet Fan Wen Chen Kung) recommended that investigation should be made and famine relief brought to the sufferers. No answer was made to this recommendation. At the next morning's audience he asked the emperor, "How would it be if the palace was without food for half a day?" This produced the desired effect, and Chung yen was sent to take control of the situation. Nothing could have pleased him better. He opened the granaries, established relief works, forbade illicit sacrifices and petitioned that the taxes should be waived, and that the pole tax for Kiangsu should be definitely done away with. This was granted. The emperor, seeing that Fan was a man of unusual ability, called him to the palace and into his private library for consultation on the general condition of the empire. Retiring from this audience he handed up a petition embodying his proposed reforms under ten heads.

It is remarkable how closely subsequent reform proposals have conformed to these proposals of Fan's.

(1) Officials should not be retired without sufficient reason.

对朝政施加影响。

范公儒雅，著述颇丰。他泛通六经，尤擅《易经》，被奉为六经权威，求教者遍及全国。他不仅传授所学，还自掏腰包，资助贫寒举子。他也利用一切机会，就时事问题或古代哲学问题，求教饱学之士。他不图安逸，勤勉不辍。其品格，其风范，其教诲，一改社会风气，成为典范。

然而，他刚正不阿，抨击腐败，无所畏惧，给自己，也给他人，惹了不少的麻烦。他经常上书弹劾官员，引经据典，大义凛然，据理力争。若无答复，他抖擞精神，再接再厉。他常常置他人打击于度外，并且不轻言败。他时遭朝廷冷落，甚至贬谪，但是无论任何职做何事都精益求精。之后，他重新被召回首都，加官晋爵，权重一时。在他担任右司谏期间，天下蝗灾肆虐，尤以江苏为甚。范仲淹（死后追谥范文正公）奏请朝廷派人视察灾情，抚恤灾民。然而他的上疏石沉大海。翌日上朝，他质问皇上："宫掖中半日不食，当何如？"这一问果然奏效，范仲淹被派去掌控局面。他欣然前往，开仓放粮，赈灾救济，禁止非法祭祀，请求朝廷免除赋税，尤其江苏的田赋应该明确予以免除。他的请求获朝廷恩准。皇帝见范公才干过人，遂召其入朝廷，任秘阁校理，征询天下大事。一日，退朝后，范上疏《答手诏条陈十事》。

令人颇为称奇的是，其后的改革提案几乎是范仲淹上书条陈的翻版。

其一：官员无充足理由不得辞官。[1]

---

[1] 明黜陟。

(2) Inefficient officials should be dismissed.

(3) Those recommended for advancement should be carefully investigated.

(4) Careful selection of higher officials should be rigidly enforced.

(5) Land should be equitably divided between the farming classes.

(6) Emphasis should be placed on agricultural pursuits, and sericulture encouraged. The Pole Tax by this time had taken the place of enforced labor for the state.

(7) Reforms should be introduced into the military affairs and the empire put in a condition of preparedness, to put down internal disturbances, and be able to meet external foes. This was a crying need at this time. It was unheeded, and the Sungs grew weaker and weaker from this time.

(8) Imperial favors should be extended only in order to show the people that faithfulness is rewarded.

(9) Imperial mandates should be issued and observed with a due sense of their importance.

(10) Taxes should be made light in all departments of the empire.

About this time the emperor became dissatisfied with his empress and put her away. Fan led the officials in petition on her behalf. For his temerity in this, he was sent as sub-prefect to Mochow (睦州). Here he remained something over a year and was sent as Prefect to Soochow and made President of the Board of Rites. While in this Prefectureship he build the first Confucian temple Soochow had ever had, and placed Hu Yuan in charge as Director of Studies for the Prefecture. From this time Soochow became the centre of literary culture of the empire. Other places followed the good example, and built Confucian temples. His short term of service as Prefect was filled with efforts for the benefit of the people, and for the elevation of the country. At the same time his opposition to Buddhism became pronounced. For he rejected the supernatural in general. He commonly said he could not believe what he could not see. But an adversary put him to rout by saying: " Nevertheless you believe what your pulse tells you as to the state of your health although you cannot see the condition thus indicated."

From his Soochow Prefectureship he was recalled to the capital and made Supervisor of Studies, and advanced to be President of the Board of Civil Appointments. He was soon appointed Governor of Kaifeng Fu. While in this

其二：应该辞退庸官。[1]

其三：被推荐升迁的官员应予以详查。[2]

其四：严格执行对职位较高官员的遴选提拔。[3]

其五：耕者公平分配土地。[4]

其六：重视农业、养蚕业。[5]田赋此时已取代徭役。

其七：进行军事改革，国家进入备战状态，平息内乱，抵御外敌。（虽是当务之急，但少有人关注。而北宋自此江河日下。）[6]

其八：皇恩只施加忠臣。[7]

其九：皇命颁布，必须遵奉。[8]

其十：国家各部门均须减轻赋税。[9]

大约此时，正值皇上对皇后不满，意欲废后。范仲淹率领群臣贸然为皇后请愿，因而被贬睦州知州。在睦州任上大约一年，范仲淹出任苏州知府、礼部员外郎。在苏州知府任上，他兴建了苏州第一座孔庙（即文庙），安排胡瑗"首当师席"，管理郡学。此后，苏州成为国家文学文化中心。各地纷纷效仿，建文庙。他在苏州任期虽短，但竭力惠及百姓，造福一方。与此同时，他明确反对佛教，排斥一切神灵鬼怪。他常说，若非亲眼所见者，断不能信。但是，有人驳斥说："譬如身体状况，试脉可知，但无法目睹。"

从苏州知府，他再次被召回朝，出任国子监，后擢升为吏部员外郎，不久出任开封府尹。开封任上，他与宰相吕夷简交恶日甚。在一次给皇帝

---

[1] 抑侥幸。
[2] 精贡举。
[3] 择官长。
[4] 均公田。
[5] 厚农桑。
[6] 修武备。
[7] 覃恩信。
[8] 重命令。
[9] 减徭役。（以上见范仲淹：《答手诏条陈十事》，载曲延庆、孙才顺著《先忧后乐范仲淹》，济南：齐鲁书社，第173—183页。）

position the ill feeling between Fan Chung-yen and the Prime Minister Lu Ich-ien（吕夷简）was intensified by Chungyen, in a petition to the emperor, comparing the then condition in the capital and empire to the time of calamity and suffering brought about by Wang Mang. (Yuan Shi-kai is spoken of as Sing Wang Mang). For his hardihood he was degraded and sent as Prefect to Jaochow in Kan Shu. The rebellion under Yuan Ho（元昊）chieftain of a Tangut tribe on the north western border broke out. This rebellion grew until the capital was compelled to take cognisance of it, and Fan Chung-yen, at his own request, was sent to put it down. He put his soldiers under rigid discipline, and reorganised the government. The celerity of his movements brought victory to his arms and the rabble of robbers was routed. The justice of his rule gained favour with friend and foe. His soldiers were treated with love and compassion, and became devoted to him. The rebels who returned to their allegiance were received and restored to their civil rights. Those who were still unsubmissive lost their ardor and Yuan Ho begged for peace. It was during this time that he became known as 小范老子 and his name was connected with that of Han Ch'i as striking terror into the hearts of the rebels of the west. (Note.—This is according to *The Annals of Soochow* but is not true as to the reason and method of peace.)

　　He was recalled to the capital and loaded with honors by the Emperor Jen Tsung. He died at the age of sixty-four, full of honors and of good deeds. In life he often said: "In the sorrows of others I first grieve, in the rejoicing of others I rejoice." In dealing with others he was always honest, keeping his word. Never choosing the easy or beneficial for itself, and avoiding the difficult, in his multitudinous life he met every situation with a bold front.

　　He was filial, loyal, faithful. When advanced in honours he still lived a frugal life, having only one kind of meat at a meal. His wife and children were provided with only sufficient food and clothing. Given to philanthropy he did much for the poor wherever he was, and added to his undying fame by establishing for the poor of his clan ancestral estates. The head office of this establishment is at Van Tsong Dzien, and was the first of the kind in the empire,—certainly the first of the kind in this part of China. He loved all and advanced not a few worthy men into positions of responsibility. The people knew his character and commented with praise on his virtues. On his death there was public mourning. The people of Wenchow and Chungchow together with former rebels erected a memorial temple to him in which his image was placed, while all classes of the people wept, as at the death of their own father, and mourned him

的上奏中，范仲淹将当时首都乃至全国状况比作王莽之乱（现在人称袁世凯为"新王莽"）。范仲淹因其刚直不阿被贬知甘肃饶州。西北边疆正值党项部落首领李元昊反叛。叛乱愈演愈烈，朝廷不得不正视。范仲淹主动请缨，被派去平息边乱。他严肃军纪，整顿吏治，率领军队，迅速出击，大获全胜，一举剿灭盗贼。他为政公平，敌友皆服。由于他爱护手下士兵，士兵对他忠心耿耿。那些叛军纷纷倒戈投诚，被妥善安置。而那些顽抗分子士气不再。李元昊被迫乞和。正是此时，人们开始称呼范仲淹为小范老子。他与韩琦齐名，威名震慑西部叛军敌胆。（注：此为《苏州府志》的说法，西部边陲安定，另有缘由。）

  他再度被召回朝，仁宗厚加褒奖。范公六十四岁时去世，一生恩遇有加，政绩善举无数。在世时，他常说："先天下之忧而忧，后天下之乐而乐。"他待人以诚，言出必行。他做事从不拈轻怕重，图谋私利，一生虽然命运多舛，但总是勇往直前。

  范公忠孝信义。备受荣宠时，他依然生活俭朴，一餐仅一荤而已。妻子儿女，衣食无余。而他所到之处，接济穷人，更因创立义庄，赡养穷困族人，而永垂不朽。义庄办公地点设在范庄前，为宋朝第一家此类机构，当然也是中国该区域第一家。他待人宽厚，德才兼备者多所遴拔。范公品格，众所周知，人人称赞其美德。他去世时，举国哀悼。润州、陈州百姓及从前叛乱者为其设立祠堂。祠堂内遗像高悬。举国上下为之恸哭，如丧考妣，

three days.

His ancestral temple is in the city on Van Tsong Dzien, where there is an image of him. During the old regime the officials, by imperial order, went twice a year to offer sacrifices in honor of this great man. His tomb is at the foot of Tien Pin Shan (天平山) and near by is another ancestral temple in which is an image of Fan Wen Chen Kung. On each side of this image, against the side wall of the building, are the images of his sons. In a rear, and therefore more honorable building, are the images of three of his ancestors, all of whom, according to the spirit tablets, were officials of high rank under various emperors. According to local tradition, when he was buried the stones on the surrounding hills stood upright, pointing to heaven in recognition of a man whose life had been in accordance with the will of heaven (God).

He was canonised 文正 and his tablet entered into the Confucian temple in 1716. He left four sons who rose to official position.

Chu Yun-min 1460-1529（祝允明枝山）. No people have given more attention to calligraphy than the Chinese, and of those who have become famous in this art Soochow has had her full share. One of the most famous of these was Chu Chi Shan. He obtained his M.A. in the fifth year of Ming Hung Chi（明宏治）and was appointed magistrate of Hsinming in Canton Province. There he became famous for putting down robbery, and brought peace to the whole prefecture.

At five years of age he was writing characters a foot square, and at nine was composing verses. An industrious student, a voracious reader, a rapid composer with flying pen, his fame as a calligraphist was soon spread over the whole empire. Like so many of China's scholars, he was fond of wine, women and gambling; while he wrote his own tunes for his attendant dancers. A reckless spendthrift, he died in great poverty, for when he had money he gave it away to someone more needy than himself.

His convivial friend and contemporary, was Tang Yin（唐寅伯虎）whose paintings rivalled those of the famous artists of the Tang and Sung dynasties.

He wrote "The Elements of History"（史学提要）and left some poetry said to be of a high order.

As is well known no names are more famous than those of Lu and Ku in Soochow. Owing to the number and prominance of these families the custom

为之举哀三日。

他的宗祠位于城内范庄前，内有塑像。按照古代帝制，官员可一年内两次奉旨祭祀这位伟人。他的墓地位于天平山脚下。不远处，另有祠堂，内悬范文正公画像。画像左右两侧，祠堂边墙上悬挂着范仲淹儿子的画像。后堂，建筑更为肃穆，悬挂范公三位先祖画像。灵牌显示，三位先祖曾为高官，效忠多位帝王。据传，范公下葬时，周围群山石头纷纷朝天矗立，以纪念这位一生遵循天道的伟人。

范仲淹谥号文正，1716年灵位入文庙。范公育有四子，皆入朝为官。

祝允明，字枝山，1460年生，1529年卒[1]。中国人最讲究书法。若论书法名家，苏州名家占有一席之地。其中，祝枝山名气最大。明宏治[2]五年中举，出任广东兴宁县知县。在其任上，因剿灭劫匪，保境安民而知名。

他五岁能写正楷，九岁能作诗文。他勤奋好学，才思敏捷，书法造诣一时名闻天下。中国历代才子，多好酒、贪色、嗜赌，祝枝山亦莫能外，他甚至为歌姬谱曲，终因挥霍无度，仗义疏财，穷困潦倒而终。

与他同一时代的好友唐寅，字伯虎，好交际，绘画比肩唐宋大家。

他编纂《史学提要》，遗诗作多篇，品格甚高。

众所周知，陆姓、顾姓为苏州名门望族。族人多，名气大，以至于当

---

[1] 祝允明生卒年应为1461—1527。
[2] 应为"明弘治"。

arose of asking in answer to a knock at the door, Lu Ku? Is it Lu or Ku? Of the Lu family probably one of the most famous in the early annals was that of Lu Chi（陆绩）3rd A.D. At the age of six he was taken to Kiu Kiang（九江）to visit Yuan Shu, who gave him some oranges to eat. He concealed one in his sleeve, which rolled out when he prostrated himself on taking his leave. His host laughingly asked "What, you hide one of my oranges?" The boy, still kneeling, answered that he wished to take one to his mother who was very fond of them. For this speech he has been enrolled as one of the twenty-four filial sons of Soochow. He grew to manhood fond of study, but his special hobby was astronomy. Though he took a military post on the borders from Sun Chuan(孙权) he nevertheless continued his studies, and constructed a map of the heavens, and annotated the *Canon of Changes*. He foretold his own death which took place at the early age of thirty-two.

Lu Chi（陆机）A.D. 261-303. The son of an official he was seven feet tall and had a voice like the toll of a great bell. Even when small (you know all the prodigies of China, and other places, must be prodigies at a very early age) he showed remarkable ability in literary attainments and military prowess. On the death of his father he took command of his soldiers. Upon the fall of the house of Wu he retired to his home and studied ten years. In 289 he went with his brother Yun to the capital at Loh Yang and on the recommendation of Chang Hwa he received an appointment and entered the services of Prince Lun of Chow（伦王）. He was soon made minister of state, and shared the downfall of his prince, but escaped death, being saved by prince Yin（颖王）, and became attached to his interests. Prince Yin's troops being defeated, an enemy reported that the defeat was brought about by the treachery of Lu Chi. The prince in a rage had him executed. On the day of his death there was a dense fog, a tree tearing wind, and a fall of several feet of snow. Among the people it was recognized that he was unjustly done to death.

Ku Ting-chen: A modern man who graduated first of the list under Hung Chi. He was gradually advanced in office until under Chen Teh became Minister of State, and was loaded with imperial favours. The emperor made a journey to the south and Ku Ting-chen was left as regent in the capital for three months. He fulfilled this regency with ability, integrity and honor.

地有一习俗，但有敲门者，必先问陆顾。即，陆还是顾？陆姓中，早年名气最大者或许当属公元三世纪的陆绩。陆绩六岁时，被带去九江拜见袁术，袁术拿出橘子招待。陆绩暗中将一颗橘子藏在袖中。临别前，跪地施礼，橘子滚落出来。主人取笑说："陆郎做客而怀橘，何为耶？"陆绩长跪不起，回答说他的母亲爱吃橘子，所以想带一个回去给母亲。因此言，陆绩位列苏州二十四孝子之一。成年后，陆绩酷爱读书，尤好天文。虽被孙权委任戍边军职，犹不辍学业。曾绘浑天图，为《易经》作注。他自卜命短，去世时，年仅三十二岁。

陆机，公元261年生，303年卒。其父为官。陆机身长七尺，声若洪钟。年少时，便展现出非凡的文学造诣与军事才干（自古英雄出少年，中外皆然）。其父去世后，陆机指挥其父部下。后孙吴灭亡，陆机隐退乡里，为学十年。公元289年，与其弟陆云至首都洛阳。经张华举荐，在赵伦王[1]手下当差。后被任命为相国[2]。司马伦覆灭，受到牵连。幸得成都王司马颖相救，逃过一死。后遂依附于司马颖。司马颖兵败，一位将军与陆机素有怨隙，趁机诬告陆机背叛导致兵败。司马颖大怒，将陆机处死。临刑之日，大雾弥合，狂风折树，平地积雪几尺厚。众人皆以为其冤死。

顾鼎臣，所处时代距今不远。弘治年间中殿试状元。累官终至正德[3]首辅，恩宠有加。皇帝南巡，留顾鼎臣在首都摄政三月。顾以其才干、品行而不辱使命。

---

[1] 应为赵王司马伦。《晋书》卷五十四《陆机传》："张华荐之诸公。"
[2] 司马伦为相国，陆机为相国参军。
[3] 此处应为嘉靖帝。

III PART

The Chinese are a people who at one time were the strongest among the nations, having founded the greatest empire in extent of territory and population ever seen in history; who have led the world in culture and in science; who have been a military people and that of a very high order; have produced some of the world's greatest scholars; who have had sages and innumerable students, yet they now present a miserable spectacle before an amazed world. For says Wells Williams concerning the Tang dynasty: "During the two hundred and eighty seven years they held the throne, China was probably the most civilized country on earth. The darkest days of the West, when Europe was wrapped in the ignorance and degredation of the Middle Ages, formed the brightest era of the east." And since Soochow has held from the very first a prominent position in the history of the whole land by reason of her learned scholars, merchant princes, and great officials, she likewise shared in the glory just referred to. But how does it come about that she is the spectacle of ineptitude, lack of initiative and general inability that we see today? For the explanation of so great a sociological condition we must go to the foundations of the life of the people; to their philosophy; to their principles of life and belief and religious systems and practice... During their rule 202 B.C. - 238 A.D. (440 years) many commentaries on the classics were issued.

But the Commentators or Han Ju were completely under the influence of the Taoist Magicians. Their speculations were Taoist and thus Taoist elements (of which Confucianism in its original condition was free) were introduced. The classics were largely written from memory by the scholars of the Former Han, and are still known as Modern Literature （今文） about the time of Wang Mang (B.C. 33-A.D. 23) "The Usurper," some books said to have been found buried were presented to the government. These contained a text with slight but vital differences from the "Modern Literature," were called "Ancient Literature (古文)". But scholars have been unable to decide the authenticity of the 古文. After the appearance of this Ku Wen a movement was set on foot to separate Taoism from Confucianism, with the result that Taoism became a separate creed, under state supervision and patronage, about the time of Huang Ti (148 A.D. to 167 A.D.); and in 165 Chang Taoling （张道陵） was appointed, by Huang Ti, the first Taoist Patriarch （天师）. Literature reached the highest point during the Han, but in spite of deleting and purging efforts the contamination of

结语

中华民族一度称雄世界。他们建立了最为强大的帝国，疆域辽阔，人口众多。中国的文化、科技曾经引领世界。中国人也曾驰骋疆场，能征惯战。这里造就了世界上最伟大的学者，这里圣哲先贤辈出，文教名人，不可胜数。而如今，天下纷乱，景象一片惨淡。因此，卫三畏谈及唐朝时曾说："两百八十七年统治期间，中国可能是当时世界上最为文明的国家。当时的欧洲为中世纪的愚昧无知、腐化堕落所困。西方处至暗之日，东方乃最亮之时。"从最初开始，苏州在整个区域历史中一直处于令人瞩目的地位，其鸿儒硕学、富商大贾、名臣廉吏，功不可没。苏州往日繁华诚如上述。可是，如今何以变成这样一番恶劣景象：粗拙、敷衍、无能。要想解释这一社会状况，我们必须探究百姓生计之本、处世之道、出世入世之宗旨……公元前202年至公元238年四百四十年间，为经学注疏蔚然成风。

但是这些评注者（或称"汉注"）完全受道教玄学影响，尊崇道家思想，因此道教元素（儒学最初并无此元素）被引入儒学。这些经书主要是西汉学者凭借记忆写成，王莽篡权（公元前33年至公元23年）[1]前后乃称"今文"。部分先前被埋书籍，发现后上交政府。这些书籍部分内容与"今文"虽略有不同，但其差异意义重大，称为"古文"。但学者们至今无法确定其真伪。古文的出现，兴起一场儒、道分离的运动。结果，大约桓帝时期（公元148年至167年）[2]，道教在朝廷监管与赞助下，成为另一门学派。公元165年，张道陵被桓帝任命为天师，即第一位道教掌门人。文学在汉朝

---

[1] 王莽篡权时间大概为公元5年至公元8年。
[2] 桓帝时期应为公元147年至167年。

Confucianism had taken place and has continued to the present. The next Great contamination and debasement took place in the Sung dynasty. The famous Sung philosophers were separated about fifteen centuries from Confucius. Many contaminations and corruptions of the text had arisen. Having been corrupted by having Taoist interpretations injected by the Han, the Sung philosophers now added the corruption of Buddhist interpretation. In their cosmogony and philosophy of nature, and attitude to ancient practices of divination they differed widely from the Great Sage. They were all thorough Buddhists and Buddhism had reached one of the lowest stages of degeneration and general decay. Confucianism pure and simple was not acceptable to the masses. Therefore the scholars reconstructed Confucianism and introduced the Map of The Great Change （太极图）. Thus they corrupted the thought of the ancients with Buddhistic speculations. They thought the highest place of honor in the Confucian world belonged to them. In their hands Heaven or the supreme Being, became:"Heaven is Reason" （天即地也）, thus, virtually denying the existence of God. Their philosophy led men away from God (for it is in every man's power to save himself, and God had nothing to do with it), retarded progress, and encouraged lying and pretence and is largely responsible for China's present weakness.—After Li Un-bin and therefore for all the namby-pamby weaknesses of the people of Soochow who are professed Confucianists but in practice from the highest to the lowest are devout Buddhists and have been from the early introduction of Buddhism to China.

Further no other philosophy is so suited to the purposes of a despotic government. The theory of Retribution is an instrument that an absolute government can handle to best advantage, and in this respect Buddhism supplies a defect which was long felt in Confucianism. In order to gain governmental favour and preferment succeed—generations have lauded and given reverence to this philosophy, and that in a manner that was in no wise its due. Here then was the fountain head of the causes of decay of Soochow. For none were so zealous as the Soochow literati in studying and carrying out the tenants of this philosophy. We are told in the introduction to the chapter "Customs and Practices" in *The Annals of Soochow*, that soon after the founding of the city "Temples and monasteries were built on every hill throughout the country of Wu." These were Taoist. As has been said Taoism was in the ascendancy during the Han dynasty, and so remained until the time of Liang Wuti (502 - 547 A. D.) when Baddhidama

登峰造极。尽管亵渎儒学的行为不断受到打击，但是这一行为从汉代开始，一直持续到今天。另一场大规模的曲解传统儒学的运动发生在宋代。宋代名儒与孔夫子已相隔大约十五个世纪。自汉代以道家阐释儒家开始，宋代经学家们开始以佛家阐释儒家，对传统儒学破坏尤甚。他们对天地起源之说，对古代祭祀神明之态度，皆与孔圣人相去甚远。他们以佛观儒，而此时佛教腐化堕落至谷底。纯朴的传统儒学反而不为大众所接受。学者因此重建儒学，并引入太极图。以佛观儒，曲解了古人的思想，他们却认为自己对儒家思想的阐释达到了新的高度。在他们的操纵下，"天（即最高存在）即地也"[1]，这一说法否认了神的存在。他们的思想使人远离神明（神不渡人，人自渡之），阻滞文化发展，怂恿谎言与虚伪。中国今日之积贫积弱，大部分原因在此。继李文彬之后，苏州百姓尽管柔弱，尽管宣称信奉儒教，但实际上，自上至下，都是虔诚的佛教徒。自佛教早期传入中国起，一贯如是。

此外，没有其他学说比得上佛教更能迎合君主专制政权。因果报应之说是专制政权可以最有效操纵的工具，这也因此成为佛教的一大缺陷。而这一缺陷也长期反映在儒学中。为了博得朝廷荣宠，一代又一代人赞颂并虔诚地信仰这一学说，此即苏州衰败的源头所在。至于研究佛教，皈依佛门，其热情无出乎苏州文人之右者。我们得知，《苏州府志》之"风俗"篇简介中记载，苏州城建成后不久，寺院庙宇遍及吴山，不过多为道观。据说，道教在汉代占据上风，一直持续到梁武帝（公元502至547年）[2]时期，

---

[1] 此处遵从原作者注文。按照字面意思以及实际情况，应该翻译为"天即理"或"理即天"。
[2] 梁武帝（公元464—549）。

(达摩) arrived. He was the sixty-first patriarch of Indian Buddhism and the first of China. He reached Canton by sea and made his way to the seat of imperial government at Nanking. This was the beginning of an infatuation with a cult that finds a parallel only in Louis XIV of France. His reign forms an important era in the history of Chinese Buddhism. Three different times he entered the Tung Tai monastery at Nanking as a Buddhist monk, and was prevailed on each time to return to state affairs only by large bribes. "Of Buddhist emperors there have been many, but in point of mad devotion Liang Wuti leads them all," says a Chinese writer. It was a time of feverish activity in building Buddhist temples. And, it should be borne in mind that Nanking was the capital of the empire, and we may justly infer that the example of the court was followed by Soochow. I only desire to show that each cult was strongly entrenched in the hearts of the people of the whole country and therefore of Soochow, and not to give a history of religion.

In China, and therefore in Soochow, superstition has always been supreme. This has led to practices that were both puerile and corrupt. Having no higher ideals than their sages and teaching who were corrupt (or at least far from perfect) their gods were corrupt with all the faults and failures of fallen man. The contrary to this has been stated and restated. But let anyone who doubts what I say, read *The Chronicles of the Deification of The Gods* （封神传） and *Travels in the West* （西游记）. In these works the delineation of the characters of the gods is given as the people believe them to be. They are startling enough.

Since man could be deceived and bribed and thereby an apparent advantage gained the same practices grew in their services to and treatment of their gods. Deception (of which there are eighty-eight varieties) and falsehood grew to such an extent that every form of service or worship or reverence became false; fear and avarice being the prompting motives to all acts of worship, selfishness became a dominant factor in the lives of the people in every walk. And to this ancestral worship, the stronghold of prejudice and opponent of change, is no exception. So deeply imbeded in the souls of the people has falsehood become that in every thing they only expect falsehood and they have become unsusceptible to the power of truth, when clearly presented to them. Truth has lost its appeal for the Soochow people.

Grinding poverty on the part of the many has always been flaunted by heartless and prodigious wealth on the part of the few who have held the power.

直到达摩出现。达摩为印度佛教第六十一祖师，第一个来到中国。他先渡海来到广州，然后北行至梁朝都城所在地南京。此即佛教崇拜之始。[1]其热烈程度，唯法国路易十四时期可与之比肩。梁武帝统治时是中国佛教史上的重要时期。梁武帝三次舍身南京同泰寺为和尚，令官员用大笔银钱为其赎身，方回朝理政。"历代帝王信奉佛教者众，但痴迷如此者，梁武帝冠绝古今。"中国一作家如是说。当时，建造佛寺，风靡一时。并且，南京是该朝首都。因此，我们有理由推断，苏州也会效仿南京朝廷。我只想以此说明，每一种学说的狂热尊崇都在天下黎民百姓心中打上深深的烙印，自然也包括苏州百姓。我无意在此讲述宗教历史。

包括苏州在内的中国，迷信一直高高在上。这导致很多既愚蠢又腐朽的做法。他们敬畏的诸位神明，其思想境界不及圣人，腐败、堕落却如凡人。当然，也有人一而再再而三地提出相反的看法。但是，假如任何人怀疑我的说法，可以去读一读《封神传》《西游记》。在这些作品中，各路神仙，各种性格，按照人们的想象，被一一勾勒出来。令人叹为观止。

因为人们可以欺骗，可以贿赂，由此获得明显优势。在祭祀神灵、对待神灵时，这些做法有增无减。欺诈（计有八十八种）、蒙蔽，以至于任何形式的仪式、礼拜、虔诚都到了假惺惺的程度。当所有的顶礼膜拜起因于恐惧、贪婪时，自私自利便主导了从事各行各业的人们的生活。对祖先的崇拜也不免固执己见、故步自封。这种说谎的习惯深深植根于民众灵魂之中，以至于他们认为凡事皆可说谎，哪怕真理清晰地呈现在眼前，他们也不为所动。对苏州百姓来说，真理毫无魅力可言。

多数百姓，一贫如洗，苦不堪言。而少数当权者，家财万贯，招摇过市，

---

[1] 佛教传入应始于西汉末东汉初，此处为原作者观点。

The principles of benevolence and rectitude that slip so readily off the teacher's tongue was (and is) given immediate contradiction by acts of crookedness and cruelty. Swarms of poor relatives, more persistant than summer flies around a cut water melon, have forced nepotism in court, council, and commercial company. Dishonesty and corruption have flourished while men of integrity and probity have usually gone begging.

......

True patriotism has not flourished because those in power, through all the ranks of officialdom, have ruled not for the good of the people, but for their own aggrandizement, and the accumulation of wealth, which was spent for the gratification of the lowest emotions.

Without copy-right, or patent laws, there has been no incentive to productive authorship or encouragement to invention.

The highest ideal of the Confucianist, who has always been the leader, was to spend his time studying and absorbing the tenets and diction of the past ages, until he could be able to produce writings that were so near like the standards that one could scarcely be told from the other. Every attempt at originality was frowned down, its author ostracized in his own time and held up to ridicule by succeeding generations. In this connection it is sufficient to site the examples of Hsun K'uang（荀况）or 荀子 and Mih Tzu（墨翟）or 墨子. Any productive effort was unworthy the superior man. On the other hand the ideal of Buddhism that has wielded such a powerful influence on the Chinese from the time of its introduction, was non-resistance, rest or inaction, contemplation, concentration of the mind on nothingness until the mind should be absorbed into nothingness.

The admixture of the principles just shewn could have only one result—the deadening of initiative and stoical acceptance of present conditions.

The form of ancestral worship that has grown out of the medly of Confucianism, Buddhism and Taoism, is a departure so far from the original that the authors would not recognise the resultant product. It sanctions polygamy and debases the home; practices idolatry while vilifying the idols; encourages deception and has no blush for the lie; while filial piety, the most lauded of all the virtues, is a one-sided obligation.

The final result being that we have a people largely void of laudable ambition steeped in ignorance, blinded by prejudice, and satisfied with tradition.

The words of a magazine writer concerning Mexico can be aptly applied

良心泯灭。为师者，满嘴的仁义道德，却一身的邪恶残忍。成群的穷亲戚，比夏天叮着切开的西瓜不放的苍蝇还难轰走。他们依靠裙带关系，入职法庭、政府、公司。狡诈堕落之徒兴旺发达，而正直诚实之辈常常沿街乞讨。

…………

真正的爱国热情并没有兴起，因为各级官吏不为百姓福祉，只为升官发财，满足最低级的欲望而已。

没有版权，没有专利法，人们既无心创作，也无意发明。

为官者多为儒家文人。他们的最高理想不过是闭门读书，在故纸堆里寻章摘句，直到写出千篇一律的文章。这些文章但有新意，必为人所厌恶；其作者必为当世所排挤，为后世所讥笑。关于这一点，仅举荀况（即荀子），墨翟（即墨子）之例足矣。但有思想，何必多产？另外，佛家思想自引入之始，即对中国人产生巨大影响。佛教倡导逆来顺受，清净无为，冥想禅定，以至四大皆空。

以上各条戒律只有一个结果：扼杀人们做事的积极性，使人禁欲克己，安于现状。

脱胎于儒释道三教杂合，祖宗崇拜早已脱离源头，面目全非。它认可一夫多妻，贬低个人家庭的地位；它时而尊崇圣贤，时而污蔑诋毁；它纵容欺诈，信口雌黄而面不改色；孝道虽为百善之首，却是单方面的责任。

最终，百姓无进取之心，愚昧无知，一叶障目，食古不化。

一位杂志作者描写墨西哥的句子可以稍加修改，拿来形容苏州，亦颇

to Soochow with only slight variations: "With violent extremes of naked poverty find incredible riches, of peons and patricians, of general illiteracy and aristocratic culture, a nation (city) that is a disorder of serfs, Croesuses, scholars, bandits, cut-throats, atheists, and saints."

In writing this paper I have made free use of Giles *Biographical Dictionary*, Martins " The Lore of Cathay," and Li's " Outlines of Chinese History."

恰切:"穷者,其穷无可掩饰;富者,其富难以置信;贱者,卖身苦力;贵者,安享荣华;一边,白丁遍地;一边,书香门第。两相对照,何其泾渭分明!一国(一城)之内,至贫至贱者与至富至贵者错杂,文人墨客与打家劫舍、杀人越货之徒并存,目无神灵者与善男信女共处。"

本文写作,参照翟理斯《古今姓氏族谱》、丁韪良《汉学菁华》和李文彬《中国历史纲要》。

Eighteen Capitals of China

中国十八省府

(盖洛 著 徐冰 译)

美国著名旅行家、人文地理学家威廉·埃德加·盖洛（William Edgar Geil）（1865—1925）著《中国十八省府》（*Eighteen Capitals of China*），由费城和伦敦利品科特公司（Philadelphia & London J. B. Lippincott Company）1911年出版。全书425页，附有139张照片。

自1903年起盖洛曾多次来中国探险，用鲜活的文字和图片生动地捕捉记录了在扬子江沿岸、长城，以及中国各大名山所考察到的中国民情，先后著成《扬子江上的美国人》《中国长城》《中国十八省府》《中国五岳》等书，受到美国读者的好评。

《中国十八省府》分"南方省府""长江流域省府""黄河流域省府"三部分。"苏州"作为第七章，出自第二部分，页码范围158—190。该章选取三大视角介绍苏州："何为'苏州'？""舟行苏州""苏州故事"。"何为'苏州'"主要介绍苏州的历史、名胜及名人；"舟行苏州"重在从水上及空中考察苏州；"苏州故事"几乎全文引用《苏州现形记》一书的"缘起"部分，展示苏州人的性格特点及所受鸦片的毒害。

盖洛在书写苏州时，广泛参考地方志、传说、史书、学术文献、文学作品等资料，力求从地貌、历史、民俗、本土文学等方面记录当时处于西化影响之下、新旧更迭的苏州的真实历史和社会风貌。虽然某些记述存在一定偏颇，但这些文字仍为今人了解、研究二十世纪初外国人眼里的苏州提供了珍贵史料。

THE YANGTZE CAPITALS
VII SOOCHOW

PART I— WHAT IS SOO?

Soo is the first of the eighteen provincial capitals to be reached from Shanghai—seat of an old kingdom, the Amsterdam-Venice of the East.

The king of Wu in the days of Pisistratus, Ezra, and Confucius was named Ho Lu,[1] who assassinated his predecessor and decided to make a new beginning. He bade his prime minister, Wu Tzǔ-hsü, design him a plan; he chose as a site an archipelago of islands among a few score of lakes some forty miles south of the Yangtze, twelve miles east of the Great Lake, and eighty miles from the sea. Geomancers were employed to consult the signs of the heavens and the winds of the earth, then to taste the waters. Then arose a rectangular wall some forty-seven li around, with nine gates, the royal number, bastions and corner forts. Within it were laid out parks, palaces, libraries, and comfortable homes; bridges links the islands, canals intersected them, eight-foot streets reticulated over them. Three former cities were depopulated to provide a people at the artificial capital; and lo, Soo-chow!

Not only did Ho Lu have Wu to make Soo, but he also had Sun, the greatest military writer of all China's ages to provide patterns for his various military manoeuvres. His use of strategy and his lessons on "The Art of War" were studied by the generals of Ch'in the Great, who made an Empire out of the fighting fragments of China. The following quotation is from the Introduction to Sun Tzǔ, by Lionel Giles, in his valuable work on "The Art of War," translated from Ssǔ-ma Ch'ien:

"Sun Tzǔ Wu was a native of the Ch'i state. His 'Art of War' brought him to the notice of Ho Lu, king of Wu. Ho Lu said to him: 'I have carefully perused your 13 chapters. May I submit your theory of managing soldiers to a slight test?'

---

[1] The name is variously given as Ho Lu (by Ssǔ-ma Ch'ien, the historian) and Ho Lü, a different character being employed in the latter case. 史学家司马迁称之为阖庐，也有用另一个字称其名的，为阖闾。——原注（本文为全书统一，译文中用"阖闾"。）

长江流域省府
第七章 苏州

第一部分 何为"苏州"?

中国十八个省府中,距离上海最近的就是苏州府——古时吴国都城,东方的阿姆斯特丹-威尼斯。

吴国君主与古希腊的庇西特拉图[1]、希伯来的以斯拉[2]及春秋末期的孔子生活在同一时代,其名阖闾,通过刺杀前吴王僚,夺取王位,开始新的统治。阖闾命令其大夫伍子胥设计修筑王城,地址选在一个由若干孤洲形成的群岛上。该群岛位于长江以南四十英里的几十个湖泊之间,太湖以东十二英里处,其八十英里之外便是大海。伍子胥请风水师一起相土尝水、象天法地。不久,一座大约周廻四十七里的矩形城墙便拔地而起,设城门九座。"九"象征帝王之尊,城门配备防御工事和角楼。城内建有园林、宫殿、藏书楼及舒适的民居。岛屿之间由桥梁连接,河道纵横交错,一条条八英尺宽的街道将这些岛屿分割为网状结构。通过归并三座旧城的人口,这座新建的都城便有了稠密的居民。瞧,苏州由此而生!

阖闾不但有伍子胥为其筑城,而且还获得了中国历史上最伟大的军事家孙武的辅佐,后者为其提供治军之法。他在《孙子兵法》中提出的战略运筹,还被秦始皇手下的将军们悉心研究过,在中国战火纷飞、四分五裂的时代,秦始皇正是依仗这些才得以统一帝国。翟林奈(Lionel Giles)把司马迁解说的《孙子兵法》译成英文,以下引文便出自他那本珍贵的译著中介绍孙子的部分[3]:

"孙子名武,齐国人。其著作《孙子兵法》为他赢得了吴王阖闾的器重。阖闾对他说:'我已仔细研读了您写的十三篇兵法。现在可否将您有关操练

---

[1] 庇西特拉图(也可拼为 Peisistratus):古雅典僭主(561B.C.—527B.C.),帕伦尼战役获胜之后,为巩固其在雅典的统治而实行保护中小土地所有者及奖励农工商业的政策。

[2] 以斯拉:公元前五世纪的以色列文士、先知和宗教改革者。

[3] 翟林奈(1875—1958):英国学者、翻译家、汉学家翟理斯(Herbert Allen Giles)之子。曾任大英博物馆图书馆助理馆长、东方图书与书写部部长,将《孙子兵法》《论语》等译成英文。以下文字摘自其译著 Sun Tzu on the Art of War(1910)引言里的"孙武及其著作"("Sun Wu and His Book")部分。《孙子兵法》在西方一度被译为《战争的艺术》(Art of War)。

Sun Tzǔ replied: 'You may.' Ho Lu asked: 'May the test be applied to women?' The answer was again in the affirmative, so arrangements were made to bring 180 ladies out of the palace. Sun Tzǔ divided them into two companies, and placed one of the King's favourite concubines at the head of each. He then bade them all take spears in their hands, and addressed them thus: 'I presume you know the difference between front and back, right hand and left hand?' The girls replied: 'yes.' Sun Tzǔ went on : 'When I say, "Eyes front," you must look straight ahead. When I say, "Left turn," you must face toward your left hand.' Again the girls assented. The words of command having been thus explained, he set up the halbreds and battle-axes in order to begin the drill. Then, to the sound of drums, he gave the order, 'Right turn!' But the girls only burst out laughing. Sun Tzǔ said: 'If words of command are not clear and distinct, if orders are not thoroughly understood, the general is to blame ... But if his orders are clear and the soldiers disobey, then it is the fault of their officers.' So saying, he ordered the leaders of the two companies to be beheaded. Now the king of Wu was watching them from the top of a raised pavilion; and when he saw that his favorite concubines were about to be executed, he was greatly alarmed and hurriedly sent down the following message: 'We are now quite satisfied as to the ability of our general to handle troops. If we are bereft of these two concubines, our meat and drink will lose their savour. It is our wish that they shall not be beheaded.' Sun Tzǔ replied: 'Having once received his Majesty's commission to be general of his forces, there are certain commands of his Majesty which, acting in that capacity, I am unable to accept.' Accordingly, he had the two leaders beheaded, and straightway installed the pair next in order as leaders in their place. When this had been done, the drum was sounded for drill once more; and the girls went through all the evolutions, turning to the right or to the left, marching ahead or wheeling back, kneeling or standing, with perfect accuracy and precision, not venturing to utter a sound. Then Sun Tzǔ sent a messenger to the king, saying: 'Your soldiers, sire, are now properly drilled and disciplined, and ready for your Majesty's inspection. They can be put to any use that their sovereign may desire; bid them go through fire and water and they will obey'... And Sun Tzǔ shared the might of the king."

士兵的方法做一个小测试呢？'孙子答：'可以。'阖闾继而又问道：'测试可否用在女子身上？'孙子予以肯定。于是吴王派人把180名宫女带到宫外，孙子将她们分为两队，让吴王的两位宠妃分别站在每个队伍的前面当队长。他令所有人持戟，并对宫女们说：'我想你们都知道向前、向后、向左、向右的区别吧？'宫女们答：'知道。'孙子继续说道：'当我让你们"向前看"时，你们必须正视前方。当我要求"向左看"，你们必须把头转向左手。'宫女们点头同意。解释清楚了口令，孙子就布置好戟和战斧以备操练。战鼓擂起，他发令：'向右看！'可宫女们非但没有按要求做，反而都大声笑起来。孙子说：'如果指令不清，士兵无法领会其意，那么责任在将领一方……但是如果所发之令意思明确，士兵却不予执行，那么他们的长官就得承担责任。'说着就命令将两位领头的宠妃拖出去杀头。吴王一直坐在高台上的亭子里观看孙子指挥操练。眼见两位爱妃即将大祸临头，吴王大为惊骇，传旨道：'我对将军指挥军队的能力非常满意，但如果将两位妃子杀死，我饮酒啖肉时便会食不甘味，还请将军刀下留情。'孙子答：'既然臣已允诺大王出任统率军队的将军，那么将心应该在军，大王所发之令，臣无法执行。'于是就命手下把两位妃子斩首示众，并立刻让其次的两名宫女顺位站到队列最前面，取而代之。调整完毕，战鼓再次响起，这一次宫女们认真操练各种队形变换，向右看、向左看、前进、后退、蹲下、立正，所有的动作都做得精确无误，其间无人胆敢发声。孙子让人向吴王禀报说：'大王，现在您的将士已经训练有素，纪律严明，时刻准备接受大王检阅。大王可以随意调遣他们，令其赴汤蹈火，他们将在所不惜。'……吴王的威权离不开孙子的大力辅佐。"[1]

---

[1] 孙子武者，齐人也。以兵法见于吴王阖闾。阖闾曰："子之十三篇，吾尽观之矣，可以小试勒兵乎？"对曰："可。"阖庐曰："可试以妇人乎？"曰："可。"于是许之。出宫中美女，得百八十人。孙子分为二队，以王之宠姬二人各为队长，皆令持戟，令之曰："汝知而心与左右手背乎？"妇人曰："知之。"孙子曰："前，则视心；左，视左手；右，视右手；后，即视背。"妇人曰："诺。"约束既布，乃设铁钺，即三令五申之。于是鼓之右，妇人大笑。孙子曰："约束不明，申令不熟，将之罪也。"复三令五申而鼓之左，妇人复大笑。孙子曰："约束不明，申令不熟，将之罪也；既已明而不如法者，吏士之罪也。"乃欲斩左右队长。吴王从台上观，见且斩爱姬，大骇，趣使使下令曰："寡人已知将军能用兵矣。寡人非此二姬，食不甘味，愿勿斩也。"孙子曰："臣既已受命为将，将在军，君命有所不受。"遂斩队长二人以徇，用其次为队长。于是复鼓之。妇人左右前后跪起皆中规矩绳墨，无敢出声。于是孙子使报王曰："兵既整齐，王可试下观之，唯王所欲用之，虽赴水火犹可也。"……孙子与有力焉。（参见司马迁著，金源编译《史记·列传》，西安：三秦出版社，2008，第22页。）

Ho Lu died[1] and was buried; his son, Fu Ch'ai, proceeded to dissipate his treasures in the usual round of Oriental dissipation—a lake of wine, a ballet troupe. The prime minister expostulated, and was sent a jewelled sword as a polite hint to cut it short. He therefore committed suicide; but the people rescued his body from the canal and made a national mourning. Since that day the city has been noted for its suicides—over the walls, down the wells, off the pagodas, into the canals; poison, dagger, and smallpox.

Changes have of course taken place. Some of the original gates have been closed, probably for "good luck" reasons, another has been opened; now there are six water gates, and six street gates, each of which has a barbican enclosing some half an acre. Outside the walls are of course extensive suburbs, with inns for late arrivals.

It is important to get hold of the fact that the land here is an accident; the water is the chief thing. There are islands, which are useful to separate the different canals and lagoons. The water-ways are as far superior to the paths as are those in Venice. And the Grand Canal in these parts dates from an ancient time, providing water-carriage from the city all over the Yangtze basin and across the country to the Hwang-ho.

The next great change in the architecture of the city is due to the arrival of Buddhism. The Indian monks were accustomed to erect dagobas, monumental spires. The Chinese idea of towers to attract "good luck" chimed in well with the new suggestion, and soon there came about the characteristic pagodas. The earliest of all is supposed to have been erected here. For the most beautiful, take the description by Dr. Hampden du Bose, of the Southern Presbyterian Mission.

"The glory of the capital is the Great Pagoda, the highest in China, and so the highest on terra firma. Stand near it and behold one of the greatest wonders of the world! Count the stories, note the verandas, see the doors, as so many pigeon-holes, and men as pigmies on those giddy heights! Consider the foundations, and what a quarry of hewn stone supports that mighty pile of masonry, which, including its spiral crown, rises to nearly two hundred and fifty feet in height. Walk round the base, which, with the shed room on the ground floor, is one hundred feet in diameter or one hundred yards around. Note the images in basso-relievo among the clouds, carved on stones, seated upon the roof, hiding in

---

[1] Ho Lu was killed in 496 B. C. 阖闾于公元前496年因重伤而死。——原注

阖闾去世，即被安葬。其子夫差继位，以各种东方常见的方式荒淫无度，挥霍父王的遗产，包括建造酒池，供养歌童舞女等。大夫伍子胥进言规劝，夫差却赐予宝剑，要他自刎。子胥听命，自绝于世。但是吴国百姓将其尸首从河中打捞上来，举国哀悼。从此以后，苏州城便因各种自杀事件频出而出名：跳城墙的、投井的、跳塔的、投河的；服毒的、割喉的，还有因染天花而殒命的。[1]

苏州自建城以来变化不断。不少初建的城门被封塞，大概出于讨吉利的缘故，另一些城门则被新辟出来。目前共有六座水门、六座陆门，每座均配有一座半英亩面积的碉楼。城墙之外自然是大片郊野，其间散落着一些客舍，供城门关闭后抵达苏州的旅人歇脚。

在苏州，陆地只是次要特征，水面才是主要特色，抓住这些特点很重要。城内岛屿颇多，将不同的河流及湖泊隔开。如同威尼斯城，在苏州，水道比陆路重要许多。流经这一地区的大运河历史悠久，为苏州与长江，直至黄河流域各地的水上运输提供了便利。

苏州城在建筑风格方面的另一显著变化，与佛教传入不无关系。印度僧侣惯常建造高耸带尖顶的舍利塔。中国人认为宝塔能集吉祥之气，这一理解与印度佛教造塔理念不谋而合，很快独具特色的宝塔就出现了。中国最早的宝塔应该就是建在苏州的。要了解苏州最美的塔，我们可以在美南长老会的杜步西（Dr. Hampden du Bose）[2]所描述的文字中一窥究竟——

"苏州府的荣耀当属北寺塔，它是中国最高的塔，也是陆地上最高之塔。站到塔边，就能仰视这座最伟大的世界奇迹之一。数数楼层，赏赏檐廊，看看那些鸽子窝般的门洞，站在令人眩晕的高处的游人就像侏儒那么小。想到它的基座要撑起包括螺旋形塔顶在内的、高达二百五十英尺的威严砖石结构，那是一块怎样被开凿出来的方形石座啊！塔的底层有廊道，设有棚屋一间，绕塔基行走，发现连廊道在内的一圈，其直径为一百英尺，或者说周长为一百码。请留意那些用浅浮雕表现的云彩浮雕，有些刻在砖上，有些置于塔顶，或隐于角落，或气势非凡地坐在神龛里。塔内供奉佛教神像，

---

[1] 此处逻辑有些荒唐，为原作者个人观点。
[2] 杜步西：美国人，在苏州工作和生活达38年之久。他与博习医院创始人柏乐文（William Hector Park）等人建立了中国禁烟会（Anti-Opium League in China），并担任首任会长，为根除鸦片对中国的危害做出贡献。撰有《中国的三教：儒、释、道》（*The Image, the Dragon, and the Demon: Or the Three Religions of China Confucianism, Buddhism and Taoism*）等著作。苏州养育巷现存的使徒堂，即由杜步西所建，堂内现有杜步西纪念碑。

the niches, and sitting majestically upon the shines.[1] Buddhist gods inside and Brahman divinities without—two hundred in number; it is a high temple of heathenism. The name of the Sir Christopher Wren who planned this tower has not come down to us, but we can admire the skill of the master hand which drew the lines. The walls are octagonal, one wall within and one without, or a pagoda within a pagoda; each wall ten feet thick, the steps rising between them by easy gradations with a walk around before the next flight is reached, the floors being paved with brick two feet square. There are eight doors to each of the nine stories, and with the cross passages the halls are full of light. And what wonderful proportions! Sixty feet in diameter at the base, it tapers to forty-five feet on the upper floor; each story slightly lower as you ascend, each door smaller, each veranda narrower. Walk round these porches; see the city lying at your feet; the Dragon Street, running south to the Confucian Temple; the Great Lake to the west; the range of hills and the picturesque pagodas that crown the jutting eminences; the plain dotted every fourth mile with hamlets. See the pagoda to the south—it marks the city of Wukiang. Follow the Shanghai canal glistening in the sunlight to the east till your eye rests on a hill—that is Quensan. At the foot of that mountain, thirty miles to the northeast, is Changsoh, a city of 100,000 inhabitants. Look northwest up the Grand Canal, thirty miles—that is Mount Wei'tsien. There is Wusih, with a population of 150,000, and within a radius of thirty miles are one hundred market-towns of from one thousand to fifty thousand inhabitants, and probably 100,000 villages and hamlets—five million within range of vision!"

Since the pagoda was built others have followed, but only six remain today, and the upper stories of some of these have been removed. Thus it is said of the South Gate Pagoda, Zay Kwaung Tah,[2] that the king built it a thirteen-story pagoda for a priest who came in 242; it was repaired twice, then torn down in 1119, and replaced by another of seven stories, which has been frequently repaired but is substantially the present building.

The walls have needed frequent attention. Then most remarkable episode is that between 581 and 610 the people deserted the city because of robbers and rebels. About 917 there was extensive fortifications, the walls being thickened to twenty-five feet and made about as lofty, while, in addition to the usual moat

---

[1] 原文为逗号，疑为印刷错误。
[2] This is of course the Soochow dialect. 这当然是苏州方言。——原注

塔外供奉印度众神，共达两百座。北寺塔是异教徒活动的重要寺庙。我们虽不知设计此塔的大师[1]姓甚名谁，却可通过丰富的建筑线条观瞻其精湛技艺。八角形的墙壁，分作内外两道；也就是说，北寺塔的结构实乃塔中有塔。每道墙厚达十英尺，台阶位于两壁之间，缓缓而上，游客要走上一圈才能到达继续登攀的另一段台阶，然后继续登攀。每层地面均由两平方英尺的砖石铺就。塔身共九层，每层八道门，因为建有相交的过道，所以塔心室内光线充足。多么美妙的宝塔构造！塔基直径六十英尺，上层直径缩到四十五英尺。越往上走，每层就比下一层低矮些，每层的门也比下面的小些，每层的回廊也会变得窄些。走在这些檐廊上，可以饱览脚下苏州的风貌：护龙街向南一直延伸到文庙；西面是太湖，连绵的群山，以及那些矗立在山顶的别致宝塔；广阔的平原上，约每隔四英里就点缀着村庄。向南可看到一座塔，它是吴江城的标志。流向上海的运河在阳光中波光粼粼，顺着它向东望，会看见一座小山，那就是昆山。昆山脚下，其东北三十英里之处即为人口已达十万的常熟。顺着大运河向西北看，三十英里处有惠山。附近就是无锡，人口十五万。以无锡为中心，方圆三十英里半径范围内，聚合着近百个集镇，居住人口从一千到五万不等。村民之数，约达十万。北寺塔所见范围内人口可达五百万之多！"[2]

继北寺塔之后，苏州又建起许多宝塔，不过今天仅存六座，其中有几座缺失了顶层结构。据传，十三层的南门塔即瑞光塔，是242年吴王（孙权）为西域僧人所建。该塔经历过两次重修，于1119年被拆毁，为另一座七层塔所取代，随后不断得到修复，但主体结构保留至今。

城墙需要不时修葺。581—610年是苏州最不可思议的时期：苏州人因城内盗贼与叛獗者猖獗而弃城逃匿。约在917年，防御性的墙垣得到进一步延伸，墙体厚度增加到二十五英尺，高度也变得更耸峙巍峨。同时，在城外已有护城河的基础上，城内又开凿了第二条护城河——这种措施仅见于河道众多的城市。1278年之后不久，蒙古人命令拆毁所有城墙，这样便无人敢据险抗拒他们的统治。然而到了约1352年他们即将失去对全国的控

---

[1] 克里斯多弗·雷恩爵士(1632—1723)：英国著名天文学家、建筑家。1966年伦敦大火烧毁了许多重要建筑，雷恩爵士提出恢复重建方案，并参与重建了包括圣保罗教堂之内的51座教堂等重要建筑。此处杜步西借用"雷恩爵士"指代"大师"，喻指北寺塔设计建造者的伟大。

[2] 此段盖洛的引文在"the Great Lake to the west"之前漏了两句："the busy north-west gate; the pile of buildings constituting the City Temple"。

outside, a second moat was constructed just inside—a procedure natural only in a city of canals. Soon after 1278 the Mongols ordered all city walls to be demolished so that there could be no further opposition to their supremacy; but when they were losing grip, about 1352, the walls here were rebuilt. When the Manchus conquered the land, they adopted an opposite policy, quartering a strong garrison in a fort alongside many cities, and so in 1662 there was a grand re-fortification. Since then the leading outward event has been the siege by the T'ai-p'ings, which led to the virtual destruction of the interior, and the speedy recovery after Gordon and his Ever Victorious Army regained it. Last of all has come the railway from Shanghai, turning north here and pointing towards Peking.

In a career of more than two millenniums Soochow has of course produced several noted men. T'ang Pah-hu, a famous artist under the Mings, lived on Peach-blossom Street; his pictures and manuscripts fetch fabulous prices to-day. Ma Liang was born near Canton, but came here to study; devoting himself to drawing, he practised assiduously on one idol at Quin Shan, to the great admiration of all who watched. A friend named Tsang Na put his autograph on the pictures, and they sold so well that his fame is recorded in the local annals. Evidently there is hope for the pavement artist with one theme.

Ts'ao, from Wusih, thirty li away, devoted himself here to the study of medicine, especially children's diseases. He hung his shingle outside the Si Men, and became so clever that he could foretell exactly the hour when health would be restored. His fame culminated when he was called in to an aged official's home to "see sickness," to prescribe for a grandchild; he preferred to begin with the official. " I am too old; my disease is incurable." "Nay, if I cannot heal the grandfather first, how can I heal the grandson?" So he had his way, and in two days had restored both patients. Then was discovered the secret of his practice, to learn the family constitution from the more developed cases.

Another Ts'ao was born at Huchow. "He picked up a pen, and it seemed to write itself." With such natural gifts he readily rose to be a Hanlin and a very high official, both a great scholar and one of the finest artists known in the Empire. Ts'ao Fu-hsing, a native of Wu (the modern Kiangsu) of the third century, was reckoned the greatest painter of his day. Commissioned by the King, Sun Ch'üan, to paint a screen, he accidentally made a blot on it, and then turned the blot into a fly so skillfully that Sun Ch'üan tried to fillip it away. He painted a picture of a red dragon which he had seen playing on the surface of a river, and later on,

制之际，苏州的城墙得以重建。满人取得政权后，推行了一种相反的政策：分屯各地，于是苏州在1662年又开始大规模重新加固城墙。自此以后，苏州最为重要的外来事件便是遭到太平军的围困，导致城内尽毁，戈登所率的"常胜军"收复苏州后，城市面貌迅速恢复。最重要的是，从上海方向来的铁路延伸到这里，一路向北，直抵北京。

在两千多年的历史长河中，苏州自然也出了不少名人。明朝著名画家唐伯虎曾居桃花坞大街，其字画现已价值不菲。马良[1]，原籍广东，却千里迢迢地来苏专攻绘画，他在昆山潜心反复临摹一尊佛像，所见者无不敬仰。一位名叫"张那"(Tsang Na)的友人在其画作上加了题款，作品马上变得十分畅销，马良的名字因此亦被载入昆山地方志。显然，此事表明致力于单一主题的街头画家，也有发展前途。

有位三十里外无锡籍的曹（音译）姓中医，专长儿科，曾在胥门外悬壶。他医术高明，能准确预测病人康复的时间。他曾被请到一位年迈官员的家中为其孙儿看病，曹中医却建议先给官员诊治。官员说："我年事已高，老病治不好啦。""不，"曹中医说，"如果我不能先治好您的病，又如何治得好您孙儿的病呢？"主人听从了他的建议。两天后，两位病人都被曹医生治愈了，他因而名声大噪。后来，人们发现了他行医的秘密，即从症状更为显著的病例身上入手，进而了解病患家族的体质特点。

另一曹姓名人生于湖州。世人评价他绘画时"提笔即成"。凭借如此天赋，他官至翰林[2]，是孙吴时期极具威望的饱学之士、著名画家。此人即曹不兴，公元三世纪吴国（今江苏）人，被视为当时最伟大的画家。一次，吴王孙权让他画一扇屏风。他不小心在上面溅了墨渍，便顺手熟练地将之画成一只苍蝇，逼真程度引得孙权举起手来要把它赶走。他曾见过水面上有红龙戏水，便将此一景象绘成图画。后来在大旱之年，有人拿来此画，

---

[1] 马良当为明朝人，其籍贯亦非广东。据《吴中人物志》（古吴轩出版社，2013年版，第189页）载："马良，字子善，临安人。来学于吴，因家焉。自幼巧慧，于绘事尤精。晚移昆山，尝作四大天王像于僧寺，甚奇特。"

[2] 三国时无翰林一职，曹不兴官职在正史中亦无记载。

during a time of drought, this dragon was brought forth and cast into the river, the result being that rain fell immediately in great quantities.

Five hundred worthies are carved in stone in the gardens of the Ts'ang Lang Pavilion. Alongside these historic heroes set a modern one, Liu Tê-Sên, or Luxuriant Virtue. A man from the anti-foreign province of Hunan had become magistrate here, and set his face against aliens acquiring land. Twice did the Southern Presbyterians attempt to buy ground for a hospital, and after expending time and money found themselves balked by him. Then Liu Tê-Sên was employed to negotiate and closed the transaction; but when the magistrate discovered for whom he had acted, he declined to stamp the deeds, and summoned Liu Tê-Sên, ostensibly to discover how much money he had pocketed. Anticipating trouble, Liu found a friend to take care of his family, and went to court, advised simply to tell the plain truth. He was obliged to kneel, and a lictor stood beside him with a bamboo. But he was able to prove that the very cheques paid over to the vandor, drawn on a native bank, had been signed by Dr. Davis. " You liar! Having a big piece of meat in your hand, surely you would take a bite of it!" But the facts were too plain, and the outwitted magistrate could secure nothing by threats and orders to beat him. After an hour the sturdy Christian was released; and after an appeal to the Foreign Office the magistrate was peremptorily ordered to do his duty and stamp the deeds.

PART II—SOO: BY BOAT

Soochow has to be explored by sections: water, earth, and sky. Water has distinctly the right of way, and we used for the main canals the "Annie Barr," a small house-boat named after an heroic missionary, while an open row-boat took us into the narrow water alleys where only paddle and punt could propel.

At the water gate toll is collected by a bag at the end of a long pole, such as cathedrals use. There is of course some delay here, and it gives opportunity to observe the cormorant fishing-boats. The birds are equipped by nature with a large pouch to deposit their catch in, and by art with a ring round the neck to prevent its slipping—accidentally—any further. They sit in double rows round the boat till the manager pushes them into the water with a bamboo; when one finds a fish, he pecks out the eye and pouches the creature; if it be too large, he invites other cormorants, and they together will lift out any fish not exceeding

投入河中,顷刻之间便招致大雨倾盆。

历史上的五百位名贤被刻碑供奉在沧浪亭里。这些名垂青史的杰出人物之中,有位现代人,名叫刘德森(Liu Tê-Sên)[1],意思是"美德丰茂"。当时有位湖南人充任苏州知府,湖南强烈排外,所以这位知府十分反对外国人来苏购置土地。美南长老会一直想在苏州购地建造医院,为此费尽时间和金钱,然而建院计划连续两次都因这位知府而遭搁置。于是,长老会众雇用刘德森从中斡旋,方得以完成相关手续。但是,当知府发现刘德森受人雇用之后,便拒绝在契约上盖章;他还传唤刘德森,声称要弄清他私吞了洋人多少好处。刘德森早预料到会遇此等麻烦,他将家人托付给友人以后,就走上公堂应询。知府命他如实陈述事件经过,他跪在庭上,身边站着手执竹杖的衙役。但他从容地证明,卖方收到的由当地票庄开出的银票,正是戴维斯博士[2]签署的那些银票。"你这个骗子!得到这么一大块肥肉,你一定会私吞一口!"知府怒斥道。然而证据俱全,事实清楚,无法否定。知府大人耗尽脑汁,乃至以当庭杖毙威吓刘德森,依然一无所获。一小时后,这位坚强的基督徒得到释放。总理各国事务衙门收到申诉,乃强令知府履行职责,在契约上盖章。

第二部分 舟行苏州

苏州得从不同角度探究:水上、陆上、空中。选择水路显然是适宜的。我们考察一些主干河道,乘坐的是"安妮·巴尔"号,那是一条以某位著名传教士[3]命名的小型住家船。而考察狭窄的河道,我们则用一条无篷手划船,此类水域唯靠划桨、撑篙方能进入。

水门边有根长杆,一端系着袋子,用于收取通行费,和教堂募集捐款的方式相同。入城放行自然会耽搁些时间,但我们却有了观看鸬鹚捕鱼的机会。这些水鸟生来就有巨大的嗉囊,可以储存所捕之鱼,渔夫在其颈项上娴熟地套上一根小圈,以防嗉囊里的鱼儿不小心滑入鸟腹之中。鸬鹚分

---

[1] 疑盖洛误,译者查阅《苏州历代人物大辞典》(李峰、汤钰林编著,上海辞书出版社,2016)"附录一清代苏州沧浪亭五百名贤祠名录",未见此名或与之同音的人名。

[2] 戴维斯:美国人,1895年与美国医生惠更生(Dr. George. R. Wilkinson, Jr.)一起在苏州齐门外创建福音医院(The Elizabeth Blake Hospital),以治疗疯癫病为特色,惠更生担任首任院长。

[3] "安妮·巴尔"号得名于 Annie Barr Wilkinson, 即惠更生医生夫人。

eleven pounds. If this be too much to swallow, remember it is a fish story.

The chief canals are laid out regularly, parallel with the great boundary moats, but of course there are blind alleys and back yards, all of water. They are designed for transportation, and in the country they serve for irrigation also, but incidentally they serve for all manners of uses. Refuse cf all kinds is tipped into them, clothes are washed, food is cleansed, fish are bred in them, and drinking water is obtained thence. To the credit of the people be it said that this is always boiled in copper kettles and converted into tea. Naturally the canals provide meat as well as drink; fish, crabs, and shrimps may be had readily. Dr. Nathaniel Gist Gee states also that an ample supply of vegetable matter is procurable here; the cyanophyceae algals are represented by nostoc and oxillaria, the latter being perennial; chlorophyceae abound, zygnema being early and hydrodictyon a late summer variety, ulothrix, cladophora and spirogyra available at all times. In the shallows there is a rich growth of drapanaldia on the rocks, with a wealth of desmids. On the rice-fields the englena often gives a green appearance to the water. For all these beautiful forms the Chinese have no distinctive names, calling them merely water-grass.

It seems rather remarkable that alongside these canals there is a separate and official system of sewers. This seems so obviously superfluous that there is an officer charged to inspect them. His method is delightfully vicarious, and consists in putting a man down at one end, then going to the other end to await his arrival and hear his report. Seldom, indeed, can the submarine passage be effected as rapidly as the inspector can be carried in the open air, but after due delay a dirty labourer duly emerges from the man-hole and narrates his adventures below. Of course it is always the same man that was put in at the other end—it can only be the dirt and discomfort of the journey that produce such changes in form and figure; did not Brother Terrapin win the great race by the aid of a numerous family? Perhaps if the inspector gave the man who went down at one end some token to carry or be imprinted on his skin, he might wait a long time before that same man emerged at the other end with the token. But can we expect better things of underground sewers in Soo than of underground conduits in New York?

为两排停在船上，主人时不时用竹竿将它们赶入水里。捉到鱼儿时，鸬鹚会啄掉鱼眼，把它吞进嗉囊；倘若鱼儿太大，它会呼唤其他鸬鹚合作捕捉，只要鱼的重量不超过11磅，它们总能把它叼出水面。如果有人说鱼太大，鸬鹚吞不下，那肯定是无稽之谈[1]。

主河道分布错落有致，常与环城的护城河平行。当然，其间也有死胡同和后院，都浸在水里。它们主要用以通航，在农村也用以灌溉。顺便提一下，这些河道实际上满足当地人的各种需求：人们把各色垃圾倒入河中，在河边洗衣服、洗食物，在河里养鱼，也从中汲取饮用水。据说苏州人总会用铜质的水壶把取自河里的水煮沸沏茶，并以此为傲。毋庸置疑，河流提供了茶饮和肉类——鱼、蟹、虾随时都能捕到。祁天锡博士（Dr. Nathaniel Gist Gee）[2]指出，在苏州水域可以获取大量水生植物：蓝藻主要以念珠藻和颤藻为代表，后者是多年生植物。绿藻极为丰富，初夏时水面到处是双星藻属植物，夏末则以网藻类的变异体为主。丝藻类、刚毛藻和水绵属绿藻四季皆有。浅水处的石头上长有丰富的竹枝藻属植物，带藻也四处皆是。稻田的水面常漂着一层绿色的裸藻。对于所有这些美丽的植物形态，中国人都没有明确的术语，而仅笼统地称之为水草。

河流沿线，有一官方修建的、独立的排水系统，似乎十分有趣。当地甚至设有专门勘察下水道的官，这一职位显然非常多余。他采用的工作方式既特别、又有趣：不用亲自钻入地下，只需找人从下水道的一头进去，他本人则走到另一头，等那人上来汇报即可。虽说在下面行走的速度当然不如在地面来得快，但地上的官员只要稍加等待，总会有一位脏兮兮的苦力从检修孔中钻出，向他陈述在地下的经历。自然，上来的人通常情况下和先前派下去的是同一位——如果此人形貌发生巨大变化，那也必定只因他身上落到污泥，在排水道里行进时痛苦不堪所致。乌龟兄弟不就是通过寻找许多家族成员帮忙，才赢了那场重要比赛的吗？[3]检察员如果在那人钻进下水道前让他带上物证，或是在其身上印个标记，他可能就要过很久才等得到同一个人钻出来了。不过，我们凭什么指望苏州的下水道检修工

---

[1] "fish story"指"夸张的叙述；吹牛"，此处有双关之意。
[2] 祁天锡（1876—1937）：美国生物学家。时任教于东吴大学（今苏州大学），并于1912年在东吴大学创建中国首个生物系，主要研究方向为华东淡水生物、鸟类及农作物。
[3] 这一版本的龟兔赛跑故事出自《东南部印第安人的神话和故事》（*Myths and Tales of the Southeastern Indians*）一书中的"乌龟赛跑"的故事（"Terrapin Races"），作者：约翰·斯万顿（John R.Swanton），美国政府出版署出版（United States Government Printing Office,1929）。

Below these deeps there are reputed to be lower still. Why or wherefore no one knows, but the legend goes that a series of sub-marine passages exists, no longer to be explored except by those who present an order with the Vermilion Pencil. Both these systems we left to their quiet seclusion, and continued our investigations on the surface of the water. All that we did in the way of delving was to examine the borings for an artesian well here. This has been put down by the Soochow University, maintained by the Methodist Episcopal Church South inside the eastern wall; the well is 333 feet deep and yields three gallons per foot per hour. Layers of brown and blue clay alternate for 292 feet, then come 11 feet of fine gray sand, and below that the 30 feet of coarse, clean gray sand, which is the stratum bringing the water.

On the bank of the inner moat, against the city wall, is to be seen a curious lantern-topped stone with seven faces, each bearing an inscription. It marks the spot where a man fell in and was drowned, and is put up to warn others to keep away, lest his spirit should drag them in too. It seems that the soul of a drowned man remains on guard till it can secure another to replace it; then it goes to its permanent abode.

Bridges of course abound, and have to be made lofty enough for the regular canal traffic to be unhindered. Some of the old ones are most picturesque in their steep rises, which yet do not hinder horses from going over. Now that new railway bridges are coming, they too have to conform to the rule of allowing proper headway for the barges below. But despite the novelties in bridge architecture, the Chinaman cannot credit that a mere Westerner can design without help from Soochow; and an account of Brooklyn Bridge evidently called forth great admiration for the powers of lying displayed.

One of the greatest bridges outside the city is renowned as the "Precious Belt," or "Fifty-three Arch," or "Bridge of the Golden Hook." This spans the river Dai-dai where it empties into the Grand Canal, and carries the tow-path of the latter; it is some three miles south of the southeast corner of the city. At the north end is a Buddhist temple, where two monks sold us tea for three and a drum for a shilling. They also furnished a tale as to the origin of the bridge. "Li was a great robber who dwelt in the hills beside the Great Lake; as his beard and whiskers were very long, they fell into his food, so he had two golden hooks to hold them up to his ears at meal-times. He commanded a thousand followers, and to those who paid blackmail he issued an exemption ticket which secured

就该比纽约的做事更加诚实呢?

管道系统之下，据说还有更为深层的结构。详情不为人知。据传那里有一系列连海的通道，除非获得皇帝朱谕，否则无人有权探查。那就任由这些水下系统尽享各自的隐秘吧，我们继续水面上的考察。大家费心检查、认真钻研的对象，是此处一口自流井周围的土样。此井由东吴大学开凿而成，长年由东面城墙内的卫理公会负责维护。井深333英尺，每英尺深度每小时的出水量为3加仑。棕色和蓝色黏土层叠交错，有292英尺深；其下为11英尺的细粒灰沙层，再向下30英尺为粗净的黏质砂，正是出水土层。

内城河岸紧靠城墙的地方，能见到一块刻成七面的怪石，每面都有题字，顶端放着灯笼。此石所立之处，曾经有人落水溺亡，立石的目的就是提醒路人及时远离，以免死者魂魄将他们也拖入水中。溺亡者的阴魂似乎始终不散，只有找到了替死鬼，他才能前往永生世界。

苏州自然有许多桥，为确保运河交通畅通无阻，桥梁都必须达到足够高度。有些古桥高高拱起，颇为陡峭，造型美观，又不会妨碍车马通行。既然这里即将新造铁路桥，那么设计时也得遵守同样规矩，留出适当的高度以便驳船能从桥下通过。尽管桥梁建构方面存在诸多新奇之处，中国人还是无法相信，一位西方人在没有苏州人的帮助之下，仅凭一己之力便能把铁路桥设计出来，与之讲述布鲁克林大桥的故事显然会令他们无比讶异，认为我们是在刻意展示高超的撒谎能力。

苏州城外最为著名的古桥之一被冠以"宝带"的美名，又叫"五十三孔桥"或"金钩桥"。石桥横跨在玳玳河（即澹台湖）上，河水在此流入京杭大运河，这里也是大运河附近的漕运纤道。宝带桥位于苏州东南角以南大约三英里之处。桥的北端有一佛寺，寺里两位僧人卖给我们一些茶水和一面鼓，分别要价三先令及一先令。他们还讲述了关于此桥来历的故事："太湖边的山里住着一位姓李的大盗。因为胡须很长，吃饭时常会垂到碗里，所以每当吃饭时，他就用两只金钩把胡须钩到耳边。他统领着一千名追随者，对那些如数支付讹金的人，他会向其签发豁免票据，令其不再遭劫。"

from robbery" —quite the method used at Western bazaars. " Nor would he rob poor people, but even distributed among them the plunder from the rich, while officials stood in awe of him. Now he desired to gain merit in heaven, so he decided to build this bridge; and under its foundations he buried precious belts and pearls. At ninety years of age he died—Where did he go? Well, I never heard of his going to heaven, nor did I hear of his going to hell. But his stomach was big, full of righteousness. If his goods[1] deeds outbalance his evil, then he will be in heaven."

A special temple and a pagoda built by Li of the Golden Hooks ensure good luck to the bridge; and this may be the reason why the Chinese surveyors wished to arrange the Foreign Concession here in 1896 after the Japanese war. But the Japanese commissioner dryly remarked it was capital for rice-growing and pheasant-hunting; so the concession was placed on the Grand Canal, opposite the south wall, with deep water frontage of a mile. A good trade has sprung up, and the customs commissioner reports eighty-seven million cigarettes imported here, with nearly two million gallons of oil, and a large export of silk goods, for which the place is famous. The Post Office handles 5,634,750 letters a year.

Bridges bridge the transition from watery Soo to earthy Soo. Pass me over.

The silken goods which form the staple export are the glory of the place, and the Imperial household gets its chief supplies hence. It is strange to see the primitive surroundings, a little hut with an earthen floor in which they are produced, with their exquisite designs and perfect workmanship. In these uncleanly surroundings a basin of water stands for the weaver to keep his hands unsoiled. He can make four or five feet daily, a yard wide, thus earning 300 or 375 cash and producing material worth nearly two shillings a foot. It is the best-paid occupation in the city.

The Fang Shêng Yüan[2], or Life-saving Institution, is unique. It does not deal with human life, and it is rather a surprise to find some 1,500 corpses stored here, and rentals varying from 600 cash to $30, prices varying with locality, fashion, and accommodation. The most expensive room had a glass window and a clock; in another there were silken scrolls with remarks on the family history and character of the dead and living; in a third there were paper servants for the use of the departed and opium utensils to keep up his earthly

[1] 此处 goods 疑为 good。
[2] "Garden for the Release of Living Creatures." "放生活物的花园。" ——原注

此法与西方集市上的做法相当一致。"大盗李非但从不掠夺穷人,还经常劫富济贫,因而官员对他颇为畏惧。后来他希望积善成德,身后升入天堂,便决定建造此桥。在桥的基座底下,埋有宝带和无数珍珠。这位大盗死时年已九十。他的灵魂究竟去了哪里?怎么说呢,我既没听说他上到天堂,也没听说他下到地狱。不过此人豪侠爽气,充满正义。如果他行的善事多于恶事,那就自然会上天堂的。"

金钩李所修建的佛寺和宝塔为宝带桥带去了好运。甲午战争后,清政府的勘测者在1896年拟将日租界勘定于此地附近,大概就是出于这个原因。但是日本使节冷漠地指出,这块土地只能靠种水稻、打野鸡赚取资本,于是日租界被改划至大运河沿岸,与南面城墙相对,前面有一英里的深水区。租界内商贸繁盛,据海关税务司记载,进口的洋烟达八千七百万支,进口的洋油达到近两百万加仑,丝织品出口量巨大,苏州的丝绸今天名扬海外。苏州大清邮局每年处理的信件多达 5 634 750 封。

桥梁将苏州的水面与陆地连接起来,以助通行。

作为苏州主要出口的商品,丝织品是苏州的荣耀。大清皇室所需的大部分绫罗绸缎均由此地提供。我们非常惊讶,缫丝的环境竟如此原始:一间泥土地面的小棚屋,而图案精美、匠心独运的丝绸就在这里生产出来。这种脏兮兮的地方常放着一盆水,供纺织工不时洗手,保持干净。纺织工每天能纺出四五英尺长、一码宽幅的绸布,可以挣到 300 或 375 美分,所产织物每英尺价值近两先令。纺织工是苏州现在报酬最高的行当。

放生园,亦称"救生局"[1],是个独一无二的所在。此处处理的事务与活人无关。我们意外地发现这里存放着约一千五百具遗体,寄存费从 600 美分到 30 美元不等,价格因寄存的地点、形式及殡室不同而不一。最贵的殡室内有一扇玻璃窗和一只钟。另一间内挂着丝质挽联,写着家属姓名及颂扬死者和生者品格的文字。还有一间内放有纸扎的仆人,供逝者在往生世界里役使,还有吸食鸦片的器具,让他在阴间也能继续保持在世时的习惯。不过,这些房屋都是附属建筑。园内有个养鳖的池塘,人们为了

---

[1] 即"昌善局",原苏州动物园前身。

habits. These apartments, however, were accessory. There is a turtle pond where people desirous of acquiring merit deposit turtles in safety; an old lady watched me fee a coolie to feed them, and congratulated me on thus amassing credit for myself. Another department is for pigs, where a patriarchal boar with a bristly back was wondering that fourteen years had not qualified him for conversion into pork and lard. Other departments benefit geese, ducks, hens, and frogs; the frogs are apparently housed apart to ensure their long life. Attached to this strange zoological garden is the inevitable tea-room, and here are scrolls with reversible sentences, like the reputed salutation to Eve of her husband, "Madam, I'm Adam"; or like Napoleon's lament, "Able was I ere I saw Elba."

The old Examination Hall still stood at my visit, a useless relic of the past. All too rapid are the changes now, and one hopes that the filial spirit will not evaporate now that the free Western air is breathing o'er the land. A typical story of the past was given by Mr. Yang:

A Chinese gentleman and his son had a fight; during the scuffle the son accidentally knocked out some of his father's front teeth. The father, though deeply offended, because of his son's superior strength was unable to punish, and so went to law. This frightened the son so much that he consulted a man named Tsu, asking him to help him out. Tsu told him to come up the next morning to a high mountain. Although in the dead of winter, the son was dressed in light-weight summer clothes. While he was sitting in the temple on top of the hill, his friend Tsu came up and demanded two thousand dollars before helping him out of the serious scrape. He paid it; then Tsu took out a knife and cut off the offending son's ear. He objected to this, but Tsu told him nothing better could have been done for him; in court the son was to say his father had bitten off his ear, and that in the mêlée the front teeth of his father had come out. The son bettered Tsu's instructions; in the scrimmage he had not knocked out his father's teeth, which would have been unfilial, but when his father bit off his ear his head rebounded up against him and knocked out his front teeth. This sounded plausible to the court, so that they both were dismissed. The father and son became friends and lived together happily. Later the father asked his son how it happened he had thought up such a good defence, as he had not bitten the ear off at all. The son told him Tsu had helped him. The father, enraged at Tsu, had him up in court, but Tsu claimed he had not helped the son. " Yes, you did," said the son. "Where do you say we met?" asked Tsu. "On the mountain, where you remember I had on

行善积德而将龟鳖在此放生。一位老妇人看到我给所带的苦力一些钱，让他喂一喂这些动物，就为我祈福，说我做的是为自己积攒功德之事。另一间屋舍里养着猪。我们看见一头年老的长鬃毛野猪，它正在纳闷，为何历经十四年依然不够变为猪肉和猪油的资格。放生园里的其他场所养着鹅、鸭、母鸡及青蛙。当然，青蛙是被分开圈养的，以确保能长命百岁。与这个怪异的动物园连在一起的是一间常见的茶室，里面挂着回文体的对联，对联的内容如同夏娃的丈夫第一次问候她的话——"女士，我是亚当"，或是像拿破仑的哀叹："落败孤岛孤败落。"

我游苏州时，原来的贡院还在，它已成为一处无用的历史遗迹。时下变化来得实在太快，自由的西风吹遍中国大地，但我们希望传统的孝道还是不要消失得无影无踪。关于孝道，杨先生给我们讲了一个经典故事：

有一对中国父子互相争执，扭打起来，儿子不小心打落了父亲几颗门牙。父亲的威严受到严重侵犯，却因儿子体力过人而无法对之实施惩罚，一气之下诉诸公堂。父亲的做法把儿子吓坏了，于是儿子向一位楚姓朋友请教，以期摆脱困境。朋友约他次日清早山顶相见。时逢严冬，四处一片肃杀死寂，但这位儿子来到约定地点时却依然身着单薄的夏装。朋友到来时，他正坐在山顶的一座寺庙里等候。朋友索要两千美元，然后才可帮他摆脱窘境。儿子如数付了钱。朋友拿出一把刀，割掉了这位逆子一只耳朵。起初儿子不同意这么做，但是朋友告诉他，除此之外，别无他法；到了公堂上，你一定要说：耳朵是父亲咬掉的，父亲的门牙也是在双方推搡时自行掉落的。儿子听从友人建议，在公堂上不仅如此应对，还添油加醋地增加了许多伪造的细节。他说，在扭打时自己没有打掉父亲的门牙，因为那是不孝之举；事实是父亲咬掉他的耳朵时用力过猛，被儿子的头回顶了一下，门牙就这样磕掉了。知县认为儿子所述颇有道理，就将父子当庭释放。爷俩从此和好如初，快乐地生活在一起。后来父亲问起儿子：既然自己根本没有咬下他的耳朵，他是如何想出如此高明的辩词来的？儿子就说了朋友相助之事。父亲勃然大怒，把楚姓朋友告上公堂。可这位朋友却声称从未帮过其子。"不对，你帮过我的，"儿子说。"那你说我们当时在哪儿碰的头？"朋友问。"在山顶，你应该记得，我那时还穿着夏衣呢。""什么？"知县插话道："大冬天会穿夏衣？""正是，冬天里我穿的是单衫。"这个细节成

summer clothes." "What, in winter?" intervened the magistrate. "Yes, in winter." But this detail was the death-blow of the case, and it was dismissed. A tale like this suggests how far we are from following the windings of the average Chinese thought, and of appreciating their standards.

Trying to understand something of the home life and the national amusements, it was with much pleasure that the opportunity was taken of helping celebrate a birthday. True, it was that of Dr. Wilkinson, but the programme was mainly native.

The Chinese students, nurses, and friends, after preparations going on for some days, made a deal of noise and good cheer. There were minstrels, an orchestra of seven men with a variety of instruments, the Victor phonograph, a present to the popular physician, a juggler who gave two exhibitions, a fine feast of say twenty courses, a mandarin and other Chinese, mostly educated, one the wife of a millionaire.

The evening opened with music by the orchestra, who were also minstrels. This was odd, but at times musical.

At one time during the splendid feast both the Victor phonograph and the native orchestra were engaged in playing at the same time. What a difference! and how superior the West over the East in this matter of music, so it seemed to me! East and West met.

The juggler played certain mystifying tricks, Oriental sleight of hand. He placed a bottle in one cylinder of card-board, a glass in another, and fired off a pistol, when behold,[1] they had exchanged places. He then spoke of the empty-headedness of the Soochow people. A Soochow man was out one night without a lantern, so he took a candle, lit it, took off his scalp, and put it in his empty head! He told a story of men arguing as to how the Great Pagoda at Soochow was built. One man said that it was begun at the top and built from the sky down to the earth; another man said from the bottom up. Another said it was built on its side and then stood up. A fourth declared it had never been built here at all, but came from another place whole! As a comment on this, he suddenly produced a pagoda of say fifteen stories, and in height about five feet.

What I particularly admired about the feast was that between shark's fins and sea cucumbers (slugs) medicine was served—the famous Chinese remedy, Boho, the immortal Boho. A fine idea,—one to be followed in the West, that of

---

[1] 此处原文为叹号,疑为印刷错误。

为此案最不靠谱的关键，楚姓朋友马上就被释放了。这类故事表明，要跟上中国人蜿蜒复杂的大脑回路，理解他们关于遵守孝道的标准，我们还差老大一截。

为深入了解当地人的家庭生活及其民族消遣娱乐，我们怀着极大的愉悦之情，获得了一个参与祝寿活动的机会。虽说寿星是惠更生医生[1]，但是庆祝形式极具本土色彩。

寿宴连续准备了好几天，参与其中的那些中国学生、护士和友人们大声说笑，喝彩声不断，煞是热闹。寿星家里请来了唱戏的，一个七人的吹打班子，演奏着很多种乐器；胜利牌留声机是这位备受爱戴的内科医生的生日礼物；还请到一位杂耍艺人，演了两场杂技；宴席上了二十道菜，十分讲究；到场的有一位高级官员，还有不少中国人，他们大都受过良好教育，其中一位还是某个百万富绅的太太。

吹打班子开始奏乐，夜晚拉开帷幕，唱戏也是他们的活儿。虽然感到有点奇怪，但其表演有时还是颇为悦耳的。

盛大的宴会举行期间，胜利牌留声机播放的音乐一度和戏班子的演奏撞到一起。多么奇特的感觉！在我看来，就音乐而言，西方不知超越东方多少！东西方文化在此相遇了。

杂耍艺人玩了几个故弄玄虚的戏法，不过都是基于东方特有的障眼法。他把一个瓶子放进一个硬纸板长筒里，把一只玻璃杯放进另一个长筒里，然后开了一枪，看呀，两个放进去的东西竟然调换了位置。然后他说苏州人都是"苏空头"[2]。说一个苏州人晚上出门忘了带灯笼，就拿了根蜡烛，点着了，摘下自己的头皮，把蜡烛放进空空如也的头颅里！还说了一个段子，有关一群人争论苏州北寺塔建成的方式：一人说先造塔顶，自上而下，一路造到塔基；另一人说塔是自下而上造出来的；第三位说先从侧面造，塔才站得稳；第四位宣称，北寺塔根本就没在苏州造，而是从别处造好了整体搬来的！为了证明第四种说法，他的手上突然托出了一座 5 英尺高的 15 层宝塔。

这场宴席尤为令我欣赏之处，在于鱼翅和海参两道菜之间，他们上了一种药膳，一味有名的中药——薄荷，永恒的薄荷。这个主意不错，西方

---

［1］　惠更生（J.R.Wilkinson 1862—1935），美国医生，1895 年与戴维斯在苏州创建"福音医院"，1919 年又单独创立了"更生医院"，即今苏州广济医院的前身。

［2］　"苏空头"，外地人给苏州人取的绰号，嘲讽他们外强中干，做事浮夸，不切实际。

providing in the midst of a banquet a medical course, real medicine, say Boho.

Dr. Wilkinson works at the Blake Hospital, where there is a fine operating-room in memory of two nurses who died after a short practice of their profession here. It is an unfortunate coincidence that the Moslem cemetery lies hard by, with its evergreens, cedars, and olive trees embowering its little burial mosque; or shall we say that the contrast is significant? ...

It is high time to pass from Soochow of the earth to Soochow of the sky. In the reality of the spirits there is firm belief. They lurk in the canals near scenes of death to drag in substitutes; they cross the bridges carrying lights; nothing scares them but the presence of a sinner. Now against all this popular superstition Confucius set the weight of his influence, ignoring the whole subject. Try, then, the Confucian Temple, and see how far his teaching and his memory are revered. There is a grandiloquent ode by Vong Gnow which announces, with the usual truthfulness of epitaphs, that "His road he spread abroad universally; by his teachings he brings heaven and earth into conjunction. He elected and spoke forth the Book of Six Odes. To myriad generations he handed down what he received in his palace, the righteousness of the Emperor Voh Hse [the first Emperor after the creation]. Him did he repay for the righteousness given him, by spreading it abroad till many have worshipped him and a hundred Emperors have paid him reverence." But the temple seems devoted chiefly to the bats, thousands of whom harbour in the ceiling, so that their manure produces a most disgusting odor. So deserted is it that a famous robber chief thirty years ago hid over the tablets and remained in perfect safety.

Contrast the present decadent state of Confucianism with the past. The following eloquent words, written twenty centuries ago by the famous historian Ssǔ-ma Ch'ien, best describe the position then held by the great sage in the hearts of the Chinese people:

"Countless are the princes and prophets that the world has seen in its time; glorious in life, forgotten in death. But Confucius, though only a humble member of the cotton-clothed masses, remains among us after many generations. He is the model for such as world be wise. By all, from the Son of Heaven down to the meanest student, the supremacy of his principles is fully and freely admitted. He may indeed be pronounced the divinest of men."

From the temple to the pagodas: three of these received our attention, two Pen and one Ink. A scholar built the Two Pen pagodas to attract the good luck

人可以学习借鉴，在宴会期间添加一道药膳，一种药物，比如薄荷。

惠更生医生服务于福音医院，那里有一间设备精良的手术室，用以纪念两位曾在苏州短暂工作后去世的护士。说来既是巧合也是不幸：医院紧挨着穆斯林的墓地，周边的常青树、雪松及橄榄树簇拥着经常举办葬礼的小清真寺。可否认为这种反差蕴含着深意？……

我们应该把视角从苏州的地面转向空中了。苏州人对鬼神的存在深信不疑。它们有的藏在发生过溺亡事件的地方，伺机拖个替身下水；有的过桥时闪着亮光。它们无所畏惧，除非遇到有罪之人。孔子不信鬼怪之说，在反对迷信方面，他发挥着举足轻重的影响力。那么，就去一趟文庙吧，看一看他的威望，以及今人对他的言说究竟尊崇到了什么程度。文庙里存有一篇夸张的孔子颂歌，作者是陈凤梧[1]，颂词透着志铭体惯有的真诚，其文如下："孔子传道于天下，其思想贯通天地。他整理并讲授六经，向千秋万代传授得自王家的风范，即帝王伏羲的凛然正气[伏羲是开天辟地以来(中国)第一位帝王]。孔子将此风范发扬光大，得到百姓爱戴，受到上百位帝王焚香顶礼，以此回报伏羲给予他的恩泽。"然而事实上，文庙现在似乎主要奉献给了蝙蝠。千百只蝙蝠栖息在屋顶上，其排泄物使得庙内的气味极其难以忍受。今日此地一片荒凉，难怪三十年前一位名盗头目藏匿于石碑之间，竟然安然无恙。

过去的儒学与其当前的颓败形成鲜明对照。以下雄辩之辞出自两千年前著名的史学家司马迁之手，这些语句极为精彩地描述了伟大的孔圣人在中国百姓心中所占据的地位：

"天下君王至于贤人众矣，当时则荣，没则已焉。孔子布衣，传十余世，学者宗之。自天子王侯，中国言六艺者，折中于夫子，可谓至圣矣！"

从文庙一路走去，看到几座宝塔，其中三座吸引了我们的注意力，它们是"两支笔"和"一方墨"。为保苏州文人辈出，某位文人建造了"双笔塔"(双塔)以集结好运，加护考生。可是，这之后多数考生却依然屡考不中。文

---

[1] 陈凤梧（1475—1541），明朝江西泰和人，官至南右都御史、巡抚应天十府。他所写的孔子赞词今刻在一座"颂圣碑"上，原文为："道冠古今，德配天地。删述六经，垂宪万世。统承羲皇，源起洙泗。报功报德，百王崇祀。"此碑今犹存于苏州文庙内的碑刻博物馆。

required to ensure good scholarship to the town; but as most of the candidates kept on failing afterwards, he consulted the geomancers, and they showed how absurd it was to provide two pens but no ink. The omission rectified, the candidates passed. We passed these by, however, in favor of the famous nine-story pagoda, with its inscription over the doorway, "From within issues precious light." All around are idols, with blue nightcaps to prevent insects from biting them, and barred in to prevent pilgrims from carrying off chips; the numbers have thus been reduced from nine hundred, and very few are now left unprotected. A Buddhist monk, telling his beads, received the copper for admission.

Fortunately the temple which long stood in front of the pagoda was destroyed by the T'ai-p'ings and never restored; thus an open space is left for observing the fine lines of the majestic structure. A queer old priest, who made the ladies "feel crawly," held two candles to light us up the first flight of wooden stairs, which otherwise would have been groped in the darkness. Up we passed from story to story until the ninth, from which elevation the city and surroundings appeared below and beyond in delightful panorama.

Toward the south lay the great city with its green trees, its green mounds higher than the roofs of the houses, the City Temple on Kwon Dzien, in the grounds of which are hawkers crying their wares, Punch and Judy shows, caged birds singing, crowds of populace—the Vanity Fair of Soo; the Soochow University, between the Ink and Twin Pagodas; the Foreign Concession, with its smoke-stacks attached to the Silk Filatures Factory, foreign method; and a great lake.

Toward the west is the wonderful Lion Mountain, the Mountain belonging to the family of Van, their burial mountain. Up to the time when Van was buried there the rocks lay about as all others do, but when the coffin of Van came the rocks all stood up in all sorts of unnatural positions, and they have been standing there ever since. A beautiful paved road was once upon a time constructed to this mountain, for the convenience of a visiting king who was on a pleasure journey and desired to view the wonders of nature from that advantageous point. Included in this view are the North-west Gate, the busiest gate of busy Soo, through which the trade of a fertile and active region flows, and the Northern Presbyterian Hospital.

人为此请教风水先生,先生表示,光有两支笔却没有墨,多么荒唐的设计。缺失的环节很快得到纠正,从此中榜考生便络绎不绝了。走过了双塔和墨塔(文星阁),我们其实更钟爱附近的另一座著名的九层宝塔,其门楣挂着大意为"祥光此出"的匾额。塔的四周都是佛像,它们戴着蓝色睡帽以防蚊虫滋扰,前面围着栏杆把香客挡在外面,以防他们带走塑像上的碎屑。佛像的数量原先有900座,现已大幅减少,而且几乎都安装了防护设施。一位僧人捻着佛珠在门口向访客收取入内参观的铜板。

  幸运的是,塔前那座历史悠久的寺庙被太平军捣毁了,从未恢复重建,因此留出了一块空旷之地,让我们得以端详这座雄伟建筑的优美线条。一个古怪的、令女士们"起鸡皮疙瘩的"老和尚,手持两根蜡烛,照着我们走上第一段木质楼梯,若是没有他,我们上楼就只能在黑暗里摸索了。爬了一层又一层,我们终于来到第九层,从这一高度俯视,整个苏州及其周边的景致尽收眼底,十分惬意。

  塔的南面,绿树掩映之间,就是古老的苏州城,苍翠连绵的树冠比普通民居的屋顶还要高;观前街玄妙观前的广场上,尽是吆喝着兜售商品的小贩、演木偶戏的艺人、歌声婉转的笼中小鸟,到处人头攒动,那里是苏州的"名利场"。文星阁和双塔之间[1]是东吴大学;烟囱连着苏州第一丝织厂的地方是日租界,这是异国的设计;远处还有一个大湖。

  往西就是神奇的狮子山[2]。此山归范氏家族所有,为其家族墓地。范仲淹下葬以前,那里的山石别无两样,当他的棺材被抬来的一刻,所有的石头竟以各种姿态竖立起来,矗立不倒,直至今日[3]。曾经,人们修了一条幽美的小路,直达此山,以便巡幸于此的皇帝突然想在山上最佳高度,饱览苏州的自然风光。朝西同样能看到西北门(阊门),繁荣的苏州城里最为熙熙攘攘的那座城门,流经此地的商贸活动源源不断,兴盛而活跃。北美长老院所建的医院(更生医院)也在附近。

---

[1] 此处为原文直译,原作者对位置的表述有误,实际应为"文星阁和双塔之南是东吴大学"。
[2] 狮子山虽在苏州西面,但与范仲淹有关的山应为天平山,亦称"范坟山"。
[3] 民间相传范仲淹被贬回到家乡后,听说如果身后葬在天平山,子孙后代便永远做不了官。这一风水意涵与他对后代所寄予的希望一致,于是他便买下这一"绝地"。他下葬的那天,山上所有的石头都竖立起来,像宰相上朝时手持的"笏"一般,形成了"天平山上万笏朝天"的奇景。

Toward the north, within the wall, is the execution ground; outside the wall, the railway station, the plant of the Southern Presbyterians, then farms and villages, each hamlet with its clump of sacred trees. When from this altitude the perspective takes in a long line of these small villages, the landscape has the aspect of a scattered forest; in reality, the hamlets, frequent and containing each a miniature forest thrown together for the eye's pleasure, please one with the sense of plenty of trees at last in China. The Leaning Pagoda stands on the Hu Cheu Shan toward the northwest. In the distance the mountains of Dzan Zhoh lie low on the horizon.

Toward the east, apart from the continuous stretch of houses out to the Leu Men, the gate Gordon came in, there is little of importance except the lake some thirty li east of Soo. The scenery was invariably beautiful, whether we looked toward the sun this afternoon or away from it, whether down toward the grounds of the pagoda or toward the distant scenes, all beautiful, and we were reminded that Soo may mean fragrant, whether to the nose or to the eyes! Beautiful Soo![1]

PART III — A SOO NOVEL

For a good literary insight into English life the high-grade novel is to be commended. The actual story is not important, but the atmosphere, the manner of talk, the ideas of conduct, the way in which people behave, these are generally true to life. So a Chinese novel may throw a very natural light on conditions. The plot may teem with improbabilities, but the dialogue dealing with Chinese scenes is likely to be faithful enough. Quite lately there has been published a novel with a purpose, to expose the evils of opium-smoking. My friend R.A.Haden, Esq., M.A., procured it for me and made the following tasty translation. It is one of a series being issued as "Books for the Awakening of the Age." The series is avowedly produced in order to promulgate reform ideas, written in a good, easy style, which can be read all over the Empire. Here is an outline of the plot, which

---

[1] A short form of the numerals, commonly used for accounts, are known to the Chinese as "Soochow characters," or "business characters." Unlike the ordinary numerals, they are written horizontally from left to right. They are said to be of Bactrian or Phoenician origin. 一种数字的缩写形式，常用于记账，中国人称之为"苏州码子"或"商业数字"。与普通的数字不同，这些符号是从左到右横写的，据说源自中亚古国大夏王国的文字或是腓尼基文。（苏州方言里"苏"和"数"的发音相似，只是音调不同，此处的 Soo 可视为双关。）——原注

往北看去，北城墙内是刑场；墙外则是火车站，还有隶属美南长老会的建筑。再远就是田野与村落了，每座村庄都被绿树环绕。从我们所站的高度看，这些小村庄排成一条长线，被星星点点的树丛分隔开来。实际上，每个村里通常都有一片小树林，赏心悦目，令我们无比快乐，在中国我们终于看到富有大片绿植感觉的景致了。虎丘山上的那座斜塔（虎丘塔）朝西北而立，再远处，常熟诸多山脉伏卧至天际。

向东望去，民房鳞次栉比，一路延伸，直到戈登进入苏州城的那座娄门。除此之外，只见苏州以东三十里开外的那个大湖，别无特别景观。风光总是无限美好，在这个午后时光，无论我们是朝着太阳的方向看，还是往相反方向看，无论是低头朝塔下的广场看，还是在塔顶向远处眺望，所见之处，景色宜人。有人告诉我们，"苏"字可以表述芳香之意，既适用于嗅觉，也适用于视觉。美丽的苏（Soo）！

第三部分　苏州故事

若要从文学的角度解读英国人的生活，人们就得从上等小说作品里去寻找。故事的情节并不重要，重要的是里面的氛围、人物交谈的仪态、行为背后的观念及行为方式，这些总体都是现实的写照。因此，一本中国小说或许能提供非常自然的视角，帮助我们了解中国人的生活。其情节也许会充满各种虚构成分，但与中国人生活场景相关的对话应该非常忠于现实。最近市面上就出了一本小说，以揭露抽鸦片的危害性为目的。我的朋友哈登先生（R.A.Haden）给我弄到一册，并做了以下流畅的翻译。该小说属于"醒世小说"系列丛书之一。这一系列的文学作品公开出版，宣扬改革思想，文风优美、轻松，大清帝国各处都能买到。以下为小说的情节概要，读来

may amuse, but will serve to introduce the powerful opening chapter:

THE HEART-BREAKING WEED

The plot opens in an opium shop in Soo where half the smokers and idlers of the city resort to exchange news and get a pipe. The prodigal hero (?) of the story is introduced here by a relative, older than himself but steeped in opium and vice. This man is the evil genius of the young prodigal, leading him deeper and deeper into the ways of wickedness.

In London there is a Soochow family with a daughter; this family are very much attached to an English family having a daughter who is much attached to the Soo people. The man has made his fortune, and when preparing to return to China, by mutual consent the families exchange daughters. This English girl is introduced to Chinese life at Soochow, and before she understands what is proposed is engaged to the above opium-smoking prodigal. She is persuaded to allow her feet to be bound. Being of a naturally dark complexion she easily passes as a full-blooded Chinese.

The young man to whom she is engaged reaches the lowest depth of a sot, and is taken with a very serious sickness. The most famous physician in the city pronounces the disease almost incurable. The only possible hope would be for him to be nourished by a young and beautiful woman. Therefore his marriage is hastened. But the supposed willing Chinese daughter gets an inkling of what is afoot, and, being really in love with a young man of standing and merit, she writes a letter to her Chinese friend in London, calling her home. This young lady has been given a thorough education, and having studied medicine is equal to the situation. She makes preparations to return home, but says nothing about her movements. In the meantime great preparations are in progress for the marriage.

The final arrangements are made and the feasting is on; the morrow is the day for the wedding. The English girl writes a letter to her real friend and lover, tells him the whole story of who she is, and states that she is going to take poison as soon as the letter is sent to him. He thereupon also takes opium. In the midst of the confusion, before the foreign doctor can arrive from the Soochow Hospital, Dr. Park being away from the city, and while they are discussing the advisability

令人忍俊不禁，将为人们理解富有力度的开始章节起到引介的作用：

《**断肠草**》[1]

小说开场于苏州一家鸦片馆，全城半数的吸食者及闲人常会聚到那里，吸上几口鸦片，互通一些消息。故事中的主人公是位浪荡公子（？），他有位年长的亲戚，终日沉迷鸦片、为非作歹，是这位亲戚把主人公带到了这间鸦片馆。此人就是主人公的恶魔，带着他在邪恶的深渊中日渐沉沦。

有一户苏州人家带了女儿住在伦敦，与一户英国人家结下深厚情谊，后者正好也育有一女，还特别喜欢和苏州人来往。男主人做生意发了财，在夫妇俩准备回国之际，两家同意互换女儿。于是中国家长教英国姑娘如何在苏州过中式生活。可姑娘还没有弄清事实真相，"父母"就把她许配给了前面那位吸食鸦片的浪荡公子。经劝说，她同意裹了小脚。由于天生肤色偏深，她轻轻松松就成了中国人家的那位血统纯正的小姐，无人对此置疑。

她的未婚夫吸食鸦片成瘾、无可救药，并且还得了重病。城里最有名的大夫声称此乃不治之症，唯一的希望就是找到一位年轻貌美的女子来滋润他。他的婚事即刻变得紧迫起来。然而，那位所谓言听计从的"中国女儿"大致了解了"父母"正在酝酿的大事，由于那时她正与一位德才兼备的青年谈恋爱，就给伦敦的中国女友写信催她回国。后者在英国接受过全面的教育，专攻医学，能力足以应对国内的情况。因此，她偷偷地做好归国准备，但对外却只字不提自己的计划。与此同时，"中国小姐"和鸦片鬼的婚礼正在紧锣密鼓地筹备中。

婚礼终于安排完毕，盛大的宴席已经开始，眼看次日就是婚礼正日。英国姑娘给挚友般的恋人写了封信，坦白自己的真实身份，声称对方收信之时，她将服毒而死。情急之下，她的恋人吞了鸦片殉情。一片混乱之中，人们对于究竟从苏州医院请哪位医生来实施救援不知所措，而帕克医生恰

---

[1] 《断肠草》一名《苏州现形记》，作者佚名，出版于光绪三十四年（1908），上海改良小说社刊印，共五册。下文所引内容均出自该书的"缘起"。

of sending for Dr. Wilkinson, who should walk in but some foreign guests from Shanghai— none other than the young and beautiful lady doctor from London! Knowing what she does already, she immediately understands the situation, and takes measures to save the opium suicides. In this she is successful.

She takes the place her English friend has been occupying, and is married to the apparently dying opium sot. So skillful is she that in a month she has her husband up and well. The English girl is married to her lover.

Very much of the book, as in the case with all this class of literature, reveals such depths of degradation, ignorance, and prejudice that one turns away with loathing from the disgusting pictures. However, there can be no doubt that the book gives a real picture of what is the condition of Soochow life at present. Also it is known that there have been foreign women deceived into marriages with Chinese abroad, and that they have been brought back to China. There is therefore some basis for that phase of the story, however startling it may be at first. But the book is not to be read for its plot; it is the tone of the writer toward the evils of opium that is important. It reveals a new spirit in the land, a spirit that is vocal, and that accounts for the ease of the suppression of the internal traffic, or at least of the consumption of the drug.

The preface is such a delightful revelation of what a Soo man thinks a Soo man is, that it may be given almost entire, with merely a sentence or two omitted:

"It has been said that the province of Kiangsu is both prosperous and beautiful, and is reckoned the Crown of the Southeast. Every one speaks of the place as containing brilliant mountains and clear streams, and it is a place where people collect in great numbers. What, then, are the most wonderful products of this wonderful district? There are three: Men who take the First Place at the Palace Examinations; Actors; and Beautiful women. These three classes are produced most in K'su. No other province equals K'su in this respect. There is even an ancient saying to that effect. When the writer first heard this statement he did not believe it, but on examination found that there was abundant evidence proving the statement. The honourable reader should know that from the

好出城去了。大家最后商定，当务之急请威尔金森医生乃明智之举，却又发现他被某位上海来的外国客人给耽搁了——来者不是别人，正是伦敦回来的那位漂亮女医生！女医生已然知道一切，立即看出事态的严重性，果断实施抢救，把吞鸦片的青年救活了。

英国友人一直在顶替她，现在中国姑娘亮出身份，嫁给了那位显然已经病入膏肓的鸦片鬼。她医术高超，一个月之后就把丈夫的病治愈了。那位英国姑娘也如愿和青年才子结为夫妇。

与同类文学作品一样，此书用相当的篇幅深刻地揭示了中国社会的堕落、无知、偏见之深刻程度，乃至读者对其中令人作呕的场景不忍直视。然而，无可非议，它又为我们了解当前苏州人的生活情况描绘出真实图景。不仅如此，据说确实还有外国女子被骗后嫁给海外的中国人，并且被丈夫带回中国的事。因此，无论小说乍一读来多么令人震惊，它所涉及的相关故事背景倒似乎也确有事实依托，而非空穴来风。不过，小说的重要性不在情节，而在于作者针对鸦片的危害性所秉持的语气。这意味着中国大地出现了一种崭新的精神，一种大声疾呼（重视鸦片危害）的精神。同时，它也表明中国放松了对国内鸦片运输的管制，至少放松了对鸦片使用的压制。

书的前言[1]读来身心愉悦，它揭示了苏州人对自我的评价，值得近乎完整地展示于此，以下引文仅省去了一两句原文：

"据说江苏省繁华美丽，被视为中国东南地区的翘楚和骄傲。大家都说此地山川秀丽、溪流清澈、人口密集。那么，这一人杰地灵的地区哪类人最多呢？有三类：状元、唱戏的、美妾。这三种人是江苏省出产最多的人物。其他省会在这几个方面都无法与之抗衡。甚至有句老话说的就是这个意思。当本书作者第一次听见这句话时并不信以为真，然而经过仔细调查，发现确有大量凭证足以印证它的正确性。尊敬的读者应该都知道，自本朝

---

[1] 即中文原著中的"缘起"。

beginning of the present dynasty to this time Soochow has produced many men who were first in the examinations. A full exposition of this is laid out in the book, 'The Flowery Sea of Sin' 〔apparently an advertisement of another book in the series〕.

"The most famous tunes known as 'Kunchong' are produced at Soochow. Practically all the actors of the Empire are Soochow men. Further, the teachers of singing, together with the instructors of actors, are Soochow men. The whole class of expectant actors, together with the amateur actors and singers, are all from here. Is this not proof that this product comes from Soochow?

"Now as to the Beautiful Women. It is not necessary to go further than the small place Shanghai. Send there one to go through the whole number of wealthy families of that place, and the conditions as to these women can be easily learned. But you answer: 'I am neither a Nun nor one of the Six Old Wives.'[1] How then shall I gain entrance to these big families? And if one did find entrance, these women are busy from morning to night doing nothing else but attending the theatre, or burning incense before the gods.' Yet if you enquire, the facts are easily learned.

" As to the First Men at the Palace Examinations. Take one generation and compare. Of the three hundred and sixty divisions of commerce and trade, where is the one that does not have its First Man? Even among the lower classes there are those who are reckoned First Man of the class. The literary style of Soochow is the best, and her essayists of fame are beyond number. For this reason the

---

[1] Literally, " I am not one of the Three Aunts (San Ku) nor one of the Six Old Wives (*Liu P'o*)." In the "Cho kêng Lu," a volume of notes and essays by T'ao Tsung-i of the Yüan dynasty, we find a paragraph on the Three Aunts and the Six Old Wives: "If one of these persons enters a house, it seldom happens that she does not introduce theft and adultery. Whenever possible, avoid them as carefully as you would a snake or scorpion. The *San Ku* are: (1) Ni Ku, the Buddhist Nun; (2) Tao Ku, the Taoist Nun; (3) Kua Ku, the female soothsayer. The *Liu p'o* are: (1) Ya p'o, the female broker; (2) Mei p'o, the marriage go-between; (3) *Shih p'o*, the sorceress; (4) *Ch'ien p'o*, the praying woman; (5) *Yao p'o*, the herb-seller; (6) *Wên p'o*, the midwife." The phrase *san ku liu p'o* is the Chinese equivalent of "women of bad character." 字面意思为 "我既非三姑之一，也非六婆之一。"在元代陶宗仪所著的《辍耕录》——关于史事的笔记和札记一书中，我们找到了一个描写"三姑六婆"的段落："三姑六婆中任何一位踏入别人家，几乎总会招来偷盗或通奸的勾当。只要可能，要像避开蛇蝎一般避开此类人。"三姑"指：（1）尼姑，佛教的修女；（2）道姑，道教的修女；（3）卦姑，女性算命者。"六婆"指：（1）牙婆，贩卖人口的女子；（2）媒婆，婚姻方面的女性介绍人；（3）师婆，女魔法师；（4）虔婆，做祈祷的女性（译者按，此解有误，实指淫媒）；（5）药婆，卖草药的女子；（6）稳婆，接生婆。"中文里的"三姑六婆"相当于英文的"不正经的女人"。——原注

开始至今,苏州出了相当多的科举状元。《孽海花》中对此有全面的说明(显然,作者顺便在为该系列的另一本书打广告)。

"苏州人创作的最有名的声腔叫'昆腔'。大清帝国内几乎所有唱昆曲的都是苏州人。不仅如此,教唱腔的先生,还有教做戏的指导师傅,也都是苏州人。整个名角的班子,以及业余表演者和演唱者,也都来自苏州。这些证据不都表明唱戏的产自苏州吗?

"至于美妾,单从小地方上海一地即可一窥究竟,不必大费周章去更远的地方调查。派个人去上海了解下那里有钱人家共有几户,轻易就能知道这些女子的处境。不过如果派的是你,你会回答:'我既非尼姑也非六婆,怎样才能名正言顺地踏进这些大户人家呢?即便真能进去,也会发现这些女子忙来忙去的,也不过尽是些听听戏、烧烧香的事,除此之外,从早到晚几乎无所事事。'但是只要你去打听,就会知道她们的真实生活。

"至于科举考试中的状元,我们就拿一代人做个比较。三百六十行,哪一行不出状元?即便在下等阶层中,也有'状元'级别的人士。苏州的

First Place is continually carried off by Soochow. But this is not to be reckoned strange.

"Why, however, should these two classes come from Soochow? There is a reason for it, which I will now give. *It is because the words in their mouths are lies.* There are none who will not flatter for their own ends. With tongues lolling in salty mouths their lips glibly bring forth right and wrong; making use of ready-made phrases they appear all the more convincing. Becoming pleased with their own efforts, they will chew maggots in order to cause others to feel that they greatly surpass ordinary men, even to the bounds of the wonderful. But in reality, with teeth strong and molars set, they only cause others to laugh at their antics.

"Look at the clothes on their backs. They speak only of what is good to look at, having fetching touches. If one should be dressed in a manner that does not shine, this is sure to cause them to look lightly on him. For this reason those of moderate means must likewise be clothed in fashion, wearing the latest pattern. Not only do great families think much of clothes and long gowns, but even their dogs make no mistakes as to whom to bark at. For when they see one in short and blue clothes, they expose their teeth in a snarl; jumping about they wag a fierce tail, and that without cessation, showing that they too have got the knack of slighting the poor and currying favour with the rich. Hence it is that men and women in the city primp, prink, and powder. Whatever the time demands, that must they do. If they are not able to afford these things, they spend a few cash and rent them. If they cannot rent, then they with an ever-ready mouth borrow.

"Their one heart's idea is that whatever happens they must attain their desires. Apparently yielding, they are not. Before the fierce every one will be a polished gentleman. Being reviled, he opens not the mouth. Being struck, he says, ' I strike not back.' If there is a method of passing a point, they use that method, whatever it may be. They have a saying, 'Don't move the heavens to obtain the possessions under heaven. Pass the day in peace.' All can show a certain amount of intelligence, but all are avaricious to get a thing a little lower than it should be,

文风最佳，著名的苏籍文人墨客不计其数。正因如此，苏州一直出状元。不过这一点也不足为奇。

"然而，为什么这两类人都出自苏州呢？背后自有原因，且听我说来。*因为苏州人嘴里谎话连篇*。没有一个苏州人不是出于个人目的而恭维他人。凭借尖酸刻薄的油滑，他们嘴皮一等，舌头一滚，就能评判是非对错，信手拈来的鬼话似乎增强了可信度。他们越说越来劲，嚼蛆的目的就想让别人觉得他们比普通人高出一筹，甚至达到了神人的境界。然而现实里，他们伶牙俐齿，说的噱头只能引起别人捧腹大笑而已。

"瞧瞧他们身上穿的衣服。他们会先伸手摸一下你衣服的质地，然后只会说它好看的一面。如果你穿得并不光鲜亮丽，他们肯定就看不起你。因此，那些小家小户之人，必须同富人一样衣着时髦，身上的服装剪裁新颖。不仅有钱人家非常看重长衫马褂的材质，就连他们家的狗也不会弄错该朝什么人狂叫。因为只要它们看到某人穿着蓝色短衫，就会咆哮着露出牙齿，上蹿下跳，乱摇尾巴，不得停歇，仿佛要表明他们和主子一样，也掌握了怠慢穷人、拍富人马屁的本事似的。因此，苏州的男男女女个个打扮考究、装腔作势、涂脂抹粉。不论时间是否来得及，打扮是一件必须做的事情。如果他们买不起这些服饰，就会花上几个铜板去租。如果连租也租不起，那么他们会大言不惭地开口问别人去借。

"他们共有的观念就是不论怎样都必须达成愿望。当然，放弃，他们是不会选的。在凶恶之人面前，每个人都是好脾气先生。即便被骂，他也不动口。如果挨打了，他则说：'我不还手。'只要有办法避免矛盾升级，苏州人就会用这个办法，不管形式如何。他们常说：'得天下的方式不必专门去搬动天。过个太平日子就行。'苏州人都有一点小聪明，对于想得到的东西，也都有些小贪心，总能以稍微低廉点的方式获得，并且都会因

and at the same time attain an apparent pleasure.

"There has never been a Soochow man with deep plans, including possibilities and looking to consequences, that urged him on to accomplish some great or worthy deed. There have been no men of noted bravery, or great strength, or broad sympathy. Of course, then, the men being fops seeking to ape the great man, they only become fit material for show, and thus become actors such as Yu and Mang [famous spendthrifts of ancient Soo]. The women are compliant, and thus collect to themselves consideration. With all diligence they show an enticing mien and become worthy to be secondary wives."

The reader who has followed thus far will understand how it is that Soo produces such articles.

"There is, however, another matter, and in this the Soo people are very greatly at fault. What would you suppose? It is a kind of heaven-born inclination to laziness. For, not willing to stand alone, they think only of relying on some one else. If he was born under the roof of a rich family, then he looks to the superfluous shadow of his ancestors and enjoys the property left by father and mother. With superfluous clothes and enticing food he simply draws in his neck and attends to nothing at all. He enjoys the present peace with wealth and honour, without thinking of using the father's position to surpass the elevation of his ancestors. If he is born under a poor roof, he hurries toward the light of, and attaches himself to, the powerful— becoming simply a parasite. Going about he whines for pity; stretching out a long neck, with eyes staring, he looks in every direction for some one to give him a rise. If by chance he has no reliable kith or workable kinfolk whereby he may gain an easy support, providing clothes to go abroad and food to fill up with, why, then, his wife and children are exposed to cold and hunger. Hating heaven and bearing a grudge against earth, he goes staggering in useless poverty until he is brought to deeds of shame, and he stops at nothing. Stealing and pilfering, he searches heaven and earth if by any means he may turn over and obtain a few filthy cash and make himself appear with the face of the rich. The Soo man guards a cash as his life. Whether there be a

为占到这种小便宜而沾沾自喜。

"苏州人做事从来没有深思熟虑后的计划，既不考虑各种可能性，也不能预见后果，因为缺乏规划，也就无从敦促他完成某些大事要事。此地一直没有出过特别英勇之士，或是强大的人，或是心胸宽广的慈悲之人。当然，由于他们尽是些只想模仿重要人物的浮夸子弟，苏州人最终只能沦为做戏的合适人选，于是就成了如优和孟一样的唱戏的（优和孟是苏州古代有名的挥霍无度者）[1]。苏州女子性格温顺，富有体贴之心。加上勤劳，她们展露出一种迷人风情，成为当二太太的合适之选。"

读者一路读到这里，就会知道这样的文章怎么会出自苏州了。

"还有一个问题，在这方面苏州人恶习不改。你们觉得是什么问题？那是一种懒惰的天性。因为他们不愿意靠自己，总想着依仗别人。如果是富家子弟，他便指望活在老祖宗奢华的蒙蔽之下，享受父母留下的家业，坐吃山空。他衣着华丽，成日美味珍馐，缩着脖子，什么事情都不管。他贪图眼前安逸，沉湎于荣华富贵和家族名望，从来不去想如何利用父亲的地位超越祖先的荣光。如果出身贫寒，那么他立刻会急着靠近、攀附到有权有势的人身边——纯粹当个寄生虫。这种人到哪儿都会用抱怨博取同情，整日伸长了脖子，瞪大了眼睛，四处找关系，以便混入上流社会。假若恰巧找不到可靠的熟人，或是得力的亲戚，助他一臂之力，比如借他几件出客可穿的衣衫，或者借他一些果腹的食物，那么此人的妻儿就只能挨饿受冻了。这种人总是怨天怨地，踉跄地徘徊在贫穷的边缘，窝囊愚蠢，直到开始做些个偷鸡摸狗之事，随后就会变得不择手段。做着小偷小摸的事，但凡他能翻身弄到几个臭钱，让自己像个阔绰之人展露头面，他是会为此想尽一切办法，钻天拱地挖空心思的。苏州人视钱如命。有时因为闹饥荒，

---

[1] 盖洛理解有误，此处的"优孟"出自成语"优孟衣冠"，指一位楚国著名艺人，因为贤明，善于模仿，常对楚王进言规劝。该成语今指人善于扮演角色做戏；也比喻一味模仿，力求形似。

demand for relief in a famine or to accomplish a public benefit, in the face of such conditions he folds his hands and looks on unconcernedly. To give away a cash is more painful than cutting off a piece of flesh. Moreover, this class of people in their regard for influence and profit have only cash in mouth and heart. If one should point to a certain family zealous in carrying out works of public benefit, they purse up the mouth in a disdainful smile and say, 'The door of charity is opened with difficulty.'

"Then, too, he who is anxious only about himself is unable to comprehend the importance of the multitudinous affairs touching the lives of the people. If the advocate says there has come a telegram calling for a convention for the discussion of public affairs, he turns up his nose in the imitation of a smile and makes answer, 'Oh, that belongs to the important affairs of the Imperial government, and it is not anything that we small people should meddle with.' Tell him a certain man is intelligent and learned, then his eyebrows are elevated in a smile all over his face, and he complacently comments, 'Essays and teaching do not answer in times of hunger the demands for rice; ceremony and economy in public business do not cloth the person in cold weather; for he who is without wealth or resources will certainly go hungry and cold.' If there should come forward a worthy affair, they are afraid it is the officials trying to squeeze them and therefore they will do nothing. But when the officials do come down on them with their authority, then they are ready to rush in. Under the impulse of fear, they wrap their cash and silver in bundles, and with both hands pass it up to the great man above. For whenever the official orders a thing done, then they rush forward and to the extent of their ability they perform what has been commanded.

"But of all things that a Soochow man fears most, there is nothing that he fears quite as much as that he will not be allowed to smoke his opium. For he has a strong and immovable determination that he will have his opium. The wealthy say: ' Let the young sons eat opium, and thus avoid the bad houses and gambling dens.' Thus they have devised a most efficacious method of protecting the family property. In order to carry out this plan, they furnish money to some friend or acquaintance with which to go and entice their own ungovernable sons to smoke opium, until the habit is fastened on them. Besides furnishing this money they thank the enticer with more money. They say he who is addicted to the use of opium loses all inclination to wild ways. Thus the reckless ways of a debauchee are avoided; but the habitué becomes indolent and useless. Day is turned into

穷人需要接受救济，还有时因其他原因需要筹集一笔公共救济金，每次遇到这些情况，他就会抱着胳膊冷眼旁观，一副事不关己的样子。要他拿出一文钱出来，简直比割掉他一块肉还要痛。此外，这个阶层的苏州人在名利方面，只愿意兑现在嘴上和心里。如果你对某个家庭说他们捐资筹募救济金的行为是出于热心，他们就会噘起嘴来，轻蔑地笑道：'慈善之举其实迫于无奈。'

"所以，这种人一心只在乎自己，是无法理解与别人生计相关的那许多事物有多重要的。如果某个发起者告诉他，有电报呼吁大家开会共议公共事务，他会鼻孔朝天，做出一副假笑的样子，答道：'哦，这种大事归大清政府所管，我等小老百姓是不可掺和进去的。'跟他说某人聪明且满腹学问，他则眉毛一扬，满脸笑意，阴阳怪气地评价道：'文章和学识在饥饿的时候不能用来当饭吃，公务上的礼仪和经济在天冷的时候不能用来当衣穿；因为无财无谋之人势必会受那熬饥挨冻之苦。'如果真有值得参与的事要他出来捐资，他们就先担心当地官员会不会从他们身上压榨金钱，于是不为所动。可是真的等到官员动了威严和真格，他们就迫不及待地乖乖掏钱了。出于害怕，他们大把大把地将金银财宝双手奉上，交给高高在上的大人物。只要衙门下令要做某件事，他们立刻一拥而上，竭尽全力，乖乖从命。

"但是在所有令苏州人害怕的事情里，没有什么比不让他抽鸦片更可怕了。他有着坚定而不可动摇的意念：必须保证有鸦片可抽。有钱人说：'儿子年轻气盛，让他们吸吸鸦片，就不会去吃喝嫖赌了。'于是他们想出了一个最为灵验的保护家产的方式。为实施这一计划，他们塞钱给朋友或熟人，让帮忙打点，把不服管教的儿子带去吸鸦片，直到后者吸上瘾为止。此外，除了提供这笔钱，他们还会给中间人支付更多费用。这些有钱人以为但凡鸦片吸出瘾来，人就不再会有胡作非为的念头。如此一来，儿子确实没有

night and night into day, and interest in everything is lost. Of course, then, they will not go to the trouble to frequent gambling dens.

" Thus their families, men and women, old and young, are as purple-faced and thin-featured as cranes. They are all the time on the opium couch, sucking the cross flute, [1] giving forth sounds not according to the laws of music. Not only do men-servants and slave girls steal their opium, but even the cats and rats in their houses have the appetite. So that whenever they are reminded that opium has been forbidden, is that not the same thing as saying that their life is in danger? Furthermore, their life is so important that they must go to any extravagance in order to pamper their appetite! Not satisfied with opium they must add to the concoction, while preparing it for smoking, some deer's horn. This addition is for tonic purposes. If one should plead with them to break the habit, they are afraid lest some disease should be induced and they lose their life, therefore they are determined at any cost to hold on to the habit. They have an expression of the heart which says, ' Break off opium, and if it is not the mistress of the house, there will be crying to heaven.' From this it may be seen that there is no more difficult question than breaking off opium.

" It is remembered that an Imperial edict was lately issued, forbidding the use of opium and fixing a time for its complete cessation. At that time in Soochow alone there were more than 3,700 dens, big and little. All these were ordered to close at once. This so frightened the smokers that their souls flew away and their spirits departed from their place. After a great consultation there were empty reports spread abroad, such as that if the many attendants at the opium dens lost their work there would be a riot and bloodshed. This was with the idea of frightening the officials into easy methods of suppressing the opium and so slackly carrying out the Imperial commands—and in the meantime they would find some easy means of subverting the same, whereby they would be enabled for a few more days to go on with their smoking. For a day more of smoking would be a day more of enjoyment. But the officials were not at all moved—

[1] This must be the instrument whose name in Chinese means "crosswise blow"—referring, I suppose, to the twisting of the performer's neck. Compare Shakespeare, "the vile squeaking of the wry-neck'd fife." The epithet "wry-necked" has been a great puzzle to commentators, who have failed to see that it is a transferred epithet, really referring to the person who plays the fife. 这一定是中国人叫作"横吹"的烟枪——之所以这么命名，我想因为吸食者用它时要扭着脖子。比较一下莎士比亚的那句台词"弯笛子的怪叫声音。"其中"弯笛子"这个词一直令评论家们困惑不解，他们没有意识到该词其实是移就的修辞手法，实指吹笛子的那个人。——原注

成为浪荡子弟,但瘾君子好逸恶劳,成了废物。夜以继日,除了鸦片,别无所好。自然对于经常逛赌窝一事也就力不从心起来。

"所以他们家里的人,男男女女、老老少少,个个面色暗沉,形容枯槁。成日躺在鸦片床上,抽着'横笛',发出毫不悦耳的声响。不但家里的男仆女佣会偷吃鸦片,就连猫和老鼠也被勾起了烟瘾,以至每当有人提醒,说鸦片已经被禁,那不就等于在警告他们要危及生命了吗?不仅如此,既然他们将性命看得格外重要,那么不惜重金,也要继续沉溺鸦片。因为不满意鸦片烟的味道,他们收膏时还必须加些鹿茸类的调和物,达到滋补的药效。如果有人劝他们戒断烟瘾,他们就会害怕戒了后反倒会得病,丢掉性命,所以想尽办法,不惜一切代价,都会继续抽大烟。这些人心里在想:'除非家里老婆哭得死去活来,否则怎可戒断鸦片。'由此可见戒烟是难上加难的事情。

"各位都记得最近颁布了一条诏书,要求禁用鸦片,并且明确了完全禁止的时间。当时在苏州,大大小小还有 3 700 多家烟馆,一下子都接到命令要求关闭。这一举措把烟鬼们吓得魂飞魄散。经过相当的商议,社会上有一些空泛的说法传播开来,比如有人指出,如果烟馆里的伙计大量失业,就会造成暴动和流血事件。这些谣言的背后其实是吸食鸦片的民众想通过吓唬官府的方式,让其采取温和手段控制鸦片,马马虎虎地去执行朝廷的命令——与此同时,他们也能找到同样简单的方法抵抗禁令,争取更多时

for the thunder rolled and the wind still blew. The doors of the recalcitrant dens were closed and those falling under the mandate were punished, so that the dens were closed both in and out of the city, even in by-ways and alleys; the whole was swept clean. Then followed some more idle reports, saying that the selling of opium by licensed shops was not to be allowed, and the habitués were sorrowful unto death.

"About this time some, thinking to take time by the forelock, bought several chests of opium and had them prepared and buried in the ground. But the most laughable case took place in a family by the name of Pan. The craving in this family was very great. Not only did they prepare opium and bury it, but besides they had a pot prepared, and took a cotton wadded robe and steeped it in the opium for three days until several pounds of opium had soaked into the cotton. It was then hung up to dry slowly. Afterwards the man began to wear the garment. Everybody was very anxious to know his meaning, but could not fathom this deep secret, over which Pan was smiling and unwilling to give it away. But his son began to talk, and said it had thus been prepared lest when the final edict of prohibition should be put into effect, and during the disturbance arising therefrom, it should not be possible to get opium; would not the craving become unbearable and his father die? Therefore he had soaked his robe in opium so that when the time came that no more opium could be secured, he would take the garment and chew a piece of it for a while and the craving would be satisfied. Why, then, should he give away this most excellent plan? I hope you who hear this will not kill yourselves laughing.

"But after all is said, the Soochow man is born with a natural weakness. He is seldom ashamed. Not only is this not enough, but he must add to this the poison of opium, and he enters deeply into its very essence. How then shall he be blamed with the laughable things he does? For the government has issued strict injunctions against smoking opium. To comply with the instructions is to bring immediate calamity on one's self. What then will be the condition of the opium fiends and what will be the world to them? If you, reader, do not believe this, just take a cursory look at these fiends. At this very time when opium is being suppressed, their mouths are full of such expressions as this: 'Suppress opium? The government taxes will be less by the the amount collected on several million of lamps, and that would not be a good riding-whip to handle.' In their hearts they really hope outside kingdom men will not agree to the prohibition and will

间吸食鸦片，多吸一天就多一天快活。不过官府雷厉风行，不为所动。那些烟馆很快就被查封，违命的即刻受到处罚。所以城内城外的烟馆，连路边的和街头巷尾的烟馆都关了门。全城烟馆被一扫而空。于是又传出了更多的谣言，说即便有资质的店也不允许卖鸦片了，这下烟鬼们变得痛不欲生。

"这种时候，有的人抓紧时机买了好几大箱鸦片，让人装好，埋入地下。最可笑的事发生在一户潘姓人家。这家人的烟瘾很大。他们不但买好鸦片埋进地里，还专门准备了一个盆子，把一件棉袍在鸦片里浸了三天，直至数磅重的鸦片尽数渗透进棉袍中。然后袍子被挂起来慢慢晾干。后来主人穿上了这件棉袍。大家都想知道他此番操作的初衷，却都无法猜出其中深意，姓潘男子微笑着不愿揭开谜底。还是他的儿子道出了原委。他说这么准备是以防禁烟的最后诏书得到执行，在随之产生的困扰中买不到鸦片，那么他的父亲不就会因为烟瘾发作得难以忍受而一命呜呼吗？所以他事先把自己的袍子浸透了鸦片，如此一来，在鸦片无所购得之际，他就可以从袍子上撕下一片来嚼一会儿，解解瘾念。难怪他不愿把这一妙招公之于众呢，各位听到这个故事可不要笑岔了气。

"不过说了这许多，苏州人还有一个天生的缺陷——不懂廉耻。非但缺乏足够的羞耻心，而且性格中还平添了鸦片的毒性，深陷毒瘾。该怎么指责他做出如此可笑之事呢？朝廷已经签发严格的禁烟命令，立刻服从就意味着自己马上遭殃。鸦片鬼的状态将会如何呢？没有了鸦片，世界对他们而言将变成什么样呢？如果各位读者不信，那就瞥一眼这些瘾君子吧。当前，鸦片正遭到管制，他们却满嘴这样的话：'禁烟的话，朝廷靠几百万盏洋油灯所收的税收就会变少，那可不是什么好使的马鞭啊。'他们真心希望外国人会不同意执行禁令，主张（大清帝国）继续进口这一毒品，

insist on importing the smoke stuff that they may control this great sluice-gate of traffic. So that when they hear that in the open ports opium-smoking is going merrily on, there is not one of them that is not secretly glad, hoping as the senile old Blossoming Talent hopes for another examination, that he may try again for his second degree.

"When he thus expresses himself, is it not deceptive beyond compare, and is it not evidence beyond question? But, dear reader, do not listen to their talk about opium and be deceived by them. For that stuff is the Heart-breaking Weed. When the poor eat it, they waste their time and lose their trade. If persons of means smoke, it is said they can thus protect their property and prevent their sons from the wild ways of youth, this being an efficacious preventive. They do not know that when opium is first eaten it is a powerful excitant to lewd ways. More than half the habitués, without sickness or pain, use the excitant of opium to become truly degraded. When they have indulged for some considerable time, they realise that there is no advantage in it. Any one with a small amount of perception may see in Soochow a class of opium-besotted prodigals who spend their time in nothing else but planning ways and means for leading astray silly women. Having become sots they can do nothing of worth. They think only of their food and how they may satisfy that fearful craving that must be satisfied. They can but devise some means for meeting this demand. There are two most used. He who has some natural good appearance endeavors to marry some rich woman; then eating her, and using her, and relying on her, he passes over a few more days of pleasure. The other is with facile tongue and enticing words and heart schemes deceitful; he only thinks of finding a rich friend, whom he deceives into gambling and leads into lewdness. With flattering sycophancy, stooping to any device in order that he may pass the days he sticks to his prey like a leach.

"Thus it is evident that opium-smoking leads to gambling and lewdness and every evil—nothing is beyond its depths of degradation. Of old it was said, 'Idleness leads to thoughts of lewdness.' Daily lolling about, smoking opium to the exclusion of everything else, how shall such idleness lead to anything else but such thoughts? Therefore biting hard on my teeth-roots I can but say, this is an injurious poison, ruining the kingdom and breaking up families. This is not because I have any enemies among this class of people. I have another reason which I will give. About ten years ago, when opium was in a most flourishing condition, there were two silly women in Soo done to death by opium sots. The

并且把控住鸦片运输的闸口。因此当听到在租界里的人还在愉快地吃着鸦片，所有人无一不是公然地表达快乐，正如年迈的秀才希望恢复科举考试，重新夺魁一般，心怀侥幸，想要再抽上几口。

"他表达出那些想法，岂不是自欺欺人？这不就是确凿无疑的证据？但是，各位看官，千万不要轻易听信他们关于鸦片烟的话。因为鸦片就是断肠草。穷人吃了，既浪费时间又丢了生意。不要以为富贵之人吸了，就能守住家产，管住不孝子，使之不至于做出许多荒唐事，把鸦片当成一剂预防良药。他们不知道的是第一次吸鸦片就会刺激人做许多下流之事。半数以上的鸦片鬼并无病痛折磨，却利用大烟的刺激自甘堕落。沉溺其中相当一段时间后，他们认识到鸦片没有一点好处。任何稍具辨识能力的人都能看到，苏州城那类瘾君子成日里无所事事，把心思尽数花在想方设法带歪傻女子上。既已成烟鬼，他们一事无成，满脑子都是鸦片，总是寻思着如何满足可怕的欲念，为满足烟瘾费尽心思。有两种方法最为常用：长相好看点的人会挖空心思娶个有钱老婆，通过吃她、用她、依赖她，多过几天快活日子；另一种烟鬼工于心计，通过花言巧语，只想结交富家子弟，骗他沉迷赌博，一路堕落。为了消磨时光，他像水蛭一样吸附在朋友身上，阿谀献媚、卑躬屈膝。

"显然，吸食鸦片会使人嗜赌成性，为非作歹，没有什么事物比鸦片令人堕落得更深的了。老话说得好：'饱食思淫欲。'终日里闲躺着抽着鸦片，万事不管，这般懒散，除了下流的念头，还能生出什么想法来？因此，我只能咬紧牙关指出，鸦片就是害人的毒药，既摧毁国家，又拆散人家。我之所以这么说不是因为吸鸦片的人里有我的仇人，实则另有一个原因，且听我说。十年前，鸦片交易十分繁荣，苏州有两个痴女子就是被鸦片鬼弄死的。当时的情况令人扼腕，引得人们纷纷叹息落泪，故事恨不得编成

whole circumstance was pitiable, productive of sighs and tears, and should be sung abroad in lays and stanzas. Therefore I have put my hand to the work of making a book, called 'THE HEART BREAKING WEED.' Whoever reads this book may know that the affections and customs of the Soo people are truly bad. And although I shall be hated by the opium-smoking class, still I should not be blamed for crying out in protest against this evil."

To such a preface, who cannot but say "Amen!" and hope that soon the drug will be removed from the land?

歌曲和诗歌传唱到外国去。因此我着手想写一本书,题目就叫《断肠草》。无论谁读了此书都会知道苏州人的喜好和风俗有多糟糕。虽然我将因此遭到抽鸦片群体的仇恨,但是为公开反对这一毒害,我不应遭受(社会的)指责。"

　　读了这样的前言,大家除了说"阿门",并且希望把鸦片尽早赶出去,还能说什么呢?

My Holidays in China
在华度假记事

(威廉·R.葛骆 著 黄洁婷 译)

《在华度假记事》(*My Holidays in China*)是英国作家威廉·R.葛骆(William R. Kahler)所著,1895年由上海戒酒会时报(Temperance Union)出版。书中记载了作者工作闲暇时的三次出游,第一次是从上海到杭州,后经宁波返回;第二次是从上海到溧阳,途经苏州和太湖;第三次是从九江到芜湖。在该书第二部分"上海到溧阳:途经苏州和太湖"的第四至七章中(原著第116页到第129页),作者记录了乘船游览苏州地区的旅途见闻,描写了苏州当地的染布、织布等传统工艺,对诸如玉峰山、苏州贡院、北寺塔、玄妙观、沧浪亭、宝带桥等名胜都有详尽的介绍。同时书中也不乏对十九世纪九十年代苏州人的生活方式、习俗信仰及当地民间传说的描述。

CHAPTER IV

While walking through one of the hamlets, an old gentleman politely offers us a mouthful of food out of his own basin, lifting the savoury morsel with his chopsticks, but it is needless to say we decline with thanks. Pah Do San Le Ting is the next place we come to and there is a mandarin tax station and a ting with a slate roof which is in excellent condition. We go for a long walk on the bank with our dogs, but the weather begins to show signs of rain, though we keep on walking as long as possible, admiring the scenery which is very pretty. Of course, the want of hills is a drawback, but as far as the eye can reach over a remarkably flat country can be seen patches of bright yellow and green of ripening corn, with darker green here and there, denoting beans. The emblem of Scotland is growing luxuriantly, as is also that of Ireland, or its Chinese substitute, while the numerous homesteads scattered about here and there peep out from among clumps of leafy tree. We meet some soldiers towing a mandarin gunboat and they civilly enquire our destination.

The people about these parts do not appear to be early risers, and we see very few boats on the move before seven o'clock when we pass a native tax station at the Sow Tung village. Here numerous small creeks have been constructed for irrigation purposes and water is raised from them by means of those primitive, but useful contrivances known as endless chain pumps, which are worked by buffaloes. Women and children also help in working these chain pumps, which are placed in the water at an angle of about twenty five degrees, though of course, the angle is much greater when the bank is high. The lower end of the pump is raised or lowered by means of a very simple contrivance, namely a rope which is attached to the lower end and wound round a bamboo which extends from the bank to an upright in the water. Cross pieces are inserted in the shore end of the bamboo which thus acts as a windlass and being twisted round as required, raises or lowers the pump. The pumping houses are thatched with straw, and if we did not know any better, we should say it is to keep the buffaloes from getting sun burnt, while people who work at some of the chain pumps frequently have no covering at all over their heads, so it appears from this that buffaloes are more cared for than human beings are. The animals have blinkers, made of tortoise shell, sometimes, over their eyes to keep them from getting giddy, it is said, while they perform their monotonous tramp round and round from early

第四章

我们走过一个村庄时,一位老先生很客气地用筷子从自己的盆里夹了一口美味的食物递给我们,当然我们婉言谢绝了。接下来我们到了三里亭摆渡[1],这里有一道官府设的税卡,还有一个完好无损、盖着石板屋顶的凉亭。我们带着几条狗在岸上走了很长一段路,天空开始有了点雨意,不过我们还是尽可能继续前行,欣赏一路的美景。当然,此处无山,稍嫌美中不足。但放眼望去,成熟的玉米地里亮黄色和绿色交会,深绿色的大豆散落在各处,一望无际的乡村美景一览无余。生机勃勃的田园风光是苏格兰和爱尔兰的一大标志,也是中国的一大标志,无数的农庄在茂密的树丛中错落隐现。我们还遇到了一队士兵拖着一艘官家炮艇,他们彬彬有礼地问我们前往何处。

这一带的人似乎并不早起,我们在七点之前经过宋塘村[2]一个当地的税卡时,就没见有几条船。这里挖了很多沟渠来灌溉农田,用水牛拉动链泵(水车)来抽水,办法虽然原始但是有效。妇女和儿童们也帮着操作这些链泵。这些链泵被放置在水中,与地面的夹角大约25度。当然,河岸越高,角度也要越大。用来抬高或者放低水泵下端的方法颇为简单,就是把绳子系在较低的一端,将绳索绕在竹竿上,再将竹竿从岸边伸出,与水中的立柱相连。竹竿位于岸上的那端插入横木后,充当了绞盘,根据需要转动,可以控制水泵的升降。泵房是间茅草屋,要是我们不了解情况的话,可能会以为它是用来防止水牛被晒伤的,而那些操作链泵的人的头上通常毫无遮挡,这样表面看来,牛比人更受到重视。有时候还会用龟壳做的眼罩遮住水牛双眼,以防止它们头晕,据说它们从早到晚就这么一直单调地一圈

---

[1] Pah Do San Le Ting,音译。
[2] Sow Tung village,音译。

morning till late at night.

As we proceed, many small bridges are passed, most of them having a single span and built of stone, three slabs being places abreast, the uprights being also of stone, and all looking very dilapidated and shaky, though this is nothing new in China.Numbers of bridges are entirely broken down and nobody seems to care whether they will ever be repaired again. It does not appear to be anybody's particular business, though it is, all the same, but the responsible parties do not want to expend money on them. Sometimes benevolent people take the matter in hand and raise subscriptions for the purpose of repairing bridges and highways. Over the Grand Canal there are also many bridges, most of them with a single arch, but the foundations have in some instances collapsed; in others, the arches are defective, and have fallen in.

All along the banks of the creek and as far back as the eye can see, patient buffaloes or cows are ploughing, and the drivers, both men and women, are over their knees in mud and water, for the women tuck up their nether garments the same way that the men do. In other places men are guiding harrows over the fields, and we see boys standing on the harrows holding on to the cows' tails to steady themselves. These harrows consist of two scantlings some foot or so, apart and kept separate by means of wooden tie pieces. The scantlings have each some fifteen iron blades about two inches broad fastened in them.

Loh Kah Pan, one hundred and twenty le from Shanghai, is next reached, and then at Muh Kah Jao, three le further on, is a high stone bridge over a creek which runs at right angles to the Soochow Creek, a long way to the left being Che Tun or "Thousand Mounds" and a pagoda. Six le from Muh Kah Jao is Loong Wong Miao, a three storied pagoda, with the lowest section solid. It is coloured bright brick-red and is at the junction of the Soochow and a smaller creek and at this place incense is offered. Formerly the pagoda stood alone, but quite recently a temple has been built in front of it, so that it cannot be seen from the Soochow Creek. A little further on are two deserted lime kilns on the left, while on the right is a creek by which one makes a short cut to Quinsan, the route by it being nine le less than by the big creek. It is distinguished by a pailou on its left bank and winds considerably, being known as the Ching Yang Kong, Tso Dong Kong and Whangpo Tso Dong in different sections. The country through which this creek passes is not uninteresting being relieved here and there by temples, bridges and hamlets. The San Kway Dong, or "Hall of Three Spirits," stands in a

圈转个不停。

我们继续航行,一路上经过了许多小桥,其中大多数都是单孔石桥,三块石板并排放置,桥墩也是石头的。这些桥看起来个个都废旧不堪、摇摇欲坠,不过这在中国早已屡见不鲜。很多桥梁已经完全断开,好像也没有人关心是不是该修一下。这似乎和任何人都没有关系,当然就算有关,他们也不想在这上面花钱。有时候会有善人出面,为修桥修路募集捐款。大运河上也有许多桥,大多为单拱桥,不过有些桥基已经塌陷,还有一些桥拱受损垮掉了。

沿着河岸向后放眼望去,只见温顺的公牛或是母牛正在犁地,赶牛的男人女人们个个都卷起裤腿,站在没膝的泥水里。另一些地方,一些男人在用犁耙耕地,还有些小男孩站在犁耙上,使劲揪着牛尾巴努力站稳。这些犁耙由两根几英尺长的小木条组成,两根木条间用木制连接件隔开。每根木条上都装有大概15个宽约2英寸的铁齿。

接着我们来到了离上海120里的陆家浜,然后又到了三里外的马家桥,此处一座高高的石桥架于河上,此河与苏州河呈直角。往左边再行上一段颇远的距离便能抵达千墩和一座宝塔。距离马家桥六里处有个龙王庙,是一座三层宝塔,塔基甚是牢固。此塔位于苏州河与一条小河的交汇处,塔身涂成鲜亮的砖红色,塔内还有檀香供应。以前这里只有一座孤零零的塔,不过最近它的前面又建了一座寺庙,所以从苏州河上就再也看不见这座塔了。再往前一点,左边是两座废弃的石灰窑,右边有一条小河,可以抄近路去昆山,比从大河走少九里的路程。河的左岸有座牌楼甚是醒目,河上风力强劲,河水各段被称为青阳港、车塘港和黄坡车塘[1]。这条河所经过的乡间散布着一些庙宇、桥梁和村庄,给它平添了几分生趣。三鬼洞蠢立

---

[1] Whangpo Tso Dong,音译。

clump of seven tall and ancient trees, and the Gno Wong Miao, a temple to Yah Foy, is next seen, and after it are the Kway Wong Miao and village. At this place there is a bridge and we find a number of lumbering straw laden boats, one of which is stuck fast under the bridge, the crew being unable to extricate it, while the villagers and the men in the other boats make no attempt to offer assistance. It is not their business; hence they do not proffer their aid, although they are themselves delayed. We set to work and with the aid of our own crew and that of the straw boat, get out ropes which being fastened to the boat, we call upon the spectators to help us haul on, the result being that we soon get all the help we want and the straw boat is successfully withdrawn from the awkward plight under the bridge. Had we not taken charge of the operations, the impinged boat would not have got clear, probably for hours, or until the crew had discharged the bulky cargo.

Arrived at Kwun San, or Quinsan as it is called by the natives, one hundred and sixty two le from Shanghai, our boat makes fast to the bank, outside one of the gates. We are beguiled by the lowdah into the belief that the hill, which gives its name to the city and inside which it is, is only one le distant, but the haziness of the native idea of time and distance is well known, so we ought not to have made the mistake in taking his statement literally. We have to pass over bridges and bridges; indeed the place is quite a second Venice, or to speak more accurately, Venice is quite a second Quinsan, for it is quite possible that the latter is the more ancient town of the two. Some of the bridges have as many as thirty seven steps to the summit, and there are lots of people on them idling about, for the good folks in this town do not appear to have much to occupy their time. We may mention in passing that there is a superstition among boatmen that it is unlucky for a boat to pass under a bridge while a woman is going over it, so that on several occasions our boatmen have rather roughly called out to some women to get off the bridges as we passed under. It is infra dig. for a woman to be "over" or above a man.

A man will not pass under a woman's clothing hanging out to dry from the upper story of a house, for a similar reason, and we have seen a mandarin stop his chair while a woman removed her belongings which had been hanging out across the street from a window of her house.

A hen, also, on the roof of a house, violates the amour propre of the Chinaman, and if the requisite remedies are not applied to counteract this

在七棵高大的古树丛中,接下来便是供奉岳飞的鄂王庙,之后是鬼王庙和一个村子。这里还有一座桥,一些装着稻草的船在水中缓慢地行驶,其中一艘牢牢地卡在桥下,船工们用尽方法也无法脱身,而村民和其他船上的人也没有帮忙的意思。这件事情与他们无关,所以没人去帮忙,但其实他们自己也被耽搁了。我们二话不说伸出援手,在我们的船工的帮助和运草船船工的努力下,我们取出了系在船上的绳索,随即号召围观的人一起拖船,很快就得到了他们的帮助,成功地把运草船从桥下拖了出来。如果我们不去帮忙,除非船工把笨重的货物卸下来,否则再过几个小时,这船也没法脱身。

到达昆山后,我们在城门外的岸边系缆停泊。此地距离上海162里。我们受船老大的蒙蔽,误以为与此城同名的那座山[1]离这只有一里远。但是众所周知,中国人对时间和距离的概念太过模糊,所以我们本不应该轻信他的话的。我们经过了一座又一座的桥;的确,这个地方简直是第二个威尼斯,或者更确切地说,威尼斯是第二个昆山,因为很可能昆山是两个城市中更为古老的那个。有些桥要爬上37级台阶才能到达桥顶,桥上有许多人在闲荡,看来这个城里似乎相当多的人都无所事事。顺便提一句,船工中有一种迷信,桥上有女人经过时,船只过桥就会倒霉。所以有好几次,我们通过桥下时,船工会粗鲁地大叫着让一些女人从桥上走开。女人在男人"上面",这可是有失身份的。

楼上如果晾着女人的衣服,男人就不会从下面经过。出于类似的原因,我们看到,一个女人从房屋窗户里去取她晒在外面的衣物时,楼下的官员便叫停了他的轿子。

同样,如果母鸡跑到了房子的屋顶上,也会伤害到中国男人的自尊心。要是不采取必要的补救措施来抵消母鸡的这种不当行为,房子就会被烧掉,

---

[1] 根据上下文,此处与"昆山"同名的山应为产昆石的玉峰山。因其形状如马鞍,又称马鞍山。

impropriety on the part of the hen, the house will be burnt down, so the biped has to be caught and summarily put to death. In the event of pigeons flying about in the vicinity of a fire, they are no longer pigeons, but "fire crows" and are the emissaries of the fire demons. The birds are supposed to be looking for some other place to burn, instead of, as is actually the case, searching for their burnt out homes.

Sometimes when fires have been more prevalent than usual in a district, the householders engage Taoist priests to invoke Ho Wong, the Fire God, to put a stop to the ravages of the fire fiends. For this purpose a procession is organized, horns are blown, gongs and drums are beaten and there is considerable commotion in order to frighten the fiends away from the locality. The fiends, however, have orders to destroy so many houses a year, though sometimes they are tender hearted and delay carrying out their instructions as long as possible, but as the year draws to a close, there are more fires than usual in consequence of the fiends completing the tale of houses to be burnt. To prevent the fire demons carrying out their orders, the natives stack tiles edgeways along the top of the roofs of their houses, thus giving the buildings the appearance of being incomplete, for the fire demons' instructions are to destroy finished houses. The owners thus think to hoodwink the demons and save their property by this ruse.

When a man's house is burnt down, he is responsible for the damage done to his neighbour's property, so he takes the earliest opportunity of getting out of the way. In the case of a fire originating in a pawnbroker's shop, the proprietor has to pay half the value of the things pawned, besides losing the sum he had advanced on them when they were pledged with him, so that the pawners get the full or nearly the full value of the things, and sometimes more. If the pawnshop gets burnt down through a fire spreading to it from another place, then the pawnbroker only pays one third of the value of the pledges, in addition to what he has already advanced.

We find Quinsan a mass of ruins, and a large portion of it is unoccupied, for when the Taipings captured it they amused themselves by killing the people and destroying the buildings, and since then the remaining inhabitants have not thought it worth their while to rebuild. The present population is scanty, and many of the women have natural sized feet, not "Golden" or "Tottering Lilies," that is feet compressed to accord with the native idea of beauty, which is said to have been inaugurated by the Lady Yow some nine hundred years ago; other say thirteen

所以得马上抓住这只鸡并且立即处死它。[1]如果鸽子在火灾附近飞来飞去，它们就不再是鸽子，而是"火鸦"，是火魔的使者。人们认为这些鸟是在找有什么地方可烧的，但实际上它们只在寻找自己被烧毁的家园。

有时候，当一个地方频繁发生火灾，房主会请道士作法，祈求火王来阻止火魔的肆虐。为此，人们会组队游行，吹响号角，敲锣打鼓，好不热闹，为的就是把火魔吓跑。不过这些火魔会收到一年要烧毁多少房屋的指令，尽管它们有时会大发善心，尽可能拖延时间，但是随着年关的临近，火魔们需要完成任务，这时候火灾就会特别多。为了阻止火魔执行任务，当地人就在屋顶把瓦片竖着堆叠起来，这样房子看起来就像是还没有完工。因为火魔得到的指令是去烧毁造好的房子，所以房主想用这种小伎俩来骗过火魔，保住他们的财产。[2]

如果有人家里房子被烧了，他还要负责赔偿邻居的财产损失，所以他会尽可能避开这种灾祸。如果火灾是由当铺引起的，店主必须在扣除典当时预支的钱以外，再赔偿相当于抵押物价值的一半，所以交当人可以得到抵押物的全部或是将近全部的价值，有时甚至更多。如果当铺是被别处蔓延而来的大火烧毁，那么除了已经预付的钱之外，店主只需再赔偿抵押物价值的三分之一。

我们发现昆山有许多废墟，大部分地方都无人居住，这是因为太平军在占领此地时，以杀人烧屋取乐。从那以后，幸存的居民便认为不值得花时间重建。现在此地人口稀少，许多女子都是天足，而非金莲小脚。所谓小脚，就是为符合中国人的审美观念而把脚缠裹起来，据说是由约900年

---

[1] 以上种种贬低女性的封建迷信行为应是原作者个人观点，不乏误解或夸张成分。
[2] 本段关于火魔的记载应为原作者对个别封建迷信行为的记录，其理解亦可能存在偏颇。

hundred. It is not the fault of the Quinsanites that their women kind have not compressed feet, but it must be laid to the charge of the Taipings, who would not allow the young girls to have their feet deformed. Yang Kway Foy, a lovely concubine of the voluptuous emperor Tang, is said to have worn shoes only three inches long, and Pan Foy is said to have danced before the last sovereign of the Tsy dynasty, and that every footstep made a lily grow. During the reign of Kang She, in A. D. 1664, an edict was promulgated forbidding foot binding under pain of blows, banishment, and the cangue (pr. kang)—or wooden collar, and the local officials were held responsible if the edict was not obeyed. It only remained in force four years, the custom being too deeply rooted to be eradicated by an edict. Since then the people have been allowed to follow their own tastes in the matter.

CHAPTER V

There are scarcely any industries in Quinsan, though we notice in one of the creeks a boatload of the C. & J. Trading Co.'s Devoe brand of kerosene. We see a man preparing native cotton cloth for figured dyeing. The cloth is covered over with a piece of flowered stencil, and the man rubs mortar through this so that some of it adheres to the cloth making flowered designs. When the mortar is dry, the cloth is steeped in the dye which does not penetrate it, and consequently does not mark the cloth, and when the latter is dry, the mortar is brushed off leaving the cloth under it white or nearly white which forms the pattern. It is rather a clumsy way of doing things, and the cloth is only marked on one side.

We reach the hill, in the side of which near the top, there is a hole, the entrance to a passage leading to Tong Sah, a hundred and twenty le distant. According to the remainder of the story, which is as true as the legend can make it, two men once entered the passage from opposite ends and are still there, as they met in the middle and neither could turn back and get out. How people found this out is another of these puzzles which we do not care to bother our heads about. The ascent to the hill is rather difficult in some places, notwithstanding that there are steps most of the way up, but many of these steps are broken and others are missing. At the summit we meet a full blown priest and a couple of acolytes and ask the priest how high the hill is, but we open our eyes when he says three le, or one mile; of course, we ought to have known that the height of a hill is designated by the time—and a le originally meant a period of time,

前（或说是 1 300 年前）的窅娘开创的。这里的女子不缠足并非昆山人自己的过错，而是因为太平军控制此地时不允许年轻女子裹脚。杨贵妃是耽于享乐的唐朝皇帝的爱妃，据说她的鞋子只有三寸长；潘妃据说曾在南齐末代皇帝面前跳舞，步步生莲花。[1] 公元 1664 年康熙统治期间，曾颁布法令禁止裹足，违者将处以鞭打、流放或者枷刑——枷是一种套在脖子上的木制刑具；如果不遵守禁令，将追究地方官的责任。这条法令只执行了四年，因为裹脚的习俗根深蒂固，一纸禁令难以根除。从此以后，人们就被允许在这件事上按照自己的喜好行事。

第五章

昆山几乎没有什么工业，不过我们在一条河上发现了一船 C. & J. 贸易公司的德富（Devoe）牌煤油。我们还看到一个男人正在准备给土棉布染色。布上覆盖着一块印花模板，然后这个人便开始刮浆，一些灰浆附着在布上，留下印花图案。浆干了以后，再将布料浸泡在染料中，染料无法渗透防染浆，这样就不会在布上留下痕迹。等到布干了以后，再把浆刮掉，布料上就形成了白色或是近乎白色的图案。这种方式有些笨拙，而且布料只有一面印了花纹。

我们到了山上，靠近山顶的地方有个洞，那是通往 120 里外的东山的通道入口。有一个流传下来的故事，也不知是真是假，说曾经有两个人分别从两端进入这个通道，直到现在还在里面，因为他们在中间相遇了，没有一个人能掉转头出来。那么这个出口是怎么发现的呢，这是另外一件令人困惑的事情，不过我们不想费神去思考这个问题。上山的路有几处相当崎岖，尽管大部分路上都有台阶，但是许多台阶已经破损，还有一些台阶不见了。在山顶上，我们遇到了一位精疲力竭的僧人和两个侍僧。我们问

---

[1]　窅娘、杨贵妃、潘妃缠足故事皆街谈巷语的传说。

but now signifies a distance—that it would take a person to reach the top. Our aneroid gives us the height as three hundred feet. "Suppose," we say to the priest, "we dig a hole right down to the bottom, how far would that be?" He replies that the depth will be forty two chang which puts his calculations out by about one hundred and twenty feet. He asks to be allowed to look through our binoculars, but as he does not know how to use them he squints through the wrong end. He is very affable and knows the Chinese names of a good many foreigners in Shanghai who have visited his temple, and he plays the host to perfection, so we are regaled with vermacelli and what looks like fish skin, a toothsome dish, although one of our party does not fancy it. The priest has a four post bell stand in his temple fitted up in winter with bedding and curtains under the bell. He sits in here in the cold weather and remains awake till 3 a.m. striking the bell by an ingenious contrivance of strings and bamboo, but with all due deference to his veracity, the snug bed and cosy curtains are more suggestive of slumber than of wakefulness.

  The panorama from the hill is a very pleasing one and the air being clear the hills near Soochow can be distinctly seen. On top of the hill there is a pagoda, which like the priest's house is in a very dilapidated condition, but both are undergoing repairs.

  The pagoda is called Ling Seah; it was built some 1,400 years ago, more or less, and destroyed by the Taipings. The story of this pagoda is that it was erected at the request of an emperor in fulfilment of a vow he had made while he was ill and he also built two other pagodas at Soochow. At the foot of the pagoda is a temple called the Whah Zung tsz, and on the hill, about the middle of it, there is a dummy pagoda of seven stories and it, too, was built in fulfilment of a vow made by a sick mandarin. At the other end of the hill there is a temple which is said to be some three hundred years old, and it was built to shelter the God of Thunder, by a teacher who felt grieved that there was no place for this worthy in the vicinity. The teacher called upon his friends and they subscribed so liberally that he was enabled to fulfil the desire of his heart and, one good turn deserving another, as the cook said to the pancake, the worthy teacher was afterwards deified. The God of Thunder, according to the image of him in this temple, has the wings and beak of a bird. Another occupant of the temple is the attendant goddess who parts the clouds for him.

僧人这座山有多高,当他说有3里(即1英里)时,我们都惊讶地睁大了眼睛;当然,我们知道他说的高度是根据一个人到达山顶的时间来确定的——"里"本来是指一段时间,但现在指的是距离,也就是说要花走3里路的时间才能抵达山顶。我们的无液气压计显示此山高度为300英尺。"假如,"我们对僧人说,"我们挖一个洞直通山底,那会有多远?"他回答说有42丈,折算过来大约是120英尺。他想看看我们的双筒望远镜,但是不知道怎么用,所以看的时候拿反了。他很和气,知道很多上海的外国人的中文名,这些人都曾到访过他的寺庙。他也很好客,招待我们吃挂面和一道看似鱼皮的菜,后者很美味,不过我们当中有个人不喜欢吃。僧人的庙里有一座四柱钟,到了冬天还会在钟的下面放上铺盖和帘子。天冷的时候,他就端坐在那儿,一直醒着,直到凌晨3点,他会用一个绳子和竹子做成的精巧装置敲响那座钟。我并非怀疑他的诚实,但恕我直言,在外人看来,那温暖的床铺和舒适的帘子更容易让人呼呼大睡,而不是保持清醒。

从山上向下俯瞰,景色宜人,晴空万里,苏州附近的群山清晰可见。山顶上有座宝塔,和僧人的房子一样破败不堪,不过二者都正在修缮中。

此塔名为凌霄,建于约1 400年前,后被太平军摧毁。关于这座塔有个故事,据说一位皇帝为了履行病中许下的誓言,下令建造了这座宝塔;除此之外,他还在苏州建了另外两座塔。塔脚下有一座庙叫华藏寺。大约在半山腰上有一座七层的模型塔,也是一名生病的官员为了履行承诺而修建的。山的另一头还有座庙,据说有300年左右的历史,是一名教师建来供奉雷神的。这位教师因为附近没有雷神庙而感到痛心,便去找他的朋友筹款建庙。朋友们纷纷慷慨认捐,最终他的心愿得以实现。所谓善有善报,这位教师后来也被人们敬奉为神仙。根据庙里的塑像,雷神长着翅膀,还有一只鸟嘴。庙里供奉的另一位神仙是雷神的侍女,负责为他分开云层。

When Buddhist priest die they are cremated; they desire during life to disassociate themselves with the world, and after death crave annihilation. To effect this their bodies are burnt and on this hill are two pagoda shaped mounds which cover the ashes of two priests.

At one of the temples on this hill our boy buys some joss sticks and burns them before the idol, the priest calling the god's attention by striking a large bell. Having finished his devotions, the boy rises from his knees and throws a few cash into a box for the benefit of the god who is informed of the gift by the noisy manner in which the cash are dashed against the bars across the top of the box, which are so placed that the coin may make a noise when thrown against them. The Chinese believe that their gods sometimes go to sleep or are engaged in other business, so, like the mandarins who have a drum placed in the front court of their yamens for the benefit of petitioners who require their aid, the gods have to be called or awakened. If the god is asleep an empty travelling chair is sometimes procured and, take in hand by vigorous natives, is shaken up and down, causing the bamboo poles to creak loudly, the noise made being sufficiently loud to awaken the slumberer who is fond of a ride. While proceeding through some lakes on one occasion we saw a crowd of people on shore, and ascertained that the gathering was in honour of Lew Wong, the god of cotton and rice. The villagers had the god in a chair and were running backwards and forwards with it, because the idol was supposed to enjoy exercise and would reward its devotees by giving them plentiful grain and cotton crops. If they reward their idols, they also punish them occasionally and cases are on record of idols being taken out of temples and dragged through the mud when there has been too much rain, or placed in the blazing sun when there has been too much heat and no rain. On one occasion when a junk had been in collision with a steamer, the old woman in the junk administered a sound spanking to her idol as if it had been a naughty child.

At the foot of Quinsan hill there are some memorial halls and one of these is in charge of a family of four—father, mother, son and daughter—and for their services they receive two piculs and a half (three cwt.) of rice a year, payment being made in kind; this with the produce of a small vegetable garden, constituting the entire income of the family. With a people who can live so frugally as this, there ought not to be much want in China.

佛教僧人去世后会被火化；他们希望自己生前能脱离尘世，死后能湮灭无余。为了实现这个愿望，他们的尸体会被焚化。这座山上就有两个宝塔形的土堆，里面埋着两位僧人的骨灰。

在山上的一座庙里，我们的男仆买了几支香，在佛像前点燃了；僧人敲响了一座大钟，以引起神仙的注意。拜完佛后，男仆站了起来，往一个箱子里扔了些铜钱。这些钱是给神仙的，铜钱撞到箱子顶上的木条发出声响，这样神仙就知道了。中国人相信神仙有时候会去睡觉或是忙于其他事务，所以，就像官员们在衙门前院放个鼓来方便告状的人那样，神仙也是需要被召唤或者唤醒的。如果神仙睡着了，人们会找来一顶空轿子，让精力充沛的当地人抬着，拼命地上下摇晃。竹竿发出响亮的嘎吱声，这样就能唤醒喜欢乘轿子的神仙了。有一次，我们经过一些湖泊，看到岸上有一群人。后来我们了解到他们聚在一起是为了纪念棉米之神——刘王。村民们把神像放在轿子里，抬着它来来回回地跑。据说神仙喜欢这种运动，也会保佑信徒五谷丰登以示嘉奖。信徒不仅会奖励神仙，偶尔也会惩罚他们。有记录显示，如果雨水连绵不绝，神像会被放到庙外的泥浆里拖行；或者碰上天气炎热干旱，神像就会被放在烈日下暴晒。有一次，一艘帆船与另一艘轮船相撞，帆船上的老妇人便狠狠地打了神像一巴掌，仿佛神仙只是个淘气的孩子。

昆山脚下有一些祠堂，其中一座祠堂由一家四口——父亲、母亲、儿子和女儿——看管。这份工作让他们每年可以得到两担[1]半（3英担[2]）大米。这笔实物报酬再加上一个小菜园子的产出，就是一家人的全部收入了。中国人的生活如此简朴，想来他们的物质需求应该不会太多。

---

[1] 重量单位，100斤等于1担。
[2] 英美制重量单位，20英担为1吨。

CHAPTER VI

We return to our boat and are soon booming along, meeting boats laden with bullocks to supply the Shanghai market and in two hours we enter a creek remarkably straight after our recent experiences. Here a boatman calls out "Foreign gentleman, what is your honorable destination?" but such politeness we do not experience at the busy village of Tah E Ding, where the boys call out "Foreign devil, cut off your heads;" together with a perfect storm of abuse. Sometimes when on our journeys we have been called "Foreign Devil" we have retaliated by applying to our revilers a word, which though harmless in itself is mighty insulting to the person to whom it is addressed. A foreigner, while proceeding along an embankment, heard a young man say "Here comes a foreign devil." He did not reply till he was passing the youth when he paused and said "The foreign devil has come," and in evidence of this gave the youth a ringing box on the ear, which, together with the fright, rolled him off the embankment to the great amusement of his own countrymen who can enjoy a joke as well as anyone. Of course, the youth would not have called out in the first instance, had he known the foreigner understood Chinese, unless he had been in a crowd and could not have been recognized. If the foreigner gives a cutting answer, the natives say loud enough to be heard, "You are very clever," the object being to soften his resentment if he has any.

Just after passing E Ding, there is a lake, on the left hand side of the creek, called the Shah Hu, or "Sand Lake." The creek in which we are was formerly a part of it, but many years ago there was a rich man who had a son, so the story goes, who had to go to Soochow to pass his literary examination, but the lake was rough at times, and fearing his young hopeful might be drowned in rough weather, he built a dyke along the northern end of the lake, leaving a channel between it and E Ding, so that the water in this channel is comparatively smooth at all times. Since then the government have kept the dyke, or more properly speaking causeway, in repair.

We come to a number of people who seem to be very busy going backwards and forwards and soon find that they are engaged in making cotton cloth. A number of slight supports rest on the ground and a woman, with a carrying pole on her shoulder from which is suspended a frame in front of her and balanced behind by means of a stone weight, is walking along spreading over the supports

第六章

我们回到船上,不久就开始快速前行,路上遇到了几艘载满小公牛的货船,这些牛是专门供应上海市场的。两个小时后,我们驶入了一条小河。就我们最近的游历而言,这么笔直的河流并不多见。河上一个船工喊道:"洋先生,阁下要前往何方啊?"在繁忙的大夷亭[1]村,我们却没有得到这样的礼遇。那里的男孩们一边喊着"洋鬼子,砍掉你们的头",一边还破口大骂。有时,在路上听到别人喊"洋鬼子",我们也会回敬一句。回敬的词虽然本身没有恶意,但对对方来说却是极大的侮辱。一个外国人在堤岸上走着,突然听到一个年轻人说:"洋鬼子来了。"他没有搭话,而是走到年轻人旁边,停下来说,"洋鬼子来了。"这显然给了年轻人一记响亮的耳光,把他吓得滚下了河堤,大大地娱乐了看热闹的乡人。当然,如果年轻人知道这个外国人懂中文,他一开始是不会大喊的,除非他躲在人群中,不可能被认出来。如果外国人的回答很尖刻,当地人就会大声说:"你真聪明。"这样对方就算有什么不满,也会缓和下来。

刚过夷亭,在河的左岸有个湖泊,叫作沙湖。我们所航行的这条河流曾经是它的一部分。据说许多年前有位富人的儿子要去苏州赶考,可是湖面间或有狂风巨浪,富人担心自己年轻有为的儿子因大风浪而死,便沿着湖的北岸建了一座堤坝,在湖泊和夷亭之间形成一条通道,这样河道里的水就总能保持相对平静。从那以后,政府便经常修缮这条堤坝,或者更确切地说是这条堤道。

我们遇到了一群人,他们看起来正来来回回忙个不停,过了一会才发现原来是在织棉布。地上放着一些细小的支架,一个妇人肩上担着根

---

[1] 大夷亭,又称夷亭(E Ding),即唯亭。

the warp from some dozen spools of cotton attached to the frame and she puts one on mind of a spider spinning its web. The warp is some two hundred and thirty four feet long and there are nine hundred threads. As soon as these have all been spread on the supports, size is put on with brushes, two persons being employed in this operation, one of the brushes being underneath and the other above the threads and the two men hold the brushes between them. Occasionally a thread breaks and many women and girls, each with smaller spools of thread, are busy repairing the damage. The first operation begins early in the morning, so that before noon, the size is dry and the threads are wound around a small windlass, the sockets for which are ropes tied round the waists of two people. When this has been tightly rolled it is placed in the loom and a woman commences to make the cloth. She works the loom with her feet and the shuttle with her hands and can make three pieces of cloth a day, each piece being thirteen feet long. All the work from cotton picking to ginning, spinning, spooling and cloth making is done on the communist principle, the machinery being of the most primitive description, but where there are so many people employed, the work is done with considerable expedition.

Five hours and a half after leaving Quinsan, we reach Way Kow Tong and in half of an hour later anchor some distance below Soochow, as the night is dark and the navigation consequently dangerous. At 7 o'clock next morning we get underway, rain having fallen during the greater part of the night, and we soon reach the outskirts of the famous city of Soochow. Along the suburbs, which extend a long way from the city, we see large bamboo rafts, and poles and bamboos piled up on shore for building purposes, and pyramids of Soochow jars and baths. We stop at the N. E. gate, but afterwards send the boat round to the S. E. gate and into the city.

Soochow is the capital of the Kiangsu province and the residence of the futai or governor, the grain commissioner, the provincial treasurer, the provincial judge and several other high officials. Soochow is also a prefectural city and in it the students in the province assemble for the annual examinations by the showtai or literary chancellor. The examination hall which we visit looks at first sight like a large stable. We enter the building by the only gate there is to the place, and looking towards the opposite end, on both sides of us are stalls with a paved passage up the centre. This passage is roofed over with matting, while the stalls have a more substantial covering of tiles. The stalls are separated from each other

扁担，前面挂着个框架，后面靠一块石砣保持平衡。她来回走动，从框架上的几打线轴上抽出经线，然后把它们铺在支架上，看上去就像蜘蛛在织网。经线大约234英尺长，有900来根线。支架上铺好了经线后，就开始刷浆，这个活儿需要两个人手持刷帚操作，一个人刷下面，另一个人刷上面。有时候会断线，这时许多妇人和女孩就会用小线轴来进行修补。第一道工序一大早就开始了，所以在中午之前浆就能干。然后把线绕在一个小绞盘上，绞盘的孔中穿入绳索，再将绳索绑在两个人的腰上。待绞盘转紧后，将其置于织布机上，接着一个妇人便开始织布。她用脚操纵织布机，用手操纵梭子，一天能织三匹布，每匹约13英尺长。所有的工序，从采摘棉花到轧棉、纺纱、绕线，一直到织布，都是分工合作共同完成。机器虽然很原始，但因为使用了大量的人力，工作完成得相当迅速。

离开昆山五个半小时后，我们到达了外跨塘。又过了半小时，由于天色已晚，航行会有危险，我们便在苏州以南不远处抛锚停泊。雨下了大半夜，第二天早上7点我们继续航行，很快就抵达了苏州这座名城的郊区。沿着远离城市的郊区一路驶来，我们看到了大竹筏，岸上堆放着建筑用的杆子和竹子，还有叠成金字塔形的一堆堆苏州产的罐子和浴盆。我们在东北门停了下来，随后又把船绕到东南门进了苏州城。

苏州是江苏省的省城，江苏抚台（即巡抚）、粮道、布政使、按察使和其他几个高级官员皆在此地驻扎。苏州也是苏州府治所在地，全省的学子每年都要齐聚此地参加由学台（即学政）主持的考试。我们参观了贡院，乍一看觉得它像一个大马厩。整栋建筑只有一道门可以出入，进了大门，向另一端望去，两侧是一个个号舍，还有一条铺好的通道直达贡院中央。通道的屋顶上有茅草覆盖，号舍顶上则铺着更加结实的瓦片。号舍之间隔

by walls about four feet high. Each stall contains three tables running parallel to the partition walls, and each table consists of a wooden platform about twelve feet long and two feet wide, mounted on two upright slabs of stone and the seats or settles are similarly constructed. On the tables are pasted strips of yellow paper, each containing a number; there are six of these to each table, to correspond with the number of students whose names are supposed to be unknown to the literary chancellor, but whose essays are marked with the numbers on their tables. There are seventy stalls with three tables in each, so that there would be accommodation for 1,260 students; but in addition to the ordinary stalls, there are a few superior ones with brick floors—the others having only a flooring of mud—nearer the chancellor's desk, so that there is room for about 200 more. The examiner has his seat at the upper end of the building, that is furthest from the gate, which is closed directly all the students have entered and not opened again till their work is done. At night the chancellor gives out the theme from the "Four Books," and it is written on a board which an attendant carries round for the students to copy off. Then they all set to work to write a dissertation on the subject. They are not supposed to receive assistance in any shape or form, but a Chinaman's sleeves are capacious and so is his ingenuity in a case like this; thus the students are able to smuggle into the hall a miniature or "sleeve" edition, as it is called by the Chinese, of the "Four Books," copies of which are openly sold in Shanghai. As the students are not allowed to go outside the building during each examination, which lasts only one day, they take their day's food in with them. At night, the essays are collected and the students are dismissed. Then the chancellor has a hard task before him in examining the treatises. Many are thrown out, while the writers of those that are accepted have to undergo a second examination. The same process is adopted here as in the first case, the writers of the best essays passing a final examination, and from this last batch are selected those who are honoured with the B.A. degree. Then during the 8th moon every third year, the successful students undergo examinations at the capital of the viceroyalty, for the second degree in the same way that they competed for the third. Finally those who succeed go to Peking where the first or highest honours are conferred, the same process of weeding prevailing there as at the other examinations. Sometimes a competitor dies while locked up in the examination hall; in this case a coffin is provided and the corpse is taken out through a hole made in the wall, or it is lifted over the wall, but on no account must it be taken out through

着大约4英尺高的墙壁。每个号舍可以放三张桌子,与隔墙平行摆放。每张桌子都由一块大约12英尺长、2英尺宽的木板装在两块竖立的石板上组成,座位的构造也是如此。桌上糊着黄纸,每张纸上写着一个号码;每张桌上贴有6个号码,对应了桌上的考生人数。考生的文章都以桌上的号码作为标记,这样学政就不会知道他的姓名。每个号舍有三张桌子,一共70个号舍,可以容纳1260名考生。除了普通的号舍外,靠近学政办公桌的地方还有一些铺着地砖的高级号舍(其他号舍都是泥地),因此还能容纳200名左右的考生。考官的座位在贡院的上首,离大门最远。所有考生进入考场后,大门立即关闭,直到考试结束才会开启。到了晚上,学政公布了出自"四书"的题目之后,随从会捧着写有题目的木板在考生间来回走动,让他们抄下试题。然后考生便开始围绕这个主题写文章。他们本不应该借助任何形式的帮助,不过中国人的袖子很大,他们的脑洞也很大,所以考生会偷偷地把微型版的"四书",即他们所谓的"袖珍本",带进考场,这种"袖珍本"在上海可以公开售卖。由于考试持续一整天,考生中途不得走出考场,所以他们会随身携带一天的食物。晚上,文章收齐后,考生离场。紧接着学政开始繁重的阅卷工作。许多考生会落榜,而那些上榜的考生还要参加第二场考试。和上一场考试的过程一样,文章做得好的人才能通过,最后被筛选出来的人获得秀才头衔。然后每三年的农历八月份,这些人赶往省城参加乡试,以同样的方式去角逐举人的头衔。最后,那些中举的人前往北京,在那儿按照同样的筛选方式,去争取最高的荣誉。如果关在贡院里的考生突然去世,这种情况下会给他提供一具棺材,但是尸体绝对不能经由唯一的大门抬出。要么在墙上打洞,把遗体从洞中运出来;

the front and only gateway. All Chinese cannot compete at the examinations, and when a candidate comes forward he must be able to prove that for three generations back his ancestors have not been barbers, play actors, yamen runners or the offspring of mesalliances.

Soochow contains five pagodas. Two are close together and not very high, but are surmounted by what appear to be inverted iron pans. Two others are of the regulation kind, while the fifth is a most unorthodox structure and is square instead of round, in fact it can hardly be called a pagoda at all. It is of recent construction comparatively and has the following history. It appears that the district where this pagoda is, was troubled by its feng-shui being out of kilter, and in consequence the unfortunate students belonging to the district who went up to the annual literary examinations were incontinently plucked. This was a disgrace which the people could not stand, so having implicit faith in their youthful prodigies, and feeling that they were not to blame, the elders came to the conclusion that something was wrong, and consulted a fortune-teller. This worthy was equal to the occasion. He knew all about it, and had he been consulted before, he could have put things to rights. It was a very simple matter too, at that, the fact being that the twin pagodas mentioned above represented pen·pencils, and the numerous creeks contained water, so they had pens and water, but no ink! How then could it be possible to write without this necessary article? They must have something to represent a slab of ink! Well, they soon had, for they went to work and built a pagoda somewhat after the shape of a slab of ink, and to heighten the resemblance, they painted it black. In consequence of this the equilibrium of the feng-shui has been restored and the students have since been able to obtain their degrees, so that it is not true, at least in China, that there is no royal road to learning. This pagoda was burnt out several years ago.

When H. E. Chang Chih-tung, viceroy of the Hu Kwang provinces, built his iron works, he naturally had some tall chimneys. These were not looked upon with favour, and a man living near to one of them, falling ill and all remedies failing to cure him, a fortune-teller gravely stated that the high chimneys of the factory were to blame. One of the magistrates, hearing of this, sent for the fortune-teller, and informed him with the aid of a little judicious application of the bamboo that he was mistaken in his prognostications. Since then high chimneys have been in favour in this locality, especially as since their erection, a dull-headed scholar, who had repeatedly failed before, has been able to pass with

要么就从墙上抬出来。不是所有的中国人都能参加科举考试,考生报考时,必须证明祖上三代没有人当过剃头匠、唱戏的或衙役,祖上婚配也无不妥。

苏州城里有五座宝塔。其中两座挨得很近,塔身并不是很高,塔顶看上去像两个倒扣的铁锅。另外两座塔的外观很普通,最不寻常的是第五座塔,是个方形塔而不是圆形塔。事实上,我们很难称其为宝塔。它的修建年份比较近,还流传着这样一个传说。宝塔所在的地方似乎曾经风水不大好,参加岁试的学子都很倒霉,无缘无故就是通过不了。这让当地的居民颜面尽失,难以接受。不过长者们对年轻人的才华深信不疑,觉得问题不在他们身上,他们断定一定有什么地方不对劲,便去问询算命先生。这对算命先生而言易如反掌,他知道怎么回事,如果之前就来向他咨询,问题可能早就解决了。这事儿说来也很简单,前面提到的双塔代表了笔,而很多河水又象征着水,所以他们有笔有水,却没有墨!那么问题来了,没有墨这件必需品,怎么可能写出文章呢?他们得找个什么东西来代表墨才行!好吧,他们很快就找到了,因为他们马上就着手造了一座形似墨的宝塔。为了加强两者的相似度,他们还把塔涂成了黑色。就这样,风水恢复了平衡,学子们从此以后也能获取功名了。所以说,"学习没有捷径"这种说法是不对的,至少在中国并非如此。这座宝塔几年前被烧毁了。

湖广总督张之洞建了一座铁厂,自然就有了一些高大的烟囱。这些烟囱可不怎么招人待见。有个住在烟囱附近的男子病倒了,怎么也治不好,一个算命先生严肃地指出,铁厂里高高的烟囱就是罪魁祸首。一位知县听说了这件事,就派人去把算命先生找来,打了他几竹板,让他明白自己的预言说错了。从那以后,当地人看这些高高的烟囱就没那么不顺眼了。特别是在烟囱建成以后,一个之前屡次科举失败的呆书生居然高分通过了考试,这更让人们对烟囱另眼相看。

flying colors.

The pagoda which is situated in the N.E. of the city, is the largest in China, is a very fine one, and is called the Po Su Tah. It has nine stories and is one hundred and fifty feet high to the top floor which is reached by two hundred and twenty eight steps. There are niches in the walls for one hundred and sixty images, though not more than one hundred are occupied, the place of honour being filled by Kwan Ying, and we find the people in charge of the pagoda have just as much inclination to "squeeze" the wayfarer as the rest of their countrymen have. A native lets us into the building and locks the door when we leave. Our servant is carrying a thousand cash on his shoulder and when he takes a hundred cash from his string and gives them to the doorkeeper, the greedy native wants a hundred more, which, however, he does not get.

In our travels we come across the scene of a recent fire and as the streets are narrow and the workmen have no other place to put the debris, the road is piled up some ten feet high with the remains of the old walls and the foundations of the burnt houses. In a temple where there are a lot of gods we see the Queen of Heaven riding on a phoenix and a god with two arms and hands sticking out of his eyes. Of course, there are numerous temples in Soochow, and we visit what may be considered a double one. It is called the Yuen Miao and each part of it contains idols in plenty. We are struck with the scene presented here as elsewhere in China, as being so much like that depicted in the Bible story at the Temple at Jerusalem, nearly nineteen hundred years ago. Here, in this Chinese temple, are stalls where all kinds of commodities are being sold, while, in the inmost courts, in company with idols, are thousands of water colour pictures exposed for sale. Some represent san shui, that is "mountains and water" or scenery; happy family relations—fathers, sons and grandsons in groups, young wives in flowing garments nursing two infant sons; other pictures representing some of the gods and mythological subjects, while painters are busy finishing other pictures. In the front building there are three large idols of the "Three Precious Ones," of the Buddhist trinity, each over twenty feet high and made of clay and mud gorgeously painted. This temple was repaired by the late Wu Sing An, the well-known Hangchow banker, at a cost of eighteen thousand taels, and foreign science was brought into requisition, for the roof and wooden pillars, the latter over two feet in diameter, were bodily raised some feet by the aid of foreign screw jacks. In the courts at the sides of the big idols are sixty small idols, each being five feet high

位于苏州城东北处的北寺塔是中国最大的宝塔，造型秀美挺拔。塔高九层，顶层离地150英尺，要爬228级台阶才能抵达。塔内有很多壁龛，可以容纳160尊佛像，但是现有的佛像不足一百，供奉的都是观音。我们发现看管这座塔的人就像他们的同乡一样，很想"敲诈"游客。一个当地人让我们进了塔，可是当我们要离开时，他却把门给锁上了。我们的仆人肩上背了一千文铜钱，他从绳子上取下一百文给了看门人，这个贪婪的家伙还想再要一百文，不过我们没有给他。

旅途中我们路过了一个最近发生过火灾的地方。街道很是狭窄，工人们没有地方放垃圾，所以被烧毁的房屋的旧墙砖和残余地基就堆在马路上，大概有十英尺高。在一座供奉了很多神仙的庙宇里，我们看到了骑在凤凰上的王母和眼睛里长出两条胳膊、两只手的神仙。当然，苏州有很多寺庙，不过我们参观的这座庙规模宏大，可以说是其他寺庙的两倍。它的名字叫作圆妙观[1]，每个殿里都有很多神像。和中国其他地方一样，这里的景象让我们印象深刻，它很像圣经故事中描述的近1 900年前耶路撒冷的圣殿。这座中国庙宇里摆满了售卖各种商品的摊位，而在最里面的大殿中，与那些神像陈列在一起的，是数千幅公开出售的水彩画。有些是描绘风景的山水画；有些是展现幸福家庭的亲情画——祖孙三代齐聚一堂，年轻的妻子衣袂飘飘，怀里抱着两个襁褓中的婴儿；有些则是神仙和神话题材绘画。还有些画家们正忙着画其他东西。前面的大殿里面有三尊巨大的佛教"三清"神像[2]，每尊神像高逾20英尺，都是泥塑彩绘。已故著名的杭州银行家胡雪岩曾耗资一万八千两白银重修了这座庙宇。修建过程中使用了外国技术，把屋顶和直径超过两英尺的木柱都用进口的螺纹千斤顶抬高了几英尺。大殿中，大神像的两边有60尊小神像，每尊5英尺高，极其丑陋，

---

[1] 即玄妙观。清代，为避康熙皇帝的名讳，改玄妙观为圆妙观，又名元妙观。民国后才恢复玄妙观的旧称。

[2] 玄妙观是道教庙宇，这里提到的神像是观中三清殿供奉的三清像，并非佛教神像。

and very ugly, representing the Chinese cycle. According to a person's age he worships one of the images, though some of the idols do duty for two years, for after the devotee has reached the end of the cycle, he has to commence again to worship the first images in it. In the rear of this building are the residences of the priests from which proceed the monotonous knocking on a wooden "fish head" bell, if such a term can be applied to the implement. One of the Soochow temples is said to contain five thousand idols; if anybody undertook to count them, it is not improbable that the number would be found to be considerably less, as we do not see anything like this number in the building.

CHAPTER VII

Stone appears to be more plentiful than wood at Soochow for the fences along the creeks are built of the former material, as are nearly all of the bridges, and of course the pailous. One of the streets in Soochow is called the "Dragon Protecting" Street, and at each end of it there is a pagoda; one represents the head and the other the tail of this peculiarly Chinese reptile which is buried or lies asleep under it. It is for this reason that the inhabitants will not pave this street with stone slabs, as they do in other parts of the city, because if they did they might hurt the creature's back, though they compromise matters by hardening the surface with stone chips and broken pottery. Outside the south west gate there is an eddy; this, we are told is where the dragon is coiled up, so that it has been reserved for Soochowites to demonstrate that the same thing can occupy two different places at one time. Near the south west gate inside the city is the Tsang Lang Garden with a large building which has gradually grown to its present extensive proportions. In this building is a place called the "Hall of Five Hundred Worthies," containing the portraits of that number of Soochowites who have become celebrated, while slabs of slate with inscriptions cut in them are let into the walls and give some account of the aforesaid worthies. On one of our visits to Soochow in 1885, there was one portrait wanting, namely that of Mr. Stevens, the then United States consul at Ningpo, who was at the time of this visit on official business and was staying in the building. It is worthy of note that he was the first consul who had ever visited Soochow officially. In addition to the other ornaments of the place, we saw the Stars and Stripes displayed in the building to denote the consul's residence there. We had seen this identical flag before

代表着中国农历的一甲子。人们可以根据自己的年龄参拜其中某尊神像,不过有些神像会代表两个年龄,因为他们的信徒在年满六十岁之后,就要重新从第一尊神像开始参拜。大殿后面是僧侣的住所,从那儿传来单调的敲木鱼的声音。据说苏州有一座庙宇,里面有五千神像;如果有人去数的话,可能会发现实际数目要小得多,至少在这座庙里我们并没有看到这么多神像。

第七章

在苏州,石头似乎比木头多。河边的栏杆都是用石头制作而成,大部分的桥是石桥,当然,牌楼也是石头做的。苏州有一条街叫"护龙"街,街道两端各有一座宝塔;一座代表龙首,一座代表龙尾,龙这种中国特有的爬行动物就埋在下面,当然也可能是在此地沉睡。正是由于这个原因,这里的居民不像本城其他地方的居民那样用石板铺路,因为如果这样做,可能会伤害到龙的背部,所以他们采用了一种折中的方式——用碎石片和破陶片来加固路面。苏州城西南门外有一处漩涡;有人告诉我们,那条龙也在此处盘旋,所以苏州人以此来证明一个神迹,同一个生物会在两个不同的地方同时出没。城内近西南门处有座园林,名为沧浪亭。此园规模颇大,经过逐年扩建而成。园内有座"五百名贤祠",祠中存有五百名吴地名人的画像,墙上嵌着刻有碑文的石板,上面写着前述名贤的生平简介。说起吴地名人,我们在 1885 年游览苏州时,时任美国驻宁波领事的司提文先生(Mr. Stevens)算得上一个,当时他正因公务在此逗留。值得一提的是,他是第一位来苏州公干的领事。除了原有的装饰以外,我们还看到园内悬挂着星条旗,显示有领事在此驻扎。我们以前在上海见过同样的旗帜,但从没想到会在苏州一座中式建筑的门

in Shanghai, but never expected to find it hoisted over the door of a Chinese building in Soochow.

We will explain how it came about that an American consul had business in Soochow. According to treaty as generally understood missionaries are allowed to buy the lease of land in the interior and the two Presbyterian missions purchased land in Soochow and commenced to build thereon. One piece of land was situated near the Confucian temple and the other close to the yamen of the imperial tailor, as he is called by foreigners. This official is the imperial commissioner whose duty it is to forward to the palace, annually, the provincial contributions of silk, satin, handkerchiefs, silk thread, etc. for which this place is celebrated. He ranks with a futai, and has all the honours attaching to such rank, but without the emoluments and authority. Some of his underlings objected to a foreign mission being so close to them, though they did not object to a colony of beggars; but foreigners—the very thought was contamination. Consequently they prevailed on their master, under the plea that the mission buildings would overlook his back yard and interfere with the privacy of his establishment, to order the work at the mission to cease at once. The authorities also stopped the operations at the other mission. The missionaries after vainly endeavouring to induce the authorities to allow them to proceed with their buildings, applied to Mr. Stahel, the United States consul-general at Shanghai, and he deputed Mr. Stevens, United Sates consul at Ningpo, to arrange matters. The Soochow authorities said the missionaries could have other pieces of land if they could find anyone willing to sell. Well, the missionaries did find people willing to sell, but the mandarins made many excuses and so delayed matters so that after fourteen days, the consul's patience was almost exhausted as the land was not transferred, though in the end the affair was settled.

The missionary hospital authorities sometimes have to deal with patients suffering from gunshot wounds inflicted by soldiers while at target practice. The soldiers are very careless; in one case at Soochow, a lad was badly wounded on the left foot, and in another a man was killed instantly by a bullet passing through his head, while in a third, a man had his shoulders shattered by a small cannon ball. It is not to be wondered at, however, that boys sometimes got wounded, as anybody can see for himself if he happens to watch native soldiers at target practice. The boys rush in to the mound or target to find the bullets that have just been fired, and the soldiers have the greatest difficulty in driving them away. The

上看到它。

我们来解释一下，一位美国领事怎么会到苏州公干。根据我们通常对条约的理解，传教士是可以在中国租借土地的。两个长老会传教团在苏州买了地开始建造教堂。其中一块地位于孔庙附近，另一块则靠近织造衙门（外国人称其为"皇室裁缝"）。织造是皇帝的钦差，负责每年为宫中采办本省的丝绸、缎子、手帕、丝线等贡品，苏州也正是因这些物件而闻名的。织造位同抚台，享有与之匹配的一切荣誉，但是俸禄和权力不一样。苏州织造的一些下属反对与外国传教士为邻，却不介意门前聚集一群乞丐；因为他们觉得外国人就是祸害。因此，他们说动了上司，以教堂会俯瞰衙门后院、干涉衙门隐私为借口，命令教堂立即停止施工。另一个教堂也被当局勒令停工。传教士们竭力劝说当局允许他们继续施工，但却徒劳无功。他们向美国驻上海总领事司塔立先生（Mr. Stahel）求助，司塔立先生便委托美国驻宁波领事司提文先生前来协商此事。苏州当局声称，如果传教士能找到愿意出手的卖家，他们可以购买其他的土地。好吧，传教士确实找到了愿意出售土地的人，但官员们又找了很多借口拖延，过了14天都没有办好土地转让手续。这几乎耗尽了领事的耐心，好在最后事情解决了。

教会医院有时还得处理病人的枪伤，这些枪伤都是练习射击的士兵造成的。士兵们很是粗心大意。有一次在苏州，一个男孩的左脚受了重伤；另一次，一个男子被子弹击穿头部当场毙命；还有一次，一名男子被一发小型炮弹击碎了肩膀。不过，这实在是不足为奇，要是有谁碰巧看过当地士兵练习打靶，就会明白为什么有时候会伤到这些人了。男孩们冲进训练场，到土堆或是靶子那儿去捡刚刚射出的子弹，士兵们根本赶不走他们。

Chinese have a fable which pokes fun at the soldiers for their want of skill in hitting the target. A general was in danger of losing a battle when a spiritual army came to his assistance and gave him the day; and on the victorious general asking the leader of the host why he had so honoured a mortal, he was informed that his ally was the God of the Target and had given his assistance out of gratitude to the soldier who, during all the years of his practice, had never hit the target. This, however, does not agree with the statements of inspecting officers, who usually inform the emperor that, having obeyed the imperial command to inspect certain troops, they have found some seventy per cent or thereabouts of the soldiers hit the target, which is usually placed about a hundred yards distant. According to the paper strength of the army there are five hundred men in each battalion, and one hundred men in each company. There are ten tents in each company, and each tent contains ten men.

In connection with the temples, we must not forget to mention one which was some time ago in a very dilapidated condition. A fortune-teller informed the then futai that if he did not have the repairs effected, some misfortune or family affliction would happen to him, so the official gave orders to have the necessary work done; but he was too late, and his mother dying soon afterwards, that is before the work was completed, he had to retire into mourning for three years, which period according to a convenient fiction is frequently reduced to twenty-seven months during which the mourner is not allowed to shave his head; he is, however, allowed to cut his hair close with a pair of scissors.

While passing along one of the streets, we come to a temple where some kind of ceremony is going on. We enter and find that the place is dedicated to one of the Gods of Riches, and the services are being conducted by a Taoist priest who is dressed in a most gorgeous robe of scarlet and gold. In his hand he holds a piece of wood about six inches long, three broad and one inch thick with which he is making passes after the style of professors of legerdemain, and at the same time repeating some cabalistic formula, first slowly, and then rapidly, as if he has a hot potato in his mouth and not another moment to live. Occasionally he knocks the piece of wood or his wand on the table in front of him, and this is the signal for a drum and two other instruments of torture to be beaten. This gives the priest time to drink a little tea, which he does frequently. In the midst of the din we are able to ascertain that the performance is paid for by a man who wants his last year's sins forgiven. This is rather an anomaly, for at the temples of the Gods

中国人有个寓言故事，嘲笑士兵们的射击水平差。有位将军快要打败仗了，这时一支神兵前来助战，帮他扭转了战局。获胜的将军问神兵首领，自己一介凡人，为何如此荣幸可以得其襄助。对方声称是靶神，因为将军多年来训练时都没射中过靶子，所以特意前来表示感谢。不过这可跟那些监察官们说的不一样。他们奉皇帝旨意视察军队后，通常回禀皇帝，他们发现大约70%的士兵能命中100码远的靶子。根据中国军队的军力报告，500人为一营，100人为一队。每队有10棚，每棚有10人。

说到庙宇，有一座庙我们不得不提。不久之前这座庙还很破旧，一个算命先生告诉当时的抚台，如果他不把庙修好，就会遭遇一些不幸或是家族灾难。于是这位官员下令进行必要的修缮工作。不过他还是迟了一步，他的母亲不久之后就去世了，这时修缮工作还没完成，他就不得不辞官守孝三年。根据惯例，孝期通常可以减少到27个月。服丧的人在守孝期间不能剃头；不过，他可以用剪刀把自己的头发剪短。

我们穿过一条街道，来到了一座寺庙前，这里正在举行某种仪式。我们进庙后才发现这地方供奉着某位财神，仪式的主持人是一位身着红色长袍的道士，袍上有金线刺绣，极其华丽。他手里拿着一块大约6英寸长、3英寸宽、1英寸厚的木头，像变戏法一样挥来挥去，同时嘴里重复念着一些神秘的咒语，先慢后快，好像嘴里有一块滚烫的山芋，一刻也停不下来。他不时地用这块木头或者说魔杖敲打面前的桌子，这是在发出信号，让人开始击鼓和敲打另外两个发出难听声音的乐器。这样道士就可以时不时地抽空喝口茶。在一片嘈杂声中，我们大致判断出这场仪式是一名男子出钱办的，他希望自己过去一年所犯的罪过能够得到宽恕。这可有点反常，因为在财神庙里，信徒们应该只会祈求财富而已。

of Riches the devotees are only supposed to pray for wealth.

We must not forget to mention that there are a great many feng-shui or ying pe or "shadow walls" in front of the principal doors of the houses of people in Soochow who pretend to any importance. These walls are intended to ward off the evil influences from the houses, and at the same time show the common people that the owners consider themselves the elite of the place. Among the charitable institutions are two refuges, one being for old and destitute men, and the other for widows. These are very large establishments, and are outside the city as are the stables of the horses used in the government courier service.

Just before leaving the city we see a large number of glazed earthenware urns, some round and others eight-sided, for holding the remains of dead people. Some of these urns have images of bald headed Buddhas and dogs on them.

Having heard that there is a celebrated bridge some seven le beyond the city, we decide to pay it a visit and after an hour's sail see in the distance what we soon find is the object of our quest. It is nearly dusk when we reach it, but it is possible to obtain a good view of this celebrated bridge which is called the Pow Tah Jao or "Precious Girdle Bridge," and it is situated at a place called Wu Kiang, locally Ung Kong or the "Five Rivers," for five large creeks meet here. At one end of the bridge there is a stone slab under a roof and on it, it is stated that the bridge is the high way to Peking from various parts of the empire. It also contains a caution to travellers to beware of robbers, the locality having a bad reputation in this respect. There are stone lions at each end of the bridge, one is nursing a cub and the other holding a tortoise. There are also two dummy pagodas, one eight sided and five stories high, with forty figures in relief, at one end of the bridge, while the other is in the water alongside the bridge about half way across. The bridge itself is noted for this peculiarity that in counting the arches there is a difference in the number, for if you count one way you will find fifty two, if from the other end, fifty three, the latter number being correct. The popular superstition about this is that when a joss was asked how many arches there were, he said fifty two, fifty three, evidently not knowing which was correct himself. Fifty two of the arches are of the same size, the other one being much larger and higher so that large junks can go through from the Tan Te Hu or "Tranquil Terrace Lake," across the entrance of which the bridge is built, the bridge running paralled to the creek.

Having read the notice on the slab with reference to robbers, our boatmen

值得一提的是，在苏州，凡是自诩有些身份的人，房子正门前都建有风水壁，或者叫影壁。这些影壁的作用是为了阻挡院外的鬼邪之气，同时也向普通百姓表明，房主自认为是精英阶层。苏州的善堂中有两个收容所，一个收容老人和贫民，另一个收容寡妇。它们设在苏州城外，规模很大，同样在城外的还有政府驿站的马厩。

离开苏州城之前，我们看到了大量的釉面陶制骨灰瓮，有圆形的，也有八边形的，用来存放死者的遗骸。有些瓮上还绘有光头佛像和狗的图案。

听说城外七里左右有座桥很出名，我们决定前去游览一番。坐了一个小时的船后，我们就远远地发现了此行的目标。我们到达时已近黄昏，但还是可以清楚地看到这座著名的"宝带桥"的全貌。这座桥坐落在一个叫吴江的地方，当地人读作 Ung Kong，意思是五条江，即有五条大江在这里汇合。桥的一端有块石碑置于亭中，据石碑记载，这座桥是全国各地通往北京的驿道。它还警告旅行者当心强盗，当地在这方面名声不太好。桥的两端各有一个石狮，一个抱着头幼狮，另一个抓着一只乌龟。还有两座模型塔，一座位于桥头，五级八面，塔上有 40 个浮雕人物；而另一座则浸在桥中段的水中。这座桥有个独特之处，就是从不同方向数，桥孔的数量是不一样的。如果从这端数，你会数出 52 个桥孔，但是换成另一端，又会发现有 53 个，第二个数字才是正确的。关于桥洞还流传着这么一个传说，说有位大佛被问到这座桥有多少桥孔时，他答道 52、53，显然他自己也不知道哪个数字是正确的。其中的 52 个桥洞大小相同，另一个则要大得多、高得多，这样从澹台湖开来的大船就可以从桥下通行无阻了。这座宝带桥横跨澹台湖口，与大运河平行。

看到石碑上有小心强盗的通告后，我们的船家和仆人不愿意继续前进。

and servant do not want to proceed and we are so informed by a deputation of three while waiting on the far end of the bridge, for them to come on. They ask to be allowed to stop and have taken the boat to the inner side of the bridge close to a mandarin gunboat, the sailors of which had at first refused to allow them to remain there, but offered no objection when the priest in charge of the Pow Tah Jao Ung Miao, the "Precious Girdle Bridge Military Temple" said they could remain.

We had on arrival visited this priest whose card shows that he is called Ven Shing or "Literary Star," and had left the usual douceur in his hands, but while returning with our men to the boat, he meets us again and asks us to go with him to his temple as he has some nice things to show us and we promise to do so after having dined. By this time it is dark, but we keep our promise and proceeding to the temple find the abbot and two others indulging in what has a suspicious resemblance to pork. We give him some bread and tell him to finish his meal, while we look round. He soon joins us, as do a number of uncouth spoken soldiers belonging to the gunboat whose rough way of speaking grates on our ears, not that they mean to be rude, but one cannot expect politeness from such people, though one sometimes gets it. The abbot, we find to be a most jolly and affable old fellow. He answers all our questions to the best of his knowledge and belief, like a willing witness and he runs on with his story as if he is delighted to have somebody to listen to him, and this reminds us he is minus the upper lobe of his right ear. He says there is not much "old time talk" about the place; all he knows is that the bridge was built some three hundred years ago by order of an emperor, and that it is a third of a le long. We find that the bridge itself is four hundred paces long, but there is a causeway at each end extending some distance. The abbot tells us the bridge is kept in repair by the local authorities, and has only recently been done up. As it is the highway to Peking from so many places in the south, there is no wonder that the temple itself should also become a celebrated place of resort and the priest shows us, with evident delight, some antithetical sentences and scrolls that have been presented by great men, such as Le Hung Chang, and others. The old fellow is a bit of a painter and shows us some of his scenery pictures.

The temple is dedicated to Kwan Te, the God of War, but there are other idols in it. Our loquacious friend shows us some smaller images, one of them being a bronze image of Indra, of foreign manufacture, and he says it is very

我们在桥的另一端等船过来时，船上派了三个人来通知我们。他们要求在此停泊，而且已经把船开到了桥的内侧，靠近一艘官方炮艇。炮艇上的水手们最初不让他们在那停靠，后来还是宝带桥武庙的住持发话让他们留下来，水手们这才没有了异议。

我们一到那儿就拜访了这位住持，他的名片上写着法号"文星"，按惯例我们给了他一些赏钱。我们带着仆人一起回船的途中，又遇见了他，他便邀请我们一道去庙里，说是有一些好东西要给我们观赏。我们答应他吃完晚饭后过去。这时天色已晚，但我们还是依约去了庙里，发现住持和另外两个人正在吃疑似猪肉的东西。我们送给他一些面包，让他先吃完饭，我们先四处看看。不久后他就赶了上来，同样加入我们的还有一些说话粗俗的炮艇士兵。这些士兵的说话方式让我们感到刺耳，他们并不是有意冒犯，但我们不能指望这些人能有什么礼貌，当然有些时候他们也会讲些礼貌。我们发现这位住持为人风趣且和蔼可亲。他尽其所知，尽其所信，回答了我们所有的问题，好像一个心甘情愿的证人。他滔滔不绝地讲述自己的故事，像是很高兴有人倾听，这也让我们发现他的右耳少了一块上耳垂。他说，这个地方没有多少旧事；他只知道这座桥大约是在300年前奉皇帝的旨意建造的，桥长约三分之一里。我们发现桥本身约有400步长，但是两端还有堤道，所以还延伸了一段距离。住持告诉我们，这座桥由当地政府负责维修，最近才修好。因为这座桥是南方各地通往北京的交通要道，所以难怪这座寺庙也成了一个著名的旅游胜地。这位僧人欣欣然地给我们展示了一些包括李鸿章在内的大人物题赠的对联和卷轴。这个老伙计有点画画的本事，还给我们看了几幅他画的风景画。

这座寺庙供奉的是战神关帝，不过里面还有其他的神像。我们健谈的朋友给我们看了一些小神像，其中一个是外国制造的因陀罗铜像。他说铜

在华度假记事

old, we are afraid to say how old. We naturally admire such a relic, whereupon he unconditionally makes us a present of it, notwithstanding our protest, but he not only renews his request that we shall take it, but gives us an image of one of the Gods of Wealth with its wealth-finding tiger. Such kindness as this is overpowering, and we tell him we cannot take them, but he says he has thirteen others of the God of Wealth "inside," so we accept his gift and at parting make him a present. He also gives us four joss sticks tied together on which were the characters meaning "year by year, peace and tranquility." When asked how he obtained his appointment to the temple he said that he was a countryman of a Shanghai taotai, who when in office gave him the place some twenty odd years ago. He used to receive a monthly allowance of ten thousand five hundred cash from the futai at Soochow, but that was stopped a long time ago, and he now depends for support on the benefactions of visitors and the proceeds of begging expeditions to the city of Soochow.

With regard to the mandarin gunboat in front of his door, its crew of thirteen men live in the temple in the daytime, but sleep on board at night, a new boat being sent each month to relieve the one on guard. We find that the captain of the gunboat is an opium smoker, and is engaged with his pipe when we call upon him. Our friend the abbot is also a votary to the drug, and has his pipe in his bedroom.

On returning to our boat one of our men tells us there is a story connected with the bridge, as follows: —It appears that an emperor desired a certain mandarin to send his son to him as he wished to see him. The mandarin replied that the boy was too ill to travel, but the emperor would accept no excuses and the son was sent, but got no further than where the bridge is now, for he died there. In commemoration of the unhappy event, the emperor caused the bridge to be built.

We return to Soochow which we leave again by the south east water gate and having entered the Grand Canal, pass Fung Jao with a peculiar grove of straight stemmed trees and a tombstone resting on the back of a stone tortoise under a shed of the same material. Next we come to Shih Tu and a great crowd are collected on the bridge to see us go under it. We pass a large tea shop with a babel of voices and soon afterwards there is an exchange of unparliamentary language between our boat men and the lowdah of an obstructionist boat and some boys call out "Foreign devil, give us some cash," but it is needless to

像非常古老,不过我们不敢说出它有多老。我们当然欣赏这样的文物,于是他打算无条件地把它赠送给我们。尽管我们谢绝了他的好意,但他不仅坚持要我们收下,还给了我们一座带有寻宝虎的财神像。这样的好意让我们承受不起,我们告诉他我们不能拿走这些神像,但他说他"里面"还有另外13座财神像,所以我们接受了他的礼物,并在分别时给了他一份回礼。他还送给我们一束香,共有四根,上面写着"岁岁平安"。当问到他怎么会到这座庙里来当住持时,他说他原是上海一个道台的同乡,这位道台20多年前在任时把他派到这儿来的。他以前每个月都能从苏州抚台那领到10 500文铜钱的补贴,但那是很久之前的事了,现在他只能靠游客捐助和自己到苏州化缘来维持生计。

至于他门前的那艘官府炮艇,船上有13名船员,他们白天待在庙里,晚上睡在船上,每个月都有一艘新的炮艇被派来换岗。我们发现炮艇的船长吸食鸦片,我们前去拜访的时候,他正在忙着弄烟枪。我们的这位住持朋友也是毒品的忠实信徒,他的烟枪就放在卧室里。

回到船上后,一个仆人告诉我们,关于这座桥还有个故事:相传有位皇帝想让某个官员把儿子送过来给他瞧瞧。官员回答说,他的孩子病得太厉害,不能远行。但皇帝不接受任何借口,最后官员的儿子还是出发了,可是才走到今天这座桥附近他就死了。为了纪念这一不幸的事件,皇帝便下令建造了这座桥。

我们回到苏州城,然后再次从东南方的水门离开,进入大运河。船经过了枫桥,那儿有一片别致的树林,林中树木笔直挺拔,还有一座石亭,内立一块墓碑置于石龟背上。接下来我们到了射渎,一大群人聚集在桥上,围观我们从桥下通过。我们经过一个人声鼎沸的大茶馆,之后不久,我们的船工就和一个故意找碴儿的船老大发生了口角。还有些孩子大声喊叫:"洋

remark that we don't. As we get clear of the place the country becomes more wooded and mulberry trees about five feet high are numerous. Stone laden boats go by bearing small yellow flags denoting that they are engaged repairing the embankments of the Canal and we soon arrive at the suburbs of Woo Se where there are a lot of brick kilns in operation. Chinese bricks which consist entirely of mud without any straw are not baked very hard and consequently are porous to a considerable extent. The kilns are circular, about twenty feet high and fired with straw, each batch of bricks requiring three days and three nights continuous firing. Idiotic beggars and mosquitoes abound about here but do not trouble us.

鬼子，给我们点钱。"不用说，我们当然一文钱都没给。我们离开此地后，乡间的树木变得越来越多，5英尺左右高的桑树比比皆是。插着黄色小旗的运石船驶过，这表明它们正忙于运河堤岸的修复工作。不久之后，我们就到了无锡的郊区，附近有很多正在工作的砖窑。中国的砖完全由泥烧制而成，不加稻草，烧得不硬，因此很是疏松。砖窑是圆形的，高约20英尺，用稻草作燃料，一炉砖需要连续烧制三天三夜。这一带有很多呆头呆脑的乞丐和蚊子，不过并没给我们带来多少苦恼。

China: Its Marvel and Mystery
中国：神奇而又神秘的国度

（李通和　著　戴莉　译）

《中国：神奇而又神秘的国度》（*China: Its Marvel and Mystery*）由英国画家李通和（T. Hodgson Liddell）撰写，1909年由乔治·艾伦与其子出版社（George Allen & Sons）在伦敦出版。书中配有40幅作者创作的彩绘，展现了二十世纪初中国主要城市和地区的自然风光。为了用画笔描绘这个神奇的国度，作者1907年来到中国，开启了为期一年的中国之行，游历了香港、广州、澳门、上海、苏州、太湖流域、杭州、北戴河、山海关、天津等地，最后到达北京，获慈禧太后特许进入颐和园作画。李通和从艺术家的视角，通过写生，向西方人传达了他对中国的印象。他希望欧洲人能看到更多以写实风格展现中国自然美景的绘画作品，以对这个伟大的国度及其文明有更深入的了解。在该书的第九章"苏州和太湖"中（原著第51页至第58页），作者记录了从苏州乘坐住家船游览太湖流域的旅途见闻，描写了江南水乡风貌及水路印象。其中的三幅插图生动展现了光福、木渎的湖光山色及横塘鸬鹚捕鱼的独特景致。

CHAPTER IX SOOCHOW AND TAHU

House-Boats—No. I Boy—The Shanghai-Nanking Railway— On our Boats— Curiosity of the Country People—My First Impressions of Chinese Waterways—Bridges—Water-raising Machines—Passing through a Village.

An expedition to Soochow and Tahu which I was asked to join, and which proved most enjoyable, was made at Easter. Two house-boats, the Togo and the Leila, provided ample accommodation for our party; one boat was quite luxuriously fitted up, and the other was quite comfortable. One could not wish for more comfortable travelling than these Shanghai house-boats afford. Of course they are specially built for foreigners' use.

The No. I Boy was instructed to make all arrangements for our journey. I may mention that the No.I Boy in a European's house in the East is the chief native servant, and occupies a similar position to the butler at home (all servants are called "boys," whatever their age); he in most cases runs the house; he engages all the other servants, and gets his squeeze (commission) from them and from the tradespeople, and although he may be paid a fair wage, his "extras" are quite considerable in a house of any size. I heard the orders given to the No. I — Yung Yung—who has been in the family nearly all his life. They were short but clear:—

"Boy, in two three day Missessee, my, young Missessee, Missessee O. and Mister T.(myself) all go house-boat, seven piecee man, you go house-boats, talkee that boatman, make all thing proper." These few instructions were quite enough to insure everything being made ready for our trip.

To save time and get quickly up country, the boats were ordered to proceed in advance to Soochow, where we would meet them, while we travelled by the new Shanghai-Nanking Railway, which is quite equal to any of our home railways in smooth running and accommodation. At Soochow we found our boats waiting for us in the creek quite near the station, which is outside the city walls. Like our own folks sixty or seventy years ago, the Chinese try to keep their railways outside the cities, and I suppose in time to come they will like ourselves be sorry for it.

We at once went on board, and were soon being quietly propelled along by our coolies with three great oars or yuloos, two to each boat with three coolies

第九章　苏州和太湖

住家船—大管家—沪宁铁路—船上见闻—好奇的村民—我对中国水路的第一印象—桥梁—翻水车—穿行村庄。

在复活节，我应邀参加了一次极其快乐愉悦的苏州及太湖之旅。两艘住家船，"多哥"号和"莱拉"号，为我们一行提供了充裕的食宿。一艘装备相当豪华，另一艘则相当舒适。没有比乘坐这些上海住家船旅行更舒适的了。当然，这些船是专门为外国人制造的。

大管家奉命为我们的旅行做好一切安排。值得一提的是，居住在东方的欧洲人家里的大管家是一位当地的主仆役，其地位相当于西方的男管家（无论年龄大小，所有仆人都被称为"boys"）。在大多数情况下，他主管整个住宅，雇用所有其他的仆人，并从仆人和商家那里拿取回扣。尽管他可能报酬一般，但无论主人家门庭大小，他的"外快"都是相当可观的。大管家荣荣几乎一生都效力于主人家，我听到主人简短而清晰地命令他道：

"管家，过两三天，夫人、我、小姐、O夫人和T先生（指我）都要乘坐住家船，共七人。你去与住家船主谈谈，把一切都安排妥当。"短短几条指令就足以确保为我们的旅行做好一切准备了。

为了节省时间尽快溯河而上，住家船受令提前赶往苏州，而我们则坐火车沿新建的沪宁铁路到苏州登船。火车运行的平稳性和舒适性与英国的火车不相上下。到了苏州，我们看到船在离车站很近的小河上等候，而车站就在城墙外。就像六七十年前的英国人一样，中国人尽量把铁路建在城外，我想将来他们会像我们一样为此而后悔。

我们立刻上了船，不一会儿，船工就划动三支摇橹悄然前行。每艘船配有两支各需三名船工推动的大橹。这是一段美好的行程，远离喧嚣的城

to each yuloo; it is a very pleasant movement, and a delightful change, after the noise of the city life, to get away quietly on the water. I in particular felt the relief of being away from the crowds of natives swarming round me as I worked.

We left Soochow at once, being anxious to get farther up to the district of the Tahu (Great Lake). Our first afternoon's journey took us above Mutu, where, near a picturesque bridge, we tied up for the night. No sooner had we come to anchor than the curious native appeared, and many crowded round on the banks watching us; they were much interested in the ladies and children of our party—we men are more common, and do not excite such curiosity.

The country folks are most inquisitive about European ladies and children, and wish to closely examine and finger their dresses. The fair, daintily-dressed children seemed specially to please them. The Chinese are very fond of children, and I have heard it said that a foreigner might go anywhere in China, not only with safety but sure of great courtesy, if accompanied by a young child.

It was on this trip that I got my first impressions of the creeks and rivers which lead into the interior, and along which for centuries has been borne the merchandise of China. Until now, water carriage has been the principal means of conveyance in this (and indeed a large) part of China, and by water one can go almost anywhere. It is like a vast network spreading all over the country, extending far and near; providing at the same time easy means of irrigation, maintaining thereby the richness and fertility of the land and a ready means of transit for its products.

The wonderful waterways of China have been a source of wealth to all and sundry, affording great employment of capital and labour; and although now railways are being rapidly built, and will doubtless prove of inestimable value, it is to be hoped that these great waterways will not be allowed to fall into disuse. Here one sees a junk deep in the quiet water moving along under her great sail, there a small sampan, and—sign of the times! —there again a noisy, puffing steam launch, towing her train of native boats, all laden to the water's edge with the various products of this rich land, or conveying inland some of the manufactures of Western countries.

We pass through many bridges built of finely dressed stone, some with one span, and others with several, and reminding one strongly of the Venetian bridges; and I could not help reflecting on how much, in the past, Southern Europe must have borrowed from China, and how things are now reversed, and

市生活,沿着河流静静前行,这种转换令人愉悦。远离了那些在我绘画时一直蜂拥在我身边的当地人,让我尤感轻松。

我们即刻离开苏州,一路向前,急切地向太湖流域驶去。第一天下午行至木渎,停泊在一座造型优美的桥边过夜。我们刚一抛锚,就吸引来了好奇的当地人。许多人围拢在岸边瞧着我们,他们对我们一行中的女士和孩子尤感兴趣——我们西方男人更常见,不会激起如此强烈的好奇心。

村民对欧洲女士和孩子最为好奇,总想仔细打量和触摸她们的衣服。那些肤色白皙、衣着讲究的孩子们似乎特别惹人喜爱。中国人非常喜欢孩子,我听说外国人如果带着一个小孩到中国的任何地方去,不仅安全,而且能尊享礼遇。

正是在这次旅行中,我对流向内陆的溪流和江河有了初步的印象。几个世纪以来,中国的货物一直沿着这些河流运输。直到现在,水运一直是中国本地区(着实广大的一片区域)主要交通运输方式,通过水路几乎可以到达任何地方。它像一个遍布全国的巨大网络,延伸到远近八方;同时提供简便的灌溉方法,从而保持土地的丰饶和肥沃,并为其产品提供现成的运输方式。

中国令人惊叹的水道极有效地利用了资本和人力,向来是所有人财富的源泉。尽管现在正加紧铺设铁路,其价值必将不可估量,但希望这些庞大的水道不会因此被废弃。近处,我们看见一艘帆船扬起巨大的风帆,沿着平静的水面平稳前行,远处有一只小舢板。远远地又驶来一艘标志着现代化的蒸汽船,发着轰响、喷着蒸汽、拖着一长列本土货船,每艘船的船舷几乎与水平齐,满载着这片富饶土地上的各种产品,或是把西方国家的一些洋货运往内地。

我们经过许多用雕琢精美的石材建造的桥梁,有的单拱,有的多拱,让人不由联想起威尼斯的桥。我不禁感慨:过去,欧洲南部国家一定向中国借鉴了不少东西,而现在,情形正好相反,中国正在向西方学习。这就

China is borrowing from the West. It is but the inevitable swing of the pendulum.

Soon after leaving Mutu, we began to approach a more hilly country, but with great tracts of flat land, through which the waterways ran, fertilising and enriching it. The rich yet tender green of springtime showed the luxuriant growth of highly cultivated land—belts of brilliant yellow, the flower of the rape—clumps of trees here and there;the whole making a beautiful landscape.

On rising ground stands a high pagoda showing out against the distant hills.

In the fields we could see the industrious people tilling their land, some hoeing and weeding, others carrying liquid from tanks, and spreading it on the soil, while the smell was wafted in the air towards us. Nothing is wasted in China.

This method of intense cultivation by the use of rank manure does not commend itself to the foreigner, who requires to be very careful as to what vegetables he eats, and is often obliged to avoid them altogether, especially salads and uncooked vegetables.

On the banks of the creeks are fitted quaintly formed machines for lifting the water up for irrigation. A long wooden trough is carried down into the water, with a continuous belt with pieces of wood fitting the trough;some of these are worked by coolies and some larger ones by water buffaloes, and the creaking noise of grinding wood is heard far off in the still evening air as the coolies or animals go their monotonous round.

Here we come to a row of quaint stone structures, widows' monuments, and entrances leading to the tombs of former great ones of the district.

Passing through one village, we had great difficulty to get our boats along between the houses on the canal; it was so narrow that at times we rubbed along touching houses on both sides, with the natives viewing us from their windows. Heated arguments arose between our coolies and others as to the best method of getting along; and people crowded on the bridges, to watch our slow progress and criticise us and our belongings. Our cook would take such an opportunity as this to go ashore and make purchases of chickens, eggs, &c., and join us farther on.

By-and-bye we reached a wide stretch of water near Kwangfoong, the character of which in the Tahu district is somewhat akin to our English Lake district. The hills are rather of the same character, soft and green, and rising to more ruggedness farther up. At Kwangfoong is a fine pagoda; the village is small and unimportant with various temples; there is a fine three-span bridge crossing

像钟摆一样必然会来回摆动。

离开木渎后不久,我们逐渐靠近一个有多处山丘但仍有着大片平地的乡村,河道穿流其间,滋养肥沃着两岸土地。春天那浓郁而又柔嫩的绿色彰显出精耕细作土地的蓬勃生机,金灿灿的油菜花片片丛生,处处绿树蓊郁,这一切构成了一幅美丽的图景。

山丘上,一座高大的宝塔在远山的映衬下巍然耸峙。

我们看到人们在田间辛勤耕种,有的在除草松土,有的从桶中舀取粪液给土壤施肥,气味弥散空中,飘向我们。在中国,一切都能物尽其用。

这种用恶臭的粪肥集约种植的方法,很不受外国人待见,因为他们需要非常小心地选择吃什么蔬菜,常常不得不放弃食用蔬菜,特别是沙拉和生蔬。

河岸上装有构造奇特的机械,用来汲水灌溉。一条长长的木制水槽伸入水中,装有一长条带着刮板的木链。一些由人踩动,另一些大一点的由牛拉动。农夫或水牛动作单调、周而复始地驱动水车,在寂静的夜空中远远就能听到木头摩擦的嘎吱声。[1]

我们经过一排古色古香被称为贞节牌坊的石头建筑,以及一道道通向当地知名先人墓地的石门。

经过一个村庄时,我们万分艰难地在运河两岸的房屋间前行。水道如此狭窄,船不时蹭到两边的房屋,当地人从窗口盯着我们看。我们的船工和当地人就如何最好地顺利通行发生了激烈的争论。人们挤在桥上,看着我们缓慢前进,对我们及随船行装评头论足。我们的厨师会利用这个机会上岸去买些鸡、鸡蛋等物品,在前方再回船同行。

不久,我们进入了光福附近的一大片水域。太湖流域这一带的特点有点类似于我们英国的湖区,山脉尤为相似,柔和而苍翠,越往上越崎岖不平。

---

[1] 作者看到的是龙骨水车,又称"翻车",是我国古代杰出的农业灌溉机械之一。

the water here, a view of which I give in my picture taken from a mandarin's grave on the hillside.

An attempt was made to shoot some snipe near here, on a flat and marshy island, but the season was late, and the birds not plentiful, so that our larder did not greatly benefit.

We stayed some days in this beautiful neighbourhood, making various excursions, examining temples, and sketching. Our two boats anchored in a snug corner under a hill, where we received visits from many natives, who were especially interested in us at meal-times, and would try to look in at our cabin windows when we were at the table. But they objected to be photographed or sketched, and a sure way to make them go off was to point a camera at them, or make a pretence of drawing them, when they would immediately hide their faces while moving away.

Our return journey was by much the same route, but it was just as interesting seeing it all again;indeed one seemed to enjoy it even more. One object which greatly attracted me was a bridge over the Canal at a small village, Wong-Dong; on the bridge was a quaint old joss-house. I was able to make a sketch of this, with some cormorant fishing-boats in the foreground. The method of catching fish with cormorants, as far as I could see, was as follows: Spars project over the side of the boat, and on these are perched the birds;the fisherman has a light cane, and with this lightly touches the bird he wishes to go, and it immediately dives for a fish;on the bird's return to the boat, the fisherman takes the fish. A ring placed round the cormorant's neck prevents it swallowing the fish.

The Woo Men Bridge at Soochow is another and one of the finest of these beautiful buildings crossing the Grand Canal, cleanly built of face stone, and taking a graceful sweep upwards and over the great arch.

Soochow is rather like Hangchow, but not, I think, so beautiful, in spite of the Chinese proverb which I mention in my Hangchow chapters. The streets are narrow, with good shops, and the usual bustling crowds. By the way these narrow streets seem to me to give a greatly exaggerated idea of the population of Chinese cities, the people being so crowded together in the narrow lanes.

We had a look at the famous pagoda in this city. It is of great age, nine storeys in height, with an immense circumference at the base. It is built with double walls, the staircase occupying the space between.

在光福有一座精美的宝塔，村庄很小，也不知名，散落着各式庙宇。一座宏丽的三孔桥横跨水面，其景色可以从我在山坡上一个官员的陵墓边拍的照片上看到。

我们试图在附近一个平坦多沼泽的小岛上打一些鹬。但时节已晚，鸟不多，所以我们的食物储存并不太丰富。

我们在这个美丽的湖区逗留了数日，远足、参观寺庙、画素描。我们的两艘船停泊在山下一个避风的角落，许多当地人来探访我们，他们特别喜欢看我们用餐。当我们进餐时，他们会设法通过船舱的窗户向里张望。但他们不让给拍照或画像，想让他们离开的有效方法就是用相机对准他们，或者假装画他们，这时他们就会立即遮着脸走开了。

回程的路线和来时差不多，不过把这一路风光重温一遍，还是一样趣味盎然。事实上，大家似乎更乐在其中。有一个景致深深吸引了我，在一个叫横塘的小村庄，有一座桥跨越运河之上，桥上有一座古色古香的老神庙。我就此景作了一幅画，前景是几艘鸬鹚捕鱼船。据我观察，用鸬鹚捕鱼的方法是这样的：船舷上架着几根竹竿，鸬鹚栖息其上；渔夫用一根轻巧的竹竿轻点，那只被点到的鸬鹚立刻潜入水中捉鱼；鸬鹚一回到船上，渔夫就把鱼取走。鸬鹚颈上戴有一环，防止它将鱼吞下。

苏州吴门桥是横跨大运河的最精美桥梁之一，由规整的石条砌置而成，坡度优美，高高的桥拱飞架水波之上。

苏州很像杭州，但我觉得并没有我在杭州章节中提到的那句中国谚语所说的那么美丽。街道狭窄，店铺林立，照例人流熙熙攘攘。顺便提一句，人群在窄窄的街巷里显得如此拥挤不堪，在我看来这些逼仄的街道极大地夸大了中国城市的人口。

我们参观了这座城市著名的宝塔。它历史悠久，塔高九层，矗立于一个巨大的基座之上。塔身由双层砖墙构造而成，楼梯盘旋其间。

The Travelers' Handbook for China
游历中国闻见撷要录

(克劳 著 蔡骏 译)

《游历中国闻见撷要录》(*The Travelers' Handbook for China*)由美国纽约多德米德出版公司(Dodd, Mead & Co.)于1925年在纽约出版,作者是近代上海的广告大亨、作家、记者、《大美晚报》(*Shanghai Evening Post and Mercury*)创办人及首任主编美国人克劳(Carl Crow,1883—1945)。作者在书中向西方游客提供了苏、锡、沪、杭等地区的游览指南。选译部分(原书第143页至第149页)较全面地介绍了苏州的地理位置、交通出行、历史沿革、古迹风景、典故特产等内容,叙述生动、行文流畅。

Soochow is 53 miles from Shanghai, on the Shanghai-Nanking Railway. Fare $2.80. Can also be reached by houseboat from Shanghai or Hangchow. A treaty port opened in 1896. Population over 500,000. Several comfortable hotels for foreigners are maintained here under Chinese management. Chinese and Japanese post offices. Carriages and ricshas are to be had at the station, but neither can be used in the walled city because of the narrow streets and the many arched bridges. Donkeys are offered at $1 a day or 20 cents an hour. The new rattan chairs are everywhere available now and may be had for a small sum for each section of the road traveled. They afford a very comfortable and pleasant way to get about.

The many canals which intersect the rich and beautiful city of Soochow have given it the name of "The Venice of the Far East," while the very high standing which its scholars have always enjoyed has made it the Athens of China. It is one of the oldest and most famous cities of China and the admiration of the Chinese for the place is expressed in the familiar quotation, "Heaven above, and below Hangchow and Soochow". The history of the city covers more than 2,000 years. In about 525 B.C. only 250 years after Rome was founded, Prince Ho Lu, of the Kingdom of Wu, ordered his prime minister to build a city for him to serve as his capital. The instructions were to build "a large and influential city where his subjects could dwell in time of danger and where his government stores could be protected from the enemies that constantly menaced his kingdom." The official decided on ambitious plans. The city was to have eight water gates, like heaven, and be square like the earth. The total length of the outer walls aggregated 47 li, about 15 miles. Inside were two inner enclosures, the larger one enclosing the Forbidden City, for the palaces and yamens, and the smaller enclosure for the personal use of the prime minister.

The city became the capital of the kingdom and grew in importance, but about 591 A.D. a new city was built for the reason that the old one was full of robbers, rebels and thieves, whose organization was so strong that it was impossible to drive them out. The walls of the new city were of wood, and the people lived within these insecure enclosures only a short time, moving back to the old city during the first years of the Tang reign. In 876, a band of robbers captured the city and again a new enclosure was built for the protection of the people. The new city took a rough wedge shape. Within the walls were many canals and 300 streets. The walls thus constructed were allowed to fall into

苏州在沪宁铁路上，离上海 53 英里，票价 2.80 元，亦可由上海或杭州乘住家船而至。苏州 1896 年开埠，人口逾 50 万，有几家由中国人管理的舒适的涉外酒店，还有中国邮局和日本邮局。火车站有马车和黄包车，但因街道狭窄、拱桥众多，此两种车辆均无法在城墙内市区使用。租用毛驴日价 1 美元或小时价 2 美分。时下藤制轿子随处可寻，按乘坐路段略收费用，以此出行，舒适惬意。

苏州富饶美丽，因河道纵横而拥有"远东威尼斯"之名，又因苏城学者自古地位颇高，使之有"中国雅典"之称。苏州乃中国最为古老、最为著名的城市之一，中国人对其仰慕之情由名谚"上有天堂，下有苏杭"可见一斑。苏城历史横跨 2 000 余年。约在公元前 525 年[1]，即罗马建立后 250 年，吴王阖闾令其大夫兴建一城为其首都，要求营建"一座庞大而有影响力的城市，其臣民可在危难之时居于城内，其官府仓库可免受时时滋扰本国之外敌"。大夫因而制定了雄心勃勃的建城规划：象天法地，此城采用方形建制，设八个水城门，其外墙方圆 47 里，约 15 英里。苏州城内建有大小两个内城，大城环抱宫城，内建宫殿和衙门；小城供大夫使用。

苏州城由此成为吴国首都，其重要性与日俱增，但大约在公元 591 年，苏州另建一座新城，究其原因乃是旧城内盗贼、叛军横行，其势力猖獗至无法驱离之境地。新城之城墙以木材构建，并不坚固，城内民众在此居住不久即于唐朝统治初年迁回旧城。876 年，一伙强徒占领了此城，因此新城墙再次营建以保护民众。此番新城略呈楔形，城墙内建众多河道和 300 条街道，营建的城墙损坏严重，多次修缮。

---

[1]　春秋时阖闾元年（公元前 514 年）吴王命伍子胥筑阖闾城。

disrepair and were restored several times.

In the 14th century, following the fall of the Mongol dynasty and while the Mings were struggling to subdue the whole country, Chang Shin Cheng attempted to re-establish the Kingdom of Wu, with himself as Emperor and Soochow as the capital. The imperial troops made short work of the city walls and the ambitious rebel was captured and executed, along with his troops. The most recent restoration of the city walls was in 1662, under the renowned Manchu Emperor, Kang Hsi. A Manchu garrison was quartered here and the town refortified. Battlements were added, rising to a height of 6 feet above the wall, which is 12 miles in circumference, 28 feet in height and 18 feet thick.

The walls as they stand today have been frequently repaired but are much the same as in 1662. The walled city is about 4 miles long from north to south and about 3 miles broad. A walk along the broad well-paved top of the wall is delightful, far away from the noise and crowds below and yet giving an excellent view of the whole city. A moat so to 100 yards wide surrounds the city and is used as a canal, connecting with the narrower intersecting canals of the city.

"At the water gate, toll is collected by a bag at the end of a long pole, such as cathedrals use. There is of course some delay here, and it gives opportunity to observe the cormorant fishing boats. The birds are equipped by nature with a large pouch to deposit their catch in, and by art with a ring round the neck to prevent its slipping—accidentally—any further. They sit in double rows round the boat till the manager pushes them into the water with a bamboo; when one finds a fish, he pecks out the eye and pouches the creature; if it be too large, he invites other cormorants and they together will lift out any fish not exceeding eleven pounds."[1]

Approaching Soochow from any direction, tall pagodas first come into view. There are five of them inside the city and three crown the near-by hills. The South Gate Pagoda is one of the many for which claims of the greatest antiquity are made, the date of construction of the original being about 248 A. D. The

---

[1] "The Eighteen Capitals of China" by William Edgar Geil. A Soochow correspondent says: "There is no regular toll for boats. Sometimes the gatekeepers do squeeze on cargo. I have never known it on passengers." 威廉·埃德加·盖尔《中国十八省府》。一名驻苏州记者说："船只不用定期缴纳过路费。有时城门看守确实会对货船雁过拔毛。我从没听说在船客身上捞油水的事。"

十四世纪，在蒙古王朝倒台，明朝征服全国之时，张士诚试图重建吴国并自立为王，以苏州为都城。朝廷大军干脆利落地攻破城墙，俘虏和处决了这个野心勃勃的叛乱分子和他的军队。城墙最近一次修复是在1662年，正值大名鼎鼎的清朝皇帝康熙统治时期。当时，一支满族军队驻扎在这里，加固了城池，加上了垛口，使城墙又高出了6英尺，形成了周长12英里，高28英尺，厚18英尺的城墙。

如今矗立着的城墙虽经频繁修复，但与1662年的城墙大致相同。墙内的城市南北长约4英里，东西宽约3英里。漫步在宽阔、平坦的城墙顶上，既能远离城下的喧嚣和人群，又能一瞰城市风光，令人心情舒畅。大约100码宽的护城河环绕古城，起到了运河的作用，还与城内交错纵横的较窄河道勾连在一起。

"拿根长杆子，一头系上个口袋，水城门的过路费就这样收到了，这种做法颇似教会收捐款。水城门处势必会有逗留，而这也有了观察鸬鹚渔船的机会。鸬鹚天生就有个存放猎物的大喉囊，有种手艺能在鸬鹚脖子上套上个环，防止鱼意外落入鸟肚。鸬鹚分成两排蹲在船沿上，渔夫会用竹竿把它们赶下水；鸬鹚发现鱼后会啄出鱼眼，然后把鱼兜在喉囊里；如果鱼太大，鸬鹚还会找来同伴，一起将不超过11磅的鱼捞出水。"

不管从哪个方向接近苏州，首先映入眼帘的总是高大的宝塔。城内有五座塔，附近的小山上还有三座。瑞光塔是众多宝塔之一，据说也是最古老的宝塔，原塔建造的年份大约是公元248年。北寺塔是中国最著名的宝

Great Pagoda, seen near the city wall from the railway station, is one of the most famous in China. It is said to have been built in 1131 A.D. The Taipings, who did not harm the pagoda, destroyed the temple which formerly stood in front of it, so that it is possible now to get a complete view of the famous structure. It consists of nine stories, 250 feet high and is a marvel of proportion. Sixty feet in diameter at the base, it is 45 feet at the top, each story being proportionately shorter, each balcony narrower, each door and window smaller. The whole is of massive construction and carries well its seven hundred years. From the upper stories an excellent view of the beautiful surrounding country can be obtained. In the vicinity are many small hills and lakes, the latter connected with each other by innumerable small canals. To the east is a level plain broken only by a number of groves planted about small villages. To the west lies the Great Lake or Ta Hu, celebrated by many Chinese poets for the beauty of its surroundings, and a famous resort for Shanghai houseboat parties. It is 40 by 50 miles in extent, dotted by many small islands which contain interesting temples and monasteries. Five million people live within the radius covered by the eye from the top balconies of the pagoda. From few other places can one view the habitations of so many of his fellow men. The old priest who opens the entrance to the pagoda for visitors expects a small tip, and the boy who carries a light through the one dark passage does so in the hope of receiving a few coppers.

The Tiger Hill Pagoda, the "leaning tower" of Soochow, was first built in 601 A.D., burned down in 1428 and the present structure was built ten years later. The Twin Pagodas, known also as the Two Pen Pagodas, stand near the Examination Halls, and to their good influence is attributed much of the fame which has come to Soochow through her scholars. Near these is the Ink Pagoda. "A scholar built the Two Pen Pagodas to attract the good luck required to insure good scholarship to the town; but as most of the candidates kept on failing afterwards, he consulted the geomancers, and they showed how absurd it was to provide two pens but no ink. The omission rectified, the candidates passed." Soochow University, an American institution, is located near the Ink Pagoda. Soochow, through many centuries, has sent more honors men to the great Metropolitan Examinations at Peking than can be claimed by any other city and it rivals Hangchow in the space it occupies in the literature of China. *The History of*

塔之一，在火车站附近的城墙边就可以望见。据说北寺塔建成于公元1131年。太平军并未毁坏这座宝塔，只是摧毁了矗立在塔前的寺庙，因而如今仍可见到这座名塔的完整风貌。塔身共有九层，高250英尺，其各层比例堪称建筑奇迹。塔底部直径60英尺，顶部直径45英尺，直径逐层缩小，露台逐层变窄，门窗逐层变小。宝塔整体规模宏大，历经七百年岁月而保存完好。从宝塔上层可以观赏四周乡野美景。宝塔附近有众多外形玲珑的丘陵、湖泊，湖泊间沟汊纵横相连，不计其数。塔东为一片平野，分布有村落若干，村外树林环绕。塔西为"大湖"，或称之为"太湖"，因其风光旖旎而为众多中国文人墨客所称道，此处也是上海住家船云集的度假胜地。太湖南北纵贯40英里，东西横跨50英里，湖内点缀众多小岛，岛上寺庙饶有趣味。从塔上最高层露台远眺，目之所及范围内住有500万人。能从一处见到如此众多的乡人之住所实乃少有。塔外有一老僧为游客开门，但其会索要少许小费；塔内有一男童掌灯引领游客穿过幽暗甬道，其亦须以若干铜板打点。

苏州的"斜塔"虎丘塔始建于公元601年[1]，1428年焚毁，现存的塔身为1438年所建。双塔，或称之为双笔塔，矗立在贡院附近，在双塔影响之下苏州出现了很多文人学士，双塔由此有了名气。双塔附近还有墨塔[2]。"一位学者修建了双笔塔以求招引好运确保苏城文运亨通；但其后多数考生连年落榜，此公遂向风水先生求教，风水先生们指出空有两笔却无墨可蘸，荒唐至极。疏漏纠正后考生们考运亨通。"美国人所建的东吴大学位于墨塔附近。数百年来，苏州向京城会试输送了大批优秀学子，其他城市无可与之比肩，其在中国文学上的地位与杭州不相上下。《苏州府

---

[1] 虎丘塔实建于公元959年。
[2] 即"文星阁"。

Soochow, a compilation begun 1,000 years ago by one of the city's most famous men, has grown to 150 volumes, through the contributions of generations of scholars.

The City Temple is one of the show places of Soochow, though infested by beggars, who annoy the foreign visitor. Within its enclosure are fourteen separate temples, containing more than two hundred principal images. Within the city walls there are several hundred temples, nunneries and monasteries. There is one large Confucian temple at which the provincial officials formerly worshiped and one smaller one where the district magistrate worshiped before going over to the large one. Near the large temple, to the east and south, are a normal school, a college, a middle school and an industrial school, all run and financed by the government. The governor's yamen is just to the north of the temple and to the west are three other interesting places, the Provincial Mint, the Horticultural Garden and the Beamless Temple. This famous building is of two stories built about 1572 A. D. and without any timber at all. There is no wood in any part of the building, the roof being supported by arches made of specially constructed brick. The roof is arched and covered with beautiful colored tiles.

The Temple of Scrolls is full of scrolls of all kinds and a walk through it gives one some idea of the various tendencies of Chinese art to run to commercialism. It is said that only countrymen go there to buy scrolls, as the best artists do their work upon order or exhibit it in private shops. On the east side of this large temple there is a smaller one that has very interesting representations of the lower regions with its varied tortures and also of saints seated upon clouds in heaven. These are in different wings of the temple.

To the south of the customs house (which is at the opposite end of the horse road from the railway station and the southeast corner of the city) is a magnificent bridge called the Precious Girdle Bridge. It consists of 53 arches and is built entirely of granite. This and many other attractive bridges in the vicinity are well worth the time taken to see them. The bridges of Soochow are famous all over China and the average Chinese finds it difficult to believe that anyone can teach the Soochow people anything about bridge building.

The gardens of Soochow could afford an interesting day's outing in themselves. There are several inside the city, but the two largest are the Loen

志》于 1 000 年前由此市最著名的人物之一开始编纂，在历代学者的贡献下，迄今已编纂达 150 卷。

玄妙观是苏州的演艺场所之一，但此地乞丐处处皆是，外国游客不胜其扰。在玄妙观围墙以内有十四座独立的庙宇，庙内供奉有两百余尊主要神像。苏州城墙内有数百座寺庙、庵堂和修道院。市内有一座大孔庙，先前省级官员在此祭奠；另有一座小孔庙，地方官员在此祭奠后再前往大孔庙朝觐。在大庙的东南两面分布有一所师范学校、一所大学、一所中学和一所工业专科学校，所有这些学校都由官府运营和资助。巡抚衙门在大孔庙的北面，再往西则是另外三个有趣的地方：省造币厂、植园和无梁殿。著名的无梁殿约建于公元 1572 年[1]，殿有两层，没有任何木制椽柱。无梁殿没有任何木制架构，其屋顶由特制的拱形砖结构支撑，上覆漂亮的五彩瓦片。

古卷庙内存有各种卷轴画，漫步其中。游客可对中国各类艺术流派，以及艺术流派的商业化进程了解一二。据说只有乡下人才会去那里买画，而顶级画家则根据委约创作，或在私家店铺展出其作品。在古卷庙东边另有一座小庙，庙内展示的地狱里各式酷刑和天堂中圣人端坐云上的画像饶有趣味，这些作品分布在庙内的不同侧翼上。

海关大楼位于城市东南角，处在连接火车站的马路的另一头，其南面是一座宏伟的桥，称为宝带桥。桥由 53 个拱组成，全部由花岗岩建造。这座桥及其附近众多其他桥梁，颇具吸引力，非常值得花时间去看一看。苏州的桥梁闻名于全中国，普通中国人很难相信还会有谁能教苏州人如何造桥。

苏州园林也值得花上一天时间在其中走走看看。苏州城内有好几座园

---

[1] 元梁殿应建于明万历四十六年（1618 年）。

Yoen and the Si Yoen (yoen means garden). One of these was formerly owned by a high Manchu official. The property was siezed by the Republican government. They are both located outside of the Northwest gate (Tsaung Mung) of the city and may be reached by carriage from the railway station. A small entrance fee is charged and one may wander at leisure through the many walks and rockeries.

To the west of the city are a number of hills a few hours journey by boat from the busy thoroughfares of the city. There one may tramp through many shaded spots rich in historic lore. An excellent little booklet, "The Hills About Soochow"[1] by Dr. J.B. Fearn, gives interesting information about the hills. They afford good climbs and excellent views.The fields of yellow rape and patches of purple clover in the early spring are well worth seeing.

Soochow has regained much of what it lost because of the Taiping rebellion and is again rich and cultured city of old, with a very large class of idle rich. In addition to its fame as the birthplace of many scholars, Soochow is also widely known in China as the birthplace of the most famous sing-song girls. Soochow women are noted for their beauty and the pleasing softness of their dialect and fashionable women from other parts of China ape the Soochow dialect. The place has not held its own, commercially, with other cities of the neighborhood, but remains the silk metropolis of the Orient, maintaining 7,000 looms for the production of brocades.

"The silken goods which form the staple export are the glory of the place, and the Imperial household formerly got its chief supplies hence. It is strange to see the primitive surroundings, a little but with an earthen floor in which they are produced, with their exquisite designs and perfect workmanship. In these uncleanly surroundings a basin of water stands for the weaver to keep his hands unsoiled. He can make four or five feet daily, a yard wide, thus earning 300 or 375 cash and producing material worth nearly two shillings a foot. It is the best paid occupation in the city."

The foreign settlement of Soochow has been built up outside the city walls, near the Customs house, and very little has been done in developing it. However the streets are wide, paved, and well cared for.

---

[1] Sold by the North China Daily News, Shanghai. 此书由华北新闻社上海分社发行。

林,最大的两座是留园和西园。其中之一以前为一位满族高官所有,后来此园为民国政府征收。两座园林都位于苏州西北门(阊门)外,可以从火车站坐马车抵达。只需支付少许门票钱,游客即可悠闲地漫步于园内众多小径和假山之中。

苏州城西有许多小山,从城内繁忙干道出发,乘船只需几个小时即可到达。在那里,游客可以漫步穿行于山丘之中,其间不起眼处往往蕴藏着丰富的历史故事。由费恩博士(Dr. J.B. Fearn)撰写的小册子《苏州的山》,堪称上乘之作,其中介绍了有关苏州山丘的有趣内容。这些山丘景色优美,值得一爬。早春金灿灿的油菜田和紫盈盈的苜蓿地非常值得观赏。

苏州已弥补因太平天国起义而造成的大部分损失,再度成为一座富有的文化古城,拥有一大批有钱的闲士。除以孕育众多学者而闻名于世外,苏州还以培养最负盛名的歌女广为中国人所知。苏州女性以其美貌和柔美悦耳的方言而有名,外地的时髦女郎乐于效仿苏州话。商业上,苏州不以一地而立,而是与周边城市并驾齐驱,但苏州是东方丝绸之都,坐拥7 000台锦缎织机。

"丝织品是苏州主要的出口商品,为地方带来了荣耀,也由此成为昔日皇室丝织品的主要来源。令人称奇的是,这里生产环境原始,在狭小的泥地上居然创造出如此精美的图案和完美的工艺。在邋遢的环境中放置一盆清水以保持织工双手洁净。一名织工一天能织四至五英尺一码宽的锦缎,能挣到300到375块钱,制造出每英尺价值将近两先令的锦缎。这是城里收入最高的职业。"

苏州的外国人定居点修建于城墙之外,在海关大楼附近,迄今定居点未有多少发展,但这里街道宽阔平整、养护良好。

To the west lies the Great Lake, one of the most beautiful places in China. It has been the scene of outings by residents of Soochow for the past 2,000 years and should be included in any houseboat trip. It can be made a part of the itinerary from Shanghai by houseboat, or local houseboats may be hired in Soochow. This is only one of the many lakes about the city.

Five American missions are represented in Soochow, viz: Southern Methodist, Northern Presbyterian, Southern Presbyterian, Southern Baptist and Protestant Hpiscopal. Probably the most important missionary enterprise is Soochow University, maintained by the Southern Methodists. This mission also has a large girls' school. The university is a thriving institution with a large foreign faculty and over 350 students. There are a number of mission hospitals, schools, etc. and a large Roman Catholic mission.

苏州西边是太湖，中国最美丽的地方之一。在过去 2 000 年间，太湖一直是苏州人的郊游胜地，也是住家船旅游必不可少的项目。游客的住家船之旅可从上海启程游览太湖，也可以在苏州当地租用住家船游览太湖。太湖只是苏州周边众多的湖泊之一。

在苏州有五个美国教会，即南卫理公会、北长老会、南长老会、南浸礼会和新教圣公会。最重要的教会事业可能是由南卫理公会运作的东吴大学，该教会还有一所大型女子学校。这所大学呈欣欣向荣之势，拥有大量外籍教职员工和 350 多名学生。苏州还有许多教会医院、学校等，还有一个大型的罗马天主教教会。

Alas Poor Soochow!
Thy Beauties Are in Shanghai

可叹啊，苏州！美人都去了上海

（伊尔丝·麦考密克　著　余利霞　译）

《可叹啊，苏州！美人都去了上海》（"Alas Poor Soochow! Thy Beauties Are in Shanghai"）选自《另眼看中国》（*Audacious Angles on China*）一书。该书由时驻上海中国报社的美国女记者伊尔丝·麦考密克（Elsie McCormick）所著，于1922年在上海由华美出版社（Chinese American Publishing Co.）出版发行。作者以诙谐幽默的笔触生动描述了其在中国（主要是上海）的所见所闻所感。书中涉及上海的有轨电车、玉石、洋泾浜英语，中国的街巷、河流、宝塔、黄包车以及车夫、裁缝、歌女等方面的内容。本文是作者的苏州游记，文中以极其夸张的笔法描写了乘坐黄包车游览苏州的体验：补的牙都被颠掉了。另外，还以较大篇幅提到苏州的众多宝塔及佛教的放生仪式等，非常有趣，值得一读。

PREVIOUS to the Chinese New Year holidays, our idea of Soochow was principally that of a place for native tourists to drop off the train and buy more watermelon seeds. We had heard indefinite rumors to the effect that the chief insect pests there were donkeys, the donkeys being so small that anyone over 110 pounds gave them curvature of the spine. We understood also that it was a favorite place for Shanghai Chinese to park Number Two wives who might otherwise turn the matrimonial duet into a trio and ruin the harmony.

When we visited the city recently, we saw the watermelon seeds and a few of the donkeys, but somehow missed the Number Two wives. From many sources we had heard that Soochow ladies are the most beautiful in China. After viewing some of the beauty-prize contestants in the streets, however, we have decided that just as all the best California oranges are in New York, so all the most charming Soochow flappers are in Shanghai. The girls we saw peeking coyly from doorways had visages of the type that look best at a masked ball, the features of most of them being as irregular as a French verb.

Our second disillusionment occurred when we cantered down the horse-road in a carriage trimmed for the holiday with flowing red streamers and shiny Christmas tree ornaments. We had not expected to travel in a carriage, our idea of sight-seeing in Soochow being mixed up with sedan-chairs and the donkeys. After passing through a gate in the wall to the city itself, we were greeted by a deputation of ricsha coolies and the information that the steps on the canal bridges having been smoothed down a few months ago, wheeled traffic could now negotiate the city streets.

Though we missed our tour on the back of Soochow's famous insects, we found out more things about the possibilities of ricsha travel than we dreamed of even on those Shanghai thoroughfares that have as many different degrees of depression as a Suicide Club. A street in Soochow is just wide enough for three eels to march abreast. In addition, it has more ups and downs than the first year of married life. It may be true that the City Fathers smoothed off the bridges, but they somehow overlooked several thousand little stone steps and others not so little that sit innocently in the middle of the thoroughfares, just waiting for a ricsha to come along. After losing two fillings from our teeth, we decided that the City Fathers and ricsha men were both subsidised by the local dentists' guild.

在中国新年假期前，我们对苏州的主要认知就是苏州是一个本土游客下火车多买点西瓜子的地方。我们曾听到一些含糊的传言，大意是苏州令人厌烦的东西主要是毛驴，那些毛驴体型很小，任何体重超过110磅的人都会压弯它们的脊柱。我们还听说苏州是上海男人安置妾室的最佳之所，因为如将妾室安置在上海，二人世界就会变成三人组合，从而毁了婚姻生活的和谐。

最近我们参观了苏州，看到了西瓜子，看到了几头毛驴，但不知怎的却没看到上海男人的妾室。我们从很多渠道听说苏州盛产美女。在街头见识了若干尚能一争美女头衔的姑娘后，我们得出如下结论：好比所有最优质的加利福尼亚橙子都卖到了纽约，苏州所有最有魅力的时髦女郎也都去了上海。我们看到女孩们在门口羞羞答答向外张望，其长相面容算是那种化装舞会上最好看的类型，大多数人的面容如法语动词般难以捉摸。

坐着马车沿着马路慢跑时，我们对苏州的另一认知也破灭了。因为节日，马车挂满了红色的飘带和亮闪闪的圣诞树装饰品。我们没料到会坐马车在苏州观光，我们想的是坐坐轿子、骑骑毛驴。结果，穿过城门进城后，迎接我们的是一群黄包车夫。从他们嘴里得知，几个月前所有桥梁的台阶都已平整，如今轮式车辆可顺利通过大街小巷。

尽管我们没能骑着臭名昭著的小毛驴游览苏州，但我们却发现乘坐黄包车可能遭遇的风险甚至比我们能想到的在上海那些大马路上的还要多，就好比自杀俱乐部有各种不同程度的抑郁症患者一样。苏州街道的宽度仅够三条鳝鱼并排而行，而且路上的高低不平处比婚姻生活第一年遇到的坎坷还要多。也许市政官员们的确平整了桥梁台阶，但不知为何他们却忽略了那些黄包车夫必须面对的数以千计的小石阶和横嵌在马路中央、个头不小的台阶。在颠簸中掉了两颗补过的牙后，我们认定市政官员和黄包车夫都拿了当地牙医协会的回扣。

Besides, every canal bridge is at the crest of hummock down which the brakeless but not unbreakable ricsha speeds at a rate of three mangled pedestrians a minute. When two ricshas meet on the highway, foot travelers take refuge in the nearest doorway while the leg-power chauffeurs decide the right of precedence by a system of geneology. The man who works back to the seventh generation first gets the right of way. We didn't do much sightseeing in ricshas, our time being taken up principally to clutching the handle of our umbrella and wondering how they would dispose of the remains, if any.

Soochow is a proud old city, conservative to a degree and ever mindful of the fact that for five hundred years it was one of the Chinese capitals. In Wusih, the residents take pride in showing visitors the city's factories; in Soochow, they show him the pagodas. The only evidence we noticed of modern commercialism was a Rice and Bean Cake Exchange, which, considering the reputation of certain local stock exchanges, may or may not be a wreath of daisies on the brow of the city.

Every time a rich man of the ancient regime had a few spare decades on his hands, he built a pagoda. Judging from the number scattered over the countryside, building pagodas must eventually get to be a habit, like having one's hair cut or going to the movies or getting dresses trimmed with monkey fur. Looking over the city from a height gives the impression that there are as many pagodas in Soochow as there are houses built in the architectural style of the Mid-Garbage Period.

The most important pagoda in the city is the Peh Sze Tah. We climbed to the top up flights of typically Chinese stairs, stopping along the way to admire mural decorations composed of Buddhas in contemplation and signatures of American sailors. From the highest gallery we saw the city through a thin veil of sleet, its widest avenue looking as narrow as a yard of baby-ribbon. On a far-off summit stood the Tiger Hill Pagoda with a slant to its length likely to make the spectator wonder whether the fault is in the horizon or in himself. It is not often, even in China, that one sees a hill with its pagoda on crooked. Farther away was a pagoda around which Chinese witches hold a party every year. On this occasion the black art ladies of Soochow roll down over the rocks and briars of a hillside without even dislocating the flowers in their hair. Their annual exercises are witnessed by large crowds who seem to be in some doubt as to whether the ladies are trying to reduce their weight or have just joined the Holy Rollers.

Close to the site of the old Examination Halls are the two Ink Pagodas,

另外，每座桥梁都位于坡道的坡顶。下桥时，没有刹车、也非牢不可破的黄包车却以每分钟能碾碎三个行人的速度冲下去。当两辆黄包车相遇时，行人躲进最近的门口避让，而车夫却以基因传承来决定道路的优先权。一位七代从业的车夫获得了优先通过的权利。坐在黄包车上，我们看不了多少风景，因为我们一直紧握伞柄，琢磨着一旦出事，他们会如何处理我们的遗体——如果尸首尚存的话。

苏州是一座保守的古城，苏州人一直引以为傲、念念不忘的是其五百年来一直是中国省府之一。无锡人会自豪地向来访者介绍他们的工厂，而苏州人则会向来访者展示他们的宝塔。我们注意到苏州现代商业的唯一佐证就是大米豆饼交易所。由于当地某些股票交易的不良声誉，大米豆饼交易所或许就是苏州的希望，也或许不是。

古代有钱人一有几十年的闲暇就会建塔。从散落在乡野的众多宝塔来看，建塔最终成了一种习惯，就像理发、看电影或用猴毛装饰衣服。从高处俯瞰苏州能见到很多宝塔，其状堪比中世纪乱糟糟的建筑遗风。

苏州最重要的宝塔是北寺塔。我们沿着典型的中式楼梯逐层爬向塔顶，沿途停下欣赏壁画，有沉思的佛像，还有美国水手到此一游的留名混杂其间。在最上面的走廊上，透过薄薄的雨夹雪，我们眺望苏州城，其最宽的大街看上去窄得像一条丝带。远处的山顶矗立着倾斜的虎丘塔，其倾斜度令观看者好奇到底是地平线歪着还是自己歪着。即便在中国也不常见山顶竖着斜塔。更远的地方还有一座塔，每年中国的神婆们会绕塔举行一次仪式。在这个仪式上，苏州的神婆们顺着山坡上的岩石和荆棘滚下，却不会弄乱她们头上插着的花儿。人们会成群结队地围观她们每年一次的活动，围观者似乎闹不明白这些女人是要减肥还是她们刚刚加入了"摇喊"教派[1]。

靠近苏州贡院旧址有两座墨塔[2]，是很久以前一位热心公益的市民建

---

[1] 美国基督教的一支，其成员做礼拜时常以喊叫和乱动来表示虔诚。
[2] 此处作者有误，应为笔塔（即双塔）。

erected long ago by a public spirited citizen who hoped to give the youth of the city better joss in their intellectual tests. After the building of the two shafts, however, the students flunked even more consistently than before. The donor of the pagodas couldn't understand the failure of his investment until a priest pointed out how futile it was to supply ink without a brush. The Soochow civic beautifier dug into his Liberty Bonds a third time and built a Brush Pagoda, after which the Soochow literati passed the tests like an Overland Limited going by Tanktown Corners.

In a birds' eye view of Soochow one is impressed by the number of small hills in the heart of the city.Though lacking in fire laws, Soochow has its own way of punishing carelessness. If several houses go up in flames the site of the building where the blaze started becomes the dumping-ground for all the burned-out neighbors. After trying in vain to clear his land of an ever-growing accumulation of ashes and unsavory food fragments, the unfortunate property-owner usually abandons his ground and lets a hill grow where his house used to be.

Soochow is one of the few cities near the Chinese coast where Buddhism is an active force. Here, for the first time since we came to the East, we saw a new temple in process of erection. Here also we saw a Buddha with a clean face and a shelf of life-sized genii who had been freshly gilded. The Sih Yuen Temple was as well-swept as if a typhoon had just blown through it and the electric bulbs that hung in the great lamps proved that the brothers of the adjoining monastery are bringing the establishment up-to-date.

Devout Buddhists of the city gain merit for the next world by buying snakes and setting them at liberty. When we suggested that this snake-liberating habit is a bit rough on the neighbors, we were told that the reptile-merchant furnishes a place for the call to freedom and then recaptures the snakes for the use of other merit-seekers later on. We heard that since the passing of the prohibition amendment, there are rattlesnakes in America dated up for six weeks ahead, but we didn't know that a similar situation obtained in Soochow.

We saw many other sights during our holiday, including the City Temple, the Liu Gardens, and the Bridge of Fifty-Three Arches, but the things we are likely to remember longest are the twisted streets, deliberately built that way because evil spirits travel only in a straight line, the tangle of soupy canals, the gray, curling roofs seen from the top of the pagoda, and the ricshaman's playful habit of dragging his vehicle over half a dozen assorted stone steps.

造的，他希望借此让苏州年轻学子在科举考试中得到佛祖庇佑。但事与愿违，两座塔建成后，考生落榜情况甚至比以前更甚。建塔者一直百思不得其解，直到一位高人指出有墨没笔[1]，他的付出自然徒劳无益。这位大善人再一次发动募捐，建了一座笔塔[2]。之后，苏州学子纷纷通过考试，就像美国大陆有限公司的火车穿城过镇一般顺利。

俯瞰苏州会对市中心众多的"小山"印象深刻。苏州虽然没有消防法，却自有一套惩治疏忽大意引起火灾的方法。如果有多家房子因火灾灰飞烟灭，那么起火点就会成为街坊邻居清理火灾废墟、堆放垃圾的地方。要清理干净越积越多的灰烬和臭不可闻的泔水往往是白费力气，倒霉的房主通常会放弃而任由垃圾越堆越高。

苏州是邻近沿海佛教盛行的几座城市之一。自我们抵达东方以来，在这里首次看到在建的一座新庙。在这里，我们还看到了一座面容端庄的佛像和一排真人大小、刚刚镀金的罗汉。西园寺打扫得干干净净，仿佛刮过台风似的，大灯笼里挂着的电灯泡证明寺庙里的和尚们正在使其现代化。

苏州虔诚的佛教徒为下一世积德而买蛇放生。当我们表示这种将蛇放生的做法对周围村民有点不太安全时，却被告知蛇贩子会提供场所放生，然后将蛇再次抓获卖给后来要积德行善的人使用。我们听说自从禁捕令修正案通过以来，在美国抓捕响尾蛇得提前六周申请，但我们却不知苏州是否也有类似情形。

此次假期我们还游玩了许多其他景点，如玄妙观、留园、五十三孔桥。但可能最难忘的是：九曲回肠的街道（故意如此修建以避邪，因邪祟只走直线），纵横交错的河道，站在塔顶望见的鳞次栉比的灰色屋顶，以及黄包车夫拉着车子、跳来跳去越过五六级石阶。

---

[1] 此处承上文之误，应为"有笔没墨"。
[2] 应为墨塔（即文星阁）。

The Venice of the Far East

东方威尼斯

(玛格丽特·耶茨·斯特林　著　余利霞　译)

《旅行杂志》(*The Travel Magazine*)刊行于二十世纪初,由纽约弗罗拉帕克出版社(Floral Park NY)出版,主要提供世界各地的旅游信息,刊登与旅游相关的各种商品广告等,其核心是各地旅游见闻和散记,供读者参考。摘译的这篇《东方威尼斯》("The Venice of the Far East")刊登在(1907—1908)月刊合订本 1908 年 6 月刊中(第 400 页至第 402 页),作者是玛格丽特·耶茨·斯特林(Margaret Yates Stirling)。文中记录了作者由上海乘船参观苏州的经历,对行驶在大运河与更小水道上的船只、北寺塔、文庙、城墙、园林与园林中的中国女子、苏州丝绸刺绣,以及巡抚衙门与巡抚夫妇的服饰都进行了较为详细的描摹,充满了对这座东方水城的好奇与赞叹。

"HEAVEN above; below Soochow;" thus read the ancient Chinese proverb. How far back in the dim annals of history this was written we cannot tell, but as the Celestial Empire knows no law of change, Soochow to-day holds the same unrivaled place among the cities of the Middle Kingdom that it enjoyed two thousand years ago. While only a few broken columns and scattered monuments of classic art bear witness to "the glory that was Greece and the grandeur that was Rome," their Chinese contemporary is the living exponent of a civilization that has been uninterrupted from 500 B.C. until the present time. Since the day it was founded during the lifetime of Confucius, the throne-less king, Soochow has been the center of culture for four hundred millions of people.

When we decided to visit this far-famed city, we engaged two house-boats which formed connecting links in the great chain of similar boats whose means of locomotion was a powerful steam tug. For three days these commodious crafts served as our hotel, and furnished us with comfortable sleeping quarters, easily converted into a spacious dining room by day. Cots, bedding provisions, and cooking utensils were carried on board while our meals were prepared by the ubiquitous Chinese "boy" who is invariably a skilled chef.

We left Shanghai at dusk one May afternoon and wound our way up a narrow creek, skirting past waving green banks, on which stood the innumerable thatched cottages of the native peasantry, until the following morning, when we came in sight of the curving roofs and towering pagodas of Soochow. No first glimpse of Venice could be more beautiful than the vision of this fair oriental city in the early dawn of a Chinese spring. Soochow, bathed in the morning light and rising from the waters of the Grand Canal, seemed the oriental Venice of a more ancient civilization. Down the Grand Canal floated the quaint junks with their square-rigged sails dyed brown in ox blood. Through the smaller waterways plied sampans or native sail-less boats, with cargoes of Celestials calmly eating their morning bowls of rice. In a country like China where such a large proportion of the population lives on the water, this river and canal life forms an interesting phase, and one can watch an entire family performing its household tasks within the restricted compass of a native junk. The sampan in Soochow takes the place of the gondola in Venice as a mode of conveyance, and is propelled in very much the same way, by a solitary boatman with single oar, used as a scull.

It was but a short distance from our mooring at the customs dock to the interior of the city which we found rife with interest, as we rode our donkeys

东方威尼斯

"上有天堂，下有苏州"，一句中国古话如是说。在朦胧的历史记录里到底多早出现这一说法我们无从得知，因天朝帝国不重变革之道，如今的苏州在中国的城市中享有和两千年前同样无可匹敌的地位。散落的断柱残碑有古典艺术之美，亦可证"希腊之荣光，罗马之辉煌"之言不虚，而当代中国人却是一个文明活生生的代表，这一文明自公元前500年一直延续至今。苏州建于素王孔子时代，一直都是四亿中国人的文化中心。

我们决定参观这一远负盛名的城市并雇用了两艘住家船。这些船与河中一长串类似的船只首尾相接，蒸汽拖船为其提供强劲动力。在三天的行程中，这些宽敞的船只就是我们的旅馆，为我们提供舒适的睡眠空间，白天又轻松变身为宽敞的餐厅。床、寝具、锅碗瓢盆也都带上了船。一位随从的中国"伙计"是位大厨，为我们准备一日三餐。

我们于五月的一个黄昏离开上海，沿着一条狭窄的溪流溯流而上。两岸绿草茵茵，坐落着无数当地农民的茅草屋。第二天早晨，苏州鳞次栉比的屋顶和高耸入云的宝塔映入我们的眼帘。第一眼所见之威尼斯也美不过春天清晨的这座美丽的东方城市。沐浴在晨曦中，苏醒于大运河上，苏州作为东方威尼斯，其文明更为古老。沿着大运河航行的是古雅的中国式帆船，挂着用牛血浸染的褐色横帆。在更小的水道上行驶的是舢板，即当地的无帆船，船上大批的中国人安静地端着饭碗，吃着早饭。中国是一个有大量人口生活在水上的国家，河上生活形成饶有趣味的片段，人们可以看到全家人在船上的狭小空间做着家务。苏州的舢板取代威尼斯的贡多拉[1]成为一种出行方式，单人单桨的推进方式也与贡多拉十分相似。

我们在离城内不远的海关码头停船，骑着毛驴穿过时不时就出现几级

---

[1] 威尼斯的一种轻快小舟，底部平坦，两头尖尖的，高高翘起。

through the narrow streets where high stone steps appear at frequent intervals. The shops have gaudy signs with great gilt characters to announce their wares, consisting principally of wonderfully carved ivories, wrought bronze and brass, rich silks, pearls, coral, and jade, which latter the Chinese consider the emblem of virtue, and a stone of happy omen. We were followed by a staring mob, who watched us curiously, gesticulated. and made many unflattering remarks about our queer clothes and queerer appearance. How round our eyes, how white our faces, and how large our feet! What they really said of us we learned later from our missionary guide. Some of the young women in our party were wearing sweaters as the day was cool. Said one gaping Chinaman, "These foreign devils change their fashions; they used to wear their flannels on the inside." "How funny to wear chicken feathers on a hat!" said another wondering Celestial. Soochow is a clean Chinese city and few of the usual objectionable sights and smells arrested our attention as our strange procession threaded its way to the Great Pagoda.

This is a vast temple of paganism, the highest in the East, and one of the wonders of the world. From its foundation it rises tapering to a height of nearly two hundred and fifty feet while images of Buddhist and Brahman deities are carved on the stones and enthroned in the shrines. We climbed the many flights of steps rising between the walls, until we reached the summit which commands a wonderful view, and on this fair spring day our eyes roamed over a smiling expanse of the Flowery Kingdom. Like a silver thread ran the Grand Canal gleaming in the sunlight, the Dragon Street winding through Soochow to the Confucian temple, the Great Lake to the west, the low-lying hills crowned by pagodas, the little villages, the larger settlements, the fertile fields—it was a bird's-eye view of a fair China.

From the Great Pagoda a short ride brought us to the Confucian temple where there is a stone map, a thousand years old, on which the street and temple sites are the same as at present. Within one of the minor temples sits enthroned a female divinity. In view of the Chinaman's supreme contempt for women, it is remarkable that his mythology should yield an equal place with that of the King of Heaven to one of the despised sex, even though divine. Yet this oriental Juno is known in the florid vernacular as "the Ruler of Earth, the Pearly Empress, and the Queen of Heaven."

One of the most interesting experiences of the day was a trip to the old wall, which has a grassy road on the summit so broad that two carriages can

很高石阶的狭窄街道,发现这座城市处处充满趣味。店铺招牌招摇惹眼,鎏金大字说明经营的商品主要有雕刻精美的象牙、精制的铜器、华丽的丝绸、珍珠、珊瑚及玉石,玉石在中国人眼中象征着美德和幸福。我们身后跟着大群围观人群,他们好奇地打量着我们,指指点点,对我们的奇装异服和更怪异的面貌说三道四。我们的眼睛多么圆,我们的脸多么白,我们的脚多么大!所有这些我们只是后来从传教士向导那里才得以知晓。我们中有几位年轻女士由于天凉穿了毛衣。一个中国人目瞪口呆地说:"这些外国佬换时尚啦,他们过去是把法兰绒穿在里面的。"另一个中国人诧异地说:"帽子上戴鸡毛,真滑稽!"苏州是一座干净的中国城市,我们一行人在前往北寺塔途中,几乎没看见令人不快的景象,也没闻到令人讨厌的气味。

这是一座巨大的异教寺庙,是东方最高的一座宝塔,堪称世界奇迹之一。塔身从基座向上逐渐收缩,高约250英尺,神龛中供奉着石雕佛像和婆罗门神像。我们沿着夹在两墙之间的楼梯向上爬到了塔顶,在晴朗的春日俯瞰苏州城,呈现在眼前的是一个花团锦簇的王国,景致美不胜收:阳光下的大运河宛如一条银链闪闪发光,护龙街蜿蜒穿越苏州直达孔庙,西边的是太湖,低矮的群山峰顶立有宝塔,还有小村落、较大居民区和肥沃的田野——好一幅美丽的中国图景。

离开北寺塔我们很快就到了孔庙。这里有一幅千年的石刻地图,图上的街寺布局一如当今。在一座小庙里供奉着一尊女神。鉴于中国人极度蔑视女性,哪怕在神界,让被蔑视的女性和天王享有同样地位也是匪夷所思的。而这位东方朱诺[1]女神在当地花哨的方言中被称为"地球的统治者、珍珠皇后、天后"。

参观古城墙是这天最有趣的体验之一。城墙顶部杂草丛生,宽得足够

---

[1] 朱诺,罗马神话中的天后,主神丘比特的妻子。

drive abreast. Think of a wall encircling with generous breadth a city, and furnishing at the same time a pleasant promenade for its inhabitants! To the casual glance it seems modeled after the pattern of the famous wall of Troy, and not until one ascends it does he realize that this is no mere skeleton of stone and mortar. We entered by means of one of the gates, and up the grassy slope our donkeys cantered merrily, until from the summit our climb repaid us with many a picturesque vista of city and winding canal.

A pleasant opportunity of seeing the Chinese under a holiday aspect was afforded us when we visited the famous mandarin's garden, which is an earthly representation of the Oriental's idea of Paradise. In these beautiful pleasure grounds there are winding paths leading to miniature lakes, which in summer reflect the delicate pink and white beauty of the lotus the emblem of Nirvana, and in whose chalice Budha is often represented as seated. Under the broad green leaves of this exquisite flower, tiny gold fish may be seen darting to and fro, while slender bridges connect artificial rookeries, crowned on their summits by fantastic pavilions. The tea houses face a charming vista of stunted pines, groves of feathery bamboo, and flowering trees, while chairs and tables beguile the pleasure seeker with their offer of quiet meditation and a cup of fragrant tea.

Here one can observe at his leisure the little Chinese lady, for she frequently leaves the seclusion of her home to take the air in her favorite gardens. She walks with difficulty in tiny embroidered satin slippers, smaller than any ever worn by Cinderella, and very pointed in the toe, as the rest of the poor woman's foot is forced into the heel. However, the abnormal shoe is the one unsensible part of the costume of the feminine Chinese. Otherwise, it is as rational as any dress reformer could desire. A loose wide sleeved coat of heavy brocade in soft delicate shades, if she is rich, and of blue linen if she is poor, is worn with ample trousers, ankle length, of black satin or sateen, with occasionally the addition of a black satin pleated skirt. She wears no hat, but her hair is parted and brushed smoothly about her ears into a low knot at her neck, while sometimes a white camellia droops in the smooth dark coils of satin-like hair. Often a closely fitting head dress of black velvet, or if she is some wealthy mandarin's wife, of pearls, forms a frame for her childlike face. Usually her round cheeks are painted; but the skin is always smooth, and in high caste women it takes the mellow shade of old ivory.

两辆马车并行。想象一下：有如此宽阔的城墙绕城一周，同时又为居民提供了漫步场所，多么惬意！乍看之下，城墙样式犹如模仿著名的特洛伊城墙，但等到登临其上，才意识到这不仅仅是石头和砂浆搭建的架构。我们进入一座城门，骑着毛驴沿着长满青草的斜坡一路欢跑，上到城墙顶部，回馈我们的是如画的城市风光和蜿蜒的护城河。

我们很高兴有机会参观一位著名官员的园林，了解中国人的度假方式。这一园林是东方人关于天堂的理想的人间代表。在这美丽乐园里，蜿蜒小径通往人工小湖，夏天湖中盛开粉白的美丽莲花。莲花象征着极乐世界，佛祖常端坐于莲花座上。宽大碧绿的荷叶下，可见小金鱼倏忽来回。小桥连接着假山，山顶立有奇异的亭子。茶室面向一片迷人的风景：矮小的松树、凤尾竹林、开满鲜花的树木，而桌椅则吸引休闲者坐下品茗静思。

在此可以悠闲地观察中国的小妇人，因其会时不时走出家门到最喜欢的花园透透气。妇人穿着一双极小的绣花缎鞋，比灰姑娘曾经穿过的任何一双鞋都要小。她行走艰难，因为鞋头很尖，脚被挤压到鞋跟部。然而，畸形鞋设计虽不合理，却是中国女性服饰的一部分。除此之外，中国妇女的服装设计总体还是非常得体的。富家之女会身穿厚缎面料的宽袖外套，散发出柔和细腻的光泽，贫寒之女所穿衣服的面料则为蓝亚麻布，下配长及脚踝的黑色缎裤，偶尔还会外罩一条百褶黑缎裙。中国妇女不戴帽子，头发分开光滑地梳向耳后，在后脖处盘成一个低髻，有时还在黑缎般的发圈上插上白色的山茶花，还经常会紧贴头发戴一个黑色天鹅绒头饰。如果是富裕的官太太，则会戴上珍珠头饰，与其娇嫩的脸庞相映衬。通常，中国妇女肤质光滑，圆润的脸颊会涂上胭脂，上流社会女性的肤色则如古老象牙般柔和醇熟。

A visit to the looms proved to us that Soochow, although the great silk center of the empire, did its manufacturing in a very primitive and laborious way. The looms are in little one-storied houses, and are worked by the feet treading on slender bamboo rods; yet among deplorably dirty surroundings are produced the richest and daintiest satins and silks. The most beautiful of Chinese embroidery is also done in this city. Costumes for the Court at Pekin, mandarins' robes, ladies' gowns, and actors' apparel, are heavily embroidered in gold and silks of many colors. Twice a year the superintendent of the silk looms sends one thousand trunks of embroidered clothing for the use of the imperial household. These gorgeous robes are sometimes worn only a few times until their beauty is marred by the upsetting of a cup of tea. Then they are sold for perhaps a third of their value, until for twenty-five or fifty Mexican dollars, they come into the possession of some foreigner, eager to carry these much prized curios to his western home.

A totally different phase of activity awaited our attention at the foreign concession, where there is a well-equipped hospital and training school for nurses in charge of a missionary and his wife, who is a physician of equal ability with her husband. One of their patients was the little daughter of the governor of the Province, whom they were treating for some spinal trouble. The success crowning their efforts made it possible for our missionary friends to gain for us a private audience in the Yamen or official residence.

We made the journey through the narrow streets in chairs each borne by two coolies, a long winding procession. From the outside this Chinese palace proved very unprepossessing, and we found the interior but slight improvement. We knocked at a large shabby but quaintly decorated gate that on opening admitted us into a court; then through another gate we passed into an enormous bare room in which their excellencies awaited us. How uncomfortable and cheerless these great gloomy Yamens, and how their poor inmates must shiver in the cold winters over their tiny charcoal fires! The governor wore the usual mandarin dress, consisting of a long richly embroidered robe and a round scarlet cap with a flowing tassel of the same color. Across his breast a square of embroidered silk had as a device a golden bird, the insignia of his rank as a civil official, while a costly necklace of large coral and jade beads fell in ample lengths over the front of his coat. His wife was dressed in the picturesque costume of the Manchu lady. The embroidered coat made of lustrous silk in the blended shades of brilliant pink

参观织机之行表明苏州虽然是清帝国的重要丝绸中心，其生产制造方式却极为原始费力。织机放置在一层楼的小房子里，需要用脚踩踏细竹竿来操作；可叹的是，在如此肮脏的环境里却生产出最富丽精美的绸缎。中国最美丽的刺绣也出自此地。北京宫廷的服饰、官员的袍服、女士们的长裙、演员的行头都是用金线及各色的丝线绣制而成。织造大人每年两次派送一千箱刺绣服装进京供皇室使用。这些富丽堂皇的衣袍有时只穿过几次后，就因打翻茶水毁其美观。随后这些衣服约以其价值的三分之一，低至25 或 50 鹰洋出售，一些外国人购买后就急不可耐地将这些珍贵的稀罕玩意儿带回西方的家中。

在外国租界，一项完全不同的活动等着我们。这里有一座设施完善的医院和一所护士培训学校，皆由一对传教士夫妇负责管理。他们都是内科医生，医术不分伯仲。他们的病人中有一位是江苏巡抚的小女儿，因脊柱疾病正接受治疗。我们传教士朋友的救治努力没有白费，使我们能够私下参观衙门或官邸。

我们坐在两个苦力抬着的轿子上如游龙般穿过狭小的街道。从外面看，这座中式宫殿很不起眼，但里面尚可观瞻。我们叩开一扇破旧却古色古香的大门进入庭院，又穿过另一扇门走进一间空旷的大房间，巡抚大人在此等着我们。这些幽暗的大衙门真是无趣又令人不自在，居住者在寒冷的冬日靠着微弱的炭火取暖必定冻得瑟瑟发抖，真是可怜！巡抚大人身穿常见的官服，一件华贵的刺绣长袍，头戴安有红缨的圆帽。胸前的方补上绣着一只金色的鸟儿以表明他的官阶，衣前还垂着一条昂贵的珊瑚朝珠。巡抚夫人穿着满族贵妇的精美服饰。散发着光泽的亮粉色和蓝色的丝绸绣花外套在左侧用金纽扣系住，下穿宽大的蓝缎裤子，天生的小脚上穿着一双绣

and blue, was fastened on the left side with small gold buttons. The wide trousers were of blue satin, and on her naturally small feet she wore embroidered satin shoes, in the center of which were large white heels in the Manchu style. Her smooth hair was arranged over a gilded wire frame which was perched on the top of her head like a huge black Alsatian bow, while from the sides emerged two gold knobs where several bright pink flowers and jade ornaments were fastened. Clinging to her side was her little daughter, a small reproduction of the mother, minus the head-dress.

After a few moments spent in the exchange of questions in regard to our age and the cost of our gowns—interrogations which form part of the punctilious etiquette of the Chinese—we were led into the banquet room where we were seated around a long table, which dispensed the hospitality of little cakes and Apollinaris, and unsweetened tea.

Through the great gates of the Yamen we passed out to our chairs, which bore us swiftly to our house-boat.

While the gray outlines of the city faded in the evening light, a vision of Soochow as one of the great centers of the Chinese Empire flashed through our minds. By means of its numerous canals, it is within easy access of Shanghai, Hangchow, and Chinkiang; it is in the heart of the silk district, and its very name has a magic sound in the ear of the Chinese. A still happier augury for its future importance is the prospect of its becoming the center of the Shanghai, Hangchow and Nanking Railway. Western enterprise has at last permeated China's oriental conservatism to good effect, and in the awakening from her long sleep, she is giving her consent to the laying of the hated railways, which will belt the empire from Canton to Peking.

With the setting sun gilding the pinnacle of the Great Pagoda, and shedding its last rays on the old wall, we turned our prow towards Shanghai, and bade a reluctant farewell to the Venice of the Far East.

花缎鞋，白色大鞋跟彰显满族风格。她梳理光滑的头发上夹着镀金发夹，在头顶扎成巨型蝴蝶结，两边各有一个金簪，上面插着亮粉色的鲜花和玉饰。身边依偎着她的小女儿，长相极像母亲，只是少了头饰。

就我们的年龄和长袍价格等一番寒暄之后——此乃中国人雷打不动的待客之道——我们被领进了宴会厅。我们围坐在一张长桌旁，桌上摆着小蛋糕、德国矿泉水和清茶。

出了衙门，我们坐上轿子，很快地回到住家船。

城市灰色的轮廓逐渐消失在暮色中，苏州，这个中华帝国伟大中心之一的形象仍在我们脑海中闪现。凭借众多的河道，苏州可轻易通达上海、杭州和镇江。处于丝绸产区的核心，苏州在中国人听来是一个有魔力的名字。更令人高兴的是，苏州未来可能成为上海—杭州—南京铁路的中心。西方企业最终瓦解了中国东方的保守主义，使其从长睡中苏醒，同意铺设其先前所憎恨的铁路，这将使清帝国从广州到北京连接起来。

当夕阳映射在北寺塔的塔尖，余晖洒向古老的城墙之时，我们调转船头，驶向上海，依依不舍地告别东方威尼斯。

Trifles of Travel

旅行琐记

(查尔斯·亨得利 著 余利霞 译)

《旅行琐记》(*Trifles of Travel*)于1924年1月在华盛顿出版发行。作者查尔斯·亨得利(Charles M. Hendley)于1922年2月至1923年3月间乘船游历美国檀香山、日本、中国、印度、印尼和埃及等地。其间以谈话式的口吻写信给在巴尔的摩的儿子,介绍自己的所见所闻。一些朋友得知后,强烈表示要一睹为快。为方便他们阅读,作者特编辑成书出版。其中的一封信(原著第61页至第66页)记录了作者游玩苏州的过程。他对苏州城外田野风貌、城墙、城内街巷及河流都有描述,对苏州城内的卫生环境颇有微词,并且将上海和苏州进行了对比。作者还较详细地描述了缫丝的全过程,对中国的丝绸生产颇为感叹。

Shanghai, China,

JUNE 4, 1922.

One day last week a party of us went to Soochow, a thoroughly native city, and spent the day. It is about fifty miles from here in the interior and about two hours ride in the cars. The country through which we passed is fertile, well cultivated, and the crops look somewhat like ours at home. There were wheat, barley, rice, and vegetables. The fields were smaller than ours, but considerably larger than those in Japan. The water buffalo take the place of the horse and are very generally used. We saw them drawing the plough in many places and frequently tramping in a small circle, turning a wheel to raise water from one of the many irrigating ditches to the fields. These water buffalo seem very docile and are treated by the natives about as we handle cattle at home. It was a common sight to see water buffalo and men walking and working in the water.

The feature of the country that was to us odd and unusual was the large number of graves and mounds. The Chinese revere and worship their ancestors. They believe that the spirit of the departed remains or hovers around the final resting place of the body and that these spirits bring bad luck if interfered with or if their resting places are disturbed. They seemed to have buried their dead wherever it was most convenient or where fancy dictated. There are single graves here and there but there are more apt to be a group of them several feet above the level of the fields. As China has been burying her dead for twenty or thirty centuries, these last resting places have accumulated until the fields are dotted with them. I should say that perhaps a fifth of the area of the country we saw is given over to burial sites. There has been a good deal said by writers upon China about the need of this land for the raising of crops, but so far the Chinese have adhered to their custom of keeping these burial places intact.

Soochow is a walled city and dates back many centuries. The wall is some fifteen or eighteen feet high, and forms a rectangle, one and a half by two and a half miles. This makes the wall about twelve miles long. The wall is surrounded completely by a wide moat filled with water and this stream is connected with canals that lead off to other sections of the country. Canals play a very important part in Chinese affairs. Large and small canals furnish means of communication and are plentiful in all the cities. They are anything but attractive to the Occidental. The water is polluted, usually filled with refuse, and has a very disagreeable odor. We would call these streams sewers' and the Board of Health

中国上海

1922年6月4号

上周我们一行人去苏州游玩了一天。苏州坐落于距上海约50英里、车程两小时左右的内地,是一座完完全全本地人的城市。途经的田野富饶肥沃,为人所精耕细作。田里的庄稼看起来与我们种的有些相似,有小麦、大麦、水稻和蔬菜。这里的农田比我们的小,但比日本的大得多。水牛取代了马匹,被广泛应用于农业生产。随处可见水牛在拉犁耕地,还经常看到它们转着圈带动水车,从遍布的灌溉渠里抽水浇地。水牛看起来很温顺,当地人对待水牛的方式跟我们差不多。水牛和男人们共同在水田中劳作的景象随处可见。

田野里有大量的坟墓,这在我们看来古怪而稀罕。中国人崇敬先人,认为逝者的灵魂会萦绕在安息之所,如果这些灵魂遭到打扰,或墓地遭到破坏,都会带来厄运。他们似乎在任何合适的地方安葬逝者,因此,一座座孤坟散落在田野里,但更多的坟墓则成组排列,有几英尺高。两三千年的时光里,中国人一直保持着这样的丧葬习俗。为此,田里的坟墓愈来愈多,直至星罗棋布。我估计我们看到的田野约两成都成了坟地。作家们一直说中国需要耕地,但时至今日中国人仍坚守着完好保护墓葬地的习俗。

苏州有城墙环绕,有好几百年的历史。城墙高约15—18英尺,形成一个约1.5×2.5英里、周长12英里左右的矩形。城墙外有宽阔的护城河环绕,与通往各地的河道相连。运河在中国举足轻重,城市中随处可见大大小小的河道,四通八达,交通便利。这些河道在西方人看来一点也不好,河水污染,垃圾淤塞,气味难闻。我们会把这些小河称作污水沟,卫生委员会

旅行琐记

would condemn them without visiting them. People in China live by them and on them, wash their clothes and their food and rear their children, their chickens and geese upon them, fish in them and go about their daily tasks in and on them and do not know that they are unsanitary or unlovely.

  Outside the wall there is a small hotel to which we repaired and where we engaged sedan chairs. These particular chairs, made of bamboo, were swung upon long poles and were carried on the shoulders of coolies, with one coolie in reserve for each chair. We made quite a procession as we were hustled along, five chairs, five of us, and fifteen coolies. Every little while at a signal from the leader, one coolie at each chair would be relieved by the extra man. It was our first experience with chairs. The sensation is not altogether agreeable. I prefer the *rickshas*. After skirting along the edge of the canal we ferried across it, passed through one of the six gates in the wall and entered the city proper. Of course this word city should not be used as it gives you an entirely wrong idea of what we saw. The streets are narrow thoroughfares or alleys which twist and wind about. You could almost touch the houses on either side by stretching out your arms. There were a few *rickshas* but as these streets or alleys are paved with small stones and are higher in the center than the sides, the *rickshas* were not comfortable. The only other means of conveyance was by small donkeys not over three feet high. Each wore bells and had small boys in attendance. We were pressed to use them but stuck to our chairs and coolie bearers.

  In the district given over to stores the street is usually canopied with a light cloth to keep out the rays of the sun. The artisans were busy in their shops which are open in front. Some were making furniture, some working in iron and brass, just as their ancestors for many generations have done. I saw one man holding a board while two other men by the use of a stout cord, one pulling one end and the other the other end, were operating a bit in order to bore a hole through the board. At another place two men were slowly and laboriously sawing a log into boards by hand.

  In many of the small two-room houses were looms upon which the family were weaving the most beautiful fabrics, brocades and tapestries. It seems that each town in China makes some distinctive thing and it is difficult to obtain that particular thing unless you visit the town where it is made. At Soochow they make a sort of golden brown tapestry, with the figures deftly sewed in usually a picture illustrating some Chinese story or legend, and these are known as Soochow tapestries. Once in a while you can find an occasional piece in

一定会宣布它们不宜游览。但中国人却枕河而居，在河里洗衣、洗菜、钓鱼，在河边养儿育女，养鸡养鹅，处理各种日常事务。他们不知道这些河道既不卫生，也不宜人。

我们下榻于城墙外的一座小旅馆，在那租了轿子。这种竹制的轿子悬吊在长杠上，由轿夫肩扛，每顶轿子有一名备用轿夫。我们五顶轿子，五个人，十五个轿夫，浩浩荡荡前行。每隔一会儿，在领头人的示意下，每顶轿子会有一名轿夫轮换休息。这是我们第一次乘轿子，并不感觉很惬意，我更喜欢黄包车。沿护城河边走了一段后，我们摆渡穿过六座城门中的一座进了苏州城。城市一词也许并不妥当，因为它会让你对我们所见产生完全错误的理解。这儿的街道狭窄、蜿蜒曲折，伸开双臂几乎能碰到两边的房子。有黄包车可代步，但街巷都是小石子铺就，中间高两边低，因此坐黄包车不舒服。另一种交通工具就是不足三英尺高的小毛驴，脖子上挂着铃铛，由小男孩牵着。我们迫不得已骑着毛驴，但仍让轿子与轿夫在旁侍候。

在商业区，街道通常用浅色的布做天篷以遮蔽阳光。商店店门敞开，匠人们在店内忙碌着，有做家具的，有打铁的，有制铜器的，一如他们的祖祖辈辈。我看到有个人手持一块木板，另两个人一人一头拉着一根粗线在木板上开孔；另一处两个人正缓慢而费力地手工锯木。

许多两居室的小房子里都有织布机，人们织着美丽的布匹和锦缎。在中国似乎每个小镇都有某些独特的商品，除非亲赴产地，否则你很难获得这些特产。苏州生产一种以苏锦为名的金褐色织锦，图案精巧，通常都是描绘中国故事或传奇。偶尔在上海也会发现此类织锦，价格相当昂贵。

Shanghai. They are quite expensive.

We were told that there are two hundred and fifty thousand people in Soochow, but there is no way to judge of the population of a place here. If I had been told that there were but twenty-five thousand I should have received the statement without surprise.

In Japan the houses are all built of wood. In China they are brick or adobe with tiled roofs. Many of them have no windows, and only one or two doors, one in front and one in the rear. You feel as if you were walking between two walls with many openings.

Probably the highest pagoda is at Soochow. It has nine stories. I do not know how many feet high but I should think several hundred. As the country is flat this pagoda can be seen for many miles.

Our caravan finally emerged through a different gate from the one by which we had entered. We were ferried across the moat, settled our bill at the hotel and returned to Shanghai.

I described in a general way in my last letter the city of Shanghai, but I said little about the native city—that part where the Chinese live—as I had not been there. Since then I have made a visit to it and found it very much like the city of Soochow. It seems remarkable that you can actually step from paved streets and modern ways into a community that has not changed its form or manner of living in hundreds of years. The example of present-day methods seems to have had no effect whatever. Soochow is fifty miles away and one would expect to find old customs and habits prevailing there, but in Shanghai, almost under the shadow of tall buildings occupied by English-speaking people, one sees life just as it is found at Soochow. The same narrow streets, the same open shops with the workmen at their tasks, the same primitive conditions, the same contrast of squalor and beautiful fabrics. While the native city is a part of Shanghai yet the English-speaking residents here seldom visit it. There are many shops in this old section, some very attractive, especially those displaying ivory, silver and silk, and they are visited by the Chinese and by tourists like ourselves. There are quite a number of tea houses and restaurants, but none of a character that could be patronized by other than natives. There is one tea house that is famous on account of its setting. It is entirely surrounded by an artificial lake or pond, not very large, and is reached by a zig-zag walk over the water. The walk is made in that form to keep out evil spirits. It seems these spirits require a straight path and cannot cross

我们得知苏州居住着 25 万人口，但在中国没有办法判断一个地方的人口数。如果早前有人告诉我苏州仅有 2.5 万人，对此说法我也不会感到惊讶。

在日本，房屋都是木质结构。在中国，房屋都是砖头或土坯垒成，上盖瓦屋顶。许多房子没有窗户，只有一前一后两扇门，感觉像是你正穿行在有很多开口的两堵墙间。

苏州可能有中国最高的宝塔，有 9 层。具体多高我不清楚，但我想总该有几百英尺高。由于该地乡野地势平坦，数英里外就能望见这座塔。

我们的旅行队伍最终从另一座城门出了市区，渡过护城河，在旅馆结清账目，返回了上海。

我上封信中大概地描述了上海，但几乎没有提及上海人的居住区，因为我从未去过。从苏州回来后我去过一次，发现那里跟苏州很像。踩着平坦的现代大马路，步入一个生活方式几百年来未曾改变过的社区，感觉很棒。当今的生活方式对此地似乎没有任何影响。苏州距上海 50 英里，我们可以料想那里古老风俗习惯盛行。但在上海，尽管有西方人居住的高楼的影响，生活却一如苏州。同样狭窄的街道，同样有工匠劳作的店铺，同样原始的条件，同样对比鲜明的脏乱环境与美丽布匹。虽然本地人居住区是上海的一部分，但西方人很少光顾。在老城区有众多店铺，有些非常吸引人，特别是那些陈列象牙、银器和丝绸的铺子，中国人和我们这样的外国游客都会光顾。另外还有大量的茶室和饭店，但只有本地人光临。有一间茶室因其环境而闻名。该茶室位于一片不大的人工湖中，经由蜿蜒曲折的步道进入。步道修成曲折的样式，是为了避邪。这些邪祟好像只能走直路，无法穿过

on this irregular one, for if they should attempt it they would be thrown into the water and drowned. The water is covered completely by the small leaf of a water plant. The buildings are very old and sadly in need of repair. At a distance it all looks very quaint and picturesque but close by it is not so attractive. May tells me that this is the famous "willow Pattern Tea House" that is on the blue and white china of that name.

There are a number of ivory stores but the work is not very fine and not nearly so good as that done by the Japanese.By the way, it is about as difficult here to make a purchase of any kind as it is to trade horses at home; you have to go through about as much finessing.If yon price an article and turn away from the salesman as if to leave he will at once inquire,"How much you give?"

I am told there are perhaps a million people in Shanghai ·and of that number only about twenty-five thousand foreigners. A good many people live on boats in the harbor. Some of the boats are as small as our rowboats. A round cover occupies the middle third. The two ends being open. They eat, sleep,and raise families upon them. I was amused to see on one boat that the family kept two geese. While I was looking at them the woman shooed them off into the water and I wondered how she would get them again, but soon discovered that they were tethered with a stout cord and after she thought they had had liberty enough, she drew them onto the boat again.

A day or two ago I went through a filature. This is a factory for winding the silk from the cocoon into a skein or hank. These cocoons are gathered in country districts and shipped here in large bags and look and feel like bags of peanuts. The laborers in the factory are nearly all children and women. The women receive twenty-five cents a day and work ten hours. I asked if they continue long at this work and was told that some of them had been in the factory thirty years.The cocoons are placed in water so hot that the operators cannot keep their fingers in it and as they work they constantly dip their fingers in a bowl of cold water which they keep by them. They run the filatures or silk from the cocoon through small holes in a piece of ivory about the size of an ordinary button,and six of these filatures are combined and twisted to make one thread. In this way they are wound around a small light frame work wheel, then taken from this and twisted in the shape of a hank. One woman manages three machines and becomes very expert. A single filature is so fine that I could not see it,even with my glasses on, but the six twisted together were plainly visible.

弯曲的道路。如果他们试图越过，则会掉进水里淹死。水面覆盖着一种小叶水生植物。茶室建筑非常老旧，且年久失修，远看古雅如画，近看却不怎么样。梅告诉我，这就是那间著名的"柳式茶室"，青花瓷茶具上就印有其名。

这儿还有很多象牙制品店，但作品不很精美，没有日货那么好。顺便提一句，在这儿购买任何一件东西都跟我们在家交易马匹一样艰难；也得要点手腕。比如你问价一件商品，然后转身假装走开，店员会马上询问："你给多少？"

有人告诉我上海约有100万人口，其中外国人只有2.5万左右。有相当多的人生活在停泊于港湾的船上。有些船和我们的手摇船一样小，中间1/3处覆盖一个圆形的顶棚，两头是露天的，他们在船上吃、住、养儿育女。好笑的是，我看到一个船家在船上养了两只鹅。我看着时，女船主正将它们赶到水中。我好奇她如何再抓住它们，但很快就发现鹅被一根结实的绳子拴住了，等她认为放够了风，就将它们拽回船上。

一两天前我去了一家缫丝厂，是一家从蚕茧中抽出丝绕成一束束、一团团的工厂。蚕茧在乡村地区收集起来装在大包里，运输至上海。那些大包看起来像装着花生似的。工厂里的劳工几乎全是妇女儿童。女工们每天工作10小时，日薪25美分。我问她们是否长期从事该行业，结果有人说已经在此工作30年了。蚕茧泡在热水中，水很烫，操作工无法将手指放进去，因此，他们工作时会不停地把手指伸进放在一旁的冷水碗里蘸一蘸。他们将丝通过约一颗普通纽扣大小的象牙上的若干小孔从蚕茧中抽出。六根这样的丝拧成一根线，丝线绕到一架小巧的纺车上，然后再绕成团。一名女工操作三台机器，非常娴熟。单根茧丝细得即使我戴上眼镜都看不清，但六根绞在一起就能清晰地看见了。

They have seasons for doing this as for most things. The season is just beginning; the cocoons are coming in from the country. As soon as the worm has spun his house around him, the cocoon is subjected to extreme heat which kills the worm as otherwise he would eat himself out of the cocoon and ruin it for silk purposes. The cocoon weighs two-thirds less after the worm is killed. This silk thread, in hanks or skeins, is baled and shipped, most of it to the United States.

There are three distinct stages in the silk business. The first is that of the farmer who raises mulberry leaves and the worms to eat them, thereby producing cocoons. The worms while making cocoons are placed on racks filled with mulberry leaves in the homes of small farmers and have to be tended carefully with regard to heat, light, etc. The next process is the filature I have described. Third is the manufacture of the skeins into silk cloth. Very little of that is done in China.

While in the native city here, I was interested in the letter writers. Rather elderly and scholarly looking men in small booths were writing letters as a means of livelihood for those who are unable to write for themselves.

We are to leave here next Tuesday afternoon by steamer and go to Chefoo. It is a two days' trip. From there we will go to Tientsin for a day or two and then to Peking.

Affectionately,
POP.

中国人做很多事情都有季节性。缫丝季此时刚开始，茧子从乡村不断地运来。蚕虫吐丝结茧后，马上用高温杀死蚕蛹，否则蚕蛹会破茧而出，就无法抽丝了。蚕蛹死后茧子重量会轻2/3。成束成团的丝线装进大包运走，大部分运往美国。

丝绸生产包含三个不同的步骤。第一步：蚕农种桑养蚕产茧。蚕虫结茧时被放置在蚕农家中铺满桑叶的架子上，此时的蚕虫光照和温度等都得仔细照料。第二步就是我刚描述过的缫丝。第三步则是将丝线加工成丝绸，这一步很少在中国完成。

在参观当地人居住区时，我对书信代写先生很感兴趣。他们看上去很老，学者气很足，坐在小亭子里代不会写字的人写信，以此谋生。

下周二下午我们会乘船离沪北上烟台，行程两天。再从烟台前往天津，逗留一两天，然后我们会去北京。

爱你的
爸爸

译后记

最早接触苏州英文史料是在 2005 年。当时，我刚从苏州大学外国语学院硕士毕业，并有幸考入苏州大学社会学院王国平先生门下，攻读博士学位。记得在一次上课时，先生对我说："上海徐家汇藏书楼有一本关于苏州的英文书，叫 Beautiful Soo，是西方人描写苏州历史风貌的，有兴趣你可以去看一看。"不久，我便怀着好奇之心踏上了寻书之旅。还记得，当我从工作人员手中小心翼翼地接过这本"尘封"了近百年的小书时，刹那间似乎有种时空穿越的感觉。细细翻阅之下，我不禁被书中内容和相片深深吸引，尤其是这些珍贵的相片真实记录了这座被誉为"东方威尼斯"古城的美丽影像，我脑海中闪过一个念头，应该让更多的人了解西方人眼中的"美丽苏州"。然而，由于种种原因，这本复印回来的小册子一直静静地躺在我的书橱里，其间我也曾想过对书中内容进行梳理，但每次都因为"太忙"而放弃，总是对自己说等空了以后再说，谁知这一等便是 10 年。

2016 年，恰逢纪念苏州建城 2 530 周年学术研讨会在我工作的苏州市职业大学召开，为参加此次会议，我终于重新拿起这本被搁置了 10 年之久的英文小书。细细研读之后，我写了一篇题为《19 世纪末美国来华传教士眼中的"美丽苏州"——以〈姑苏景志〉（"Beautiful Soo" the Capital of Kiangsu）为例》的参会论文，也算是完成了先生 10 年前布置给我的作业。2016 年底，该篇论文获"江苏省哲学社会科学界第十届学术大会优秀论文"二等奖。此后，我陆续搜集了一些有关苏州的英文史料。2019 年我撰写的论文《晚清英文史料中的"苏州形象"研究——以〈教务杂志〉为中心》又获"江苏省哲学社会科学界第十三届学术大会优秀论文"二等奖。这两篇文章也分别发表在《苏州教育学院学报》和《城市史研究》上，这也让我对苏州英文史料的搜集、研究有了初步设想。2019年，由先生担任总主编的十六卷本《苏州通史》出版面世，一时轰动学界，堪称苏州的第一部"史记"。先生在一次闲谈中对我说，《苏州通史》虽然完成，但有关苏州的外文史料很多并未收录其中，这对苏州历史文化研究而言颇为遗憾。此后，先生与我就苏州外文史料的整理和翻译又有过数次交流，我于是决定先行翻译《姑苏景志》（*"Beautiful Soo" The Capital of Kiangsu*）。由于前期对《姑苏景志》有过一番较为深入的阅读和研究，因此整个翻译过程比较顺畅，译稿也得到了先生和其他专家的认可，这也更加坚定了我做好苏州外文史料整理与翻译这个项目的决心。

2021年9月30日，苏州外文史料整理与翻译项目在苏州市职业大学外国语学院正式启动，先生亲临会场对参与项目的团队成员给予鼓励和支持。此后，团队成员们积极投入外文史料翻译。由于这些外文史料大多写于十九世纪末二十世纪初，很多地名都是沿用当时的名称；此外，很多西方人对中国以及苏州历史文化存在误读，这些都给阅读和翻译造成不少困扰。尽管如此，团队成员们克服种种困难，通过各种途径遍查、研读、共享相关资料，甚至很多成员踏上"访古之旅"，亲临书中所提及之场所，进行现场实地考察，其态度之严谨、钻研之深入令人感动！在翻译过程中，大家本着既尊重原文，又尊重史实的原则，除个别篇章有省略外，尽量将原文完整呈现，对译文亦反复酌酌，通过加脚注等方式力求提供相对准确的信息给读者，但原文中作者道听途说或者难以查证之处，不一而足。译稿初成之后，为确保译文准确，团队成员又进行交互阅读、校对，不留情面地提出批评和修改意见，多次开会共同商议，有时甚至为了一个词的翻译就"争执"半日，希望能给读者呈现出最为准确、流畅的译文。正是在团队成员共同努力、精诚合作之下，这本译著才得以顺利面世。

本辑共收入译稿九篇，具体如下：杜步西（H. C. Du Bose）的《姑苏景志》("Beautiful Soo" The Capital of Kiangsu，全本，卞浩宇译）；哈登（R. A. Haden）的《苏州历史见闻》（Some Notes from the History of Soochow，全本，孟祥德译）；威廉·埃德加·盖洛（W. E. Geil）的《中国十八省府》（Eighteen Capitals of China，节译本，徐冰译）；威廉·R. 葛骆（W. R. Kahler）的《在华度假记事》（My Holidays in China，节译本，黄洁婷译）；李通和（T. H. Liddell）的《中国：神奇而又神秘的国度》（China: Its Marvel and Mystery，节译本，戴莉译）；克劳（Carl Crow）的《游历中国闻见撷要录》（The Travelers' Handbook for China，节译本，蔡骏译）；伊尔丝·麦考密克（Elsie McCormick）的《可叹啊，苏州！美人都去了上海》（"Alas Poor Soochow! Thy Beauties Are in Shanghai"，单篇文本，余利霞译）；玛格丽特·耶茨·斯特林（Margaret Yates Stirling）的《东方威尼斯》（"The Venice of the Far East"，单篇文本，余利霞译）；查尔斯·亨得利（Charles M. Hendley）的《旅行琐记》（Trifles of Travel，节译本，余利霞译）。

最后，还要特别感谢徐欣晔先生无偿为我们提供多篇珍贵史料和诸多建议，感谢杜祯彬先生为我们解答有关苏州地理、历史方面的难题，感谢苏州大学李峰教授、顾卫星教授、孟祥春教授对译文提出的修改意见，感谢苏州市职业大学钮雪林书记、曹毓民校长对本项目的支持和鼓励，感谢苏州大学出版社李寿春副总编、沈琴编辑对本书出版付出的辛苦努力！译文不当之处，敬请读者批评指正！

卞浩宇

2022 年 7 月于越来溪畔